HEY RUB-A-DUB-DUB

A BOOK OF THE MYSTERY AND
WONDER AND TERROR
OF LIFE

I0754403

BOOKS BY
THEODORE DREISER

SISTER CARRIE
JENNIE GERHARDT
THE FINANCIER
THE TITAN
THE GENIUS
A TRAVELER AT FORTY
A HOOSIER HOLIDAY
PLAYS OF THE NATURAL AND SUPERNATURAL
THE HAND OF THE POTTER
FREE AND OTHER STORIES
TWELVE MEN

HEY RUB-A-DUB-DUB

A BOOK OF THE MYSTERY AND WONDER AND TERROR OF LIFE

By THEODORE DREISER

AUTHOR OF "SISTER CARRIE," "THE HAND OF THE POTTER," "FREE AND OTHER STORIES," "JENNIE GERHARDT," ETC.

BONI AND LIVERIGHT
NEW YORK 1920

Copyright, 1920,
By BONI & LIVERIGHT, Inc.

First printing, December, 1919
Second printing, February, 1920

Printed in the United States of America

CONTENTS

HEY RUB-A-DUB-DUB

HEY, RUB-A-DUB-DUB!

(Taken from the notes of the late John Paradiso)

I HAVE lived now to my fortieth year, and have seen a good deal of life. Just now, because of a stretch of poverty, I am living across the river from New York, in New Jersey, in sight of a splendid tower, the Woolworth Building on the lower end of Manhattan, which lifts its defiant spear of clay into the very maw of heaven. And although I am by no means as far from it as is Fifth Avenue, still I am a dweller in one of the shabbiest, most forlorn neighborhoods which the great metropolis affords. About me dwell principally Poles and Hungarians, who palaver in a lingo of which I know nothing and who live as I would despise to live, poor as I am. For, after all, in my hall-bedroom, which commands the river over the lumberyard, there is some attempt at intellectual adornment, whereas outside and around me there is little more than dull and to a certain extent aggrieved drudgery.

Not so very far from me is a church, a great yellow structure which lifts its walls out of a ruck of cheap frame houses, and those muddy, unpaved streets which are the pride of Jersey City and Hoboken. Here, if I will, I can hear splendid masses intoned, see bright altars and stained glass windows and people going to confession and burning votive candles before images. And if I go of a Sunday, which I rarely do, I can hear regularly that there is a Christ who died for men, and that He was the son of the living God who liveth and reigneth world without end.

I have no quarrel with this doctrine. I can hear it in a hundred thousand churches throughout the world. But I am one of those curious persons who cannot make up their minds about anything. I read and read, almost everything that I can lay hands on—history, politics, philosophy, art. But I find that one history contradicts another, one philosopher drives out another. Essayists, in the main, point out flaws and paradoxes in the current conception of things; novelists, dramatists and biographers spread tales of endless disasters, or silly illusions concerning life, duty, love, opportunity and the like. And I sit here and read and read, when I have time, wondering.

For, friends, I am a scrivener by trade—or try to be. Betimes, trying to make up my mind what to say about life, I am a motorman on a street-car at three dollars and twenty cents a day. I have been a handy man in a junk shop, and wagon driver, anything you will, so long as thereby I could keep body and soul together. I am not handsome, and therefore not attractive to women probably—at any rate I appear not to be—and in consequence am very much alone. Indeed, I am a great coward when it comes to women. Their least frown or mood of indifference frightens me and makes me turn inward to myself, where dwell innumerable beautiful women who smile and nod and hang on my arm and tell me they love me. Indeed, they whisper of scenes so beautiful and so comforting that I know they are not, and never could be, true. And so, in my best moments, I sit at my table and try to write stories which no doubt equally necessitous editors find wholly unavailable.

The things which keep me thinking and thinking are, first, my social and financial state; second, the difference between my point of view and that of thousands of other respectable citizens, who, being able to make up their minds, seem to find me queer, dull, recessive, or at any rate unsuited to their tastes and pleasures. I look at them, and while I say, "Well, thank heaven I am not like that," still I immediately ask myself, "Am I not all wrong? Should I not be happier if I, too, were like John Spitovesky, or Jacob Feilchenfeld, or Vaclav Melka?" —some of my present neighbors. For Spitovesky, to grow a little personal, is a small dusty man who has a tobacco store around the corner, and who would, I earnestly believe, run if he were threatened with a bath. He smokes his own three-for-fives (Flor de Sissel Grass), and deposits much of the ashes between his waistcoat and his gray striped cotton shirt. His hair, sticking bushily out over his ears, looks as though it were heavily peppered with golden snuff.

"Mr. Spitovesky," I said to him one day not long since, "have you been reading anything about the Colorado mining troubles?"

"I never read de papers," he said with a shrug of his shoulder.

"No? Not at all?" I pursued.

"Dere is nodding in dem—lies mosdly. Somedimes I look ad de baseball news in sommer."

"Oh, I see," I said hopelessly. Then, apropos of nothing, or because I was curious as to my neighbors, "Are you a Catholic?"

"I doaned belong to no church. I doaned mix in no politics, neider. Some hof de men aboud here get excided aboud politics; I got no time. I 'tend to mine store."

Seeing him stand for hours against his doorpost, or sitting out front smoking while his darksome little wife peels potatoes or sews or fusses with the children, I could never understand his "I got no time."

In a related sense there are my friends Jacob Feichenfeld and Vaclav Melka, whom I sometimes envy because they are so different. The former, the butcher to whom I run for chops and pigs' feet for my landlady, Mrs. Wscrinkuus; the latter the keeper of a spirituous emporium whose windows read "Vynas, Scnapas." Jacob, like every other honest butcher worthy the name, is broad and beefy. He turns on me a friendly eye as he inquires, "About so thick?" or suggests that he has some nice fresh liver or beef tongue, things which he knows Mrs. Wscrinkuus likes. I can sum up Mr. Feilchenfeld's philosophy of life when I report that to every intellectual advance I make he exclaims in a friendly enough way, "I dunno," or "I ain't never heard about dot."

My pride in a sturdy, passive acceptance of things, however, is nearly realized in Vaclav Melka, the happy dispenser of "Vynas, Scnapsas." He also is frequently to be found leaning in his doorway in summer, business being not too brisk during the daytime, surveying the world with a reflective eye. He is dark, stocky, black-haired, black-eyed, a good Pole with a head like a wooden peg, almost flat at the top, and driven firmly albeit not ungracefully into his shoulders. He has a wife who is a slattern and nearly a slave, and three children who seem to take no noticeable harm from this saloon life. Leaning in coatless ease against his sticky bar of an evening, he has laid down the law concerning morals and ethics, thus: no lying or stealing—among friends; no brawling or assaults or murdering for any save tremendous reasons of passion; no truckling to priests or sisters who should mind their own business.

"Did you ever read a book, Melka?" I once asked him. It was apropos of a discussion as to a local brawl.

"Once. It was about a feller wot killed a woman. Mostly I ain't got no time to read. Once I was a bath-rubber, and I had time then, but that was long ago. Books ain't nutting for me."

Melka states, however, that he was a fool to come here. "A feller wanted me to take dis saloon, and here I am. I make a living. If my wife died I would go back to my old job, I think." He does not want his wife to die, I am sure. It does not make that much difference.

But over the river from all this is another picture which disturbs me even more than my present surroundings, because, as seen from here, it is seemingly beautiful and inviting. Its tall walls are those of a fabled city. I can almost hear the tinkle of endless wealth in banks, the honks of automobiles, the fanfare of a great constructive trade life. At night all its myriad lights seem to wink at me and exclaim, "Why so incompetent? Why so idle, so poor? Why live in such a wretched neighborhood? Why not cross over and join the great gay throng, make a successful way for yourself? Why sit aside from this great game of materiality and pretend to ignore it or to feel superior?"

And as I sit and think, so it seems to me. But, alas, I haven't the least faculty for making money, not the least. Plainly beyond are all these wonderful things which are being done and made by men with that kind of ability which I appear to lack. I have no material, constructive sense. I can only think and write, in a way. I see these vast institutions (there are great warehouses on this side, too) filled to overflowing apparently with the financially interested and capable, but I—I have not the least idea how to do anything likewise. Yet I am not lazy. I toil over my stories or bounce out of bed and hurry to my work of a morning. But I have never earned more than thirty-five dollars a week in my whole life. No, I am not brilliant financially.

But the thing that troubles me most is the constant palaver going on in the papers and everywhere concerning right, truth, duty, justice, mercy and the like, things which I do not find expressed very clearly in my own motives nor in the motives of those immediately about me; and also the apparently earnest belief on the part of ever so many editors, authors, social reformers, et cetera, that every person, however weak or dull-appearing externally, contains within himself the seed or the mechanism for producing endless energy and ability, providing he can only be made to realize that he has it. In other words we are all Napoleons, only we don't know it. We are lazy Napoleons, idle Hannibals, wasteful and indifferent John D. Rockefellers. Turn the pages of any magazine—are there not advertisements of and treatises on How To Be Successful, with the authors thereof offering to impart their knowledge of how so to be for a comparative song?

Well, I am not one who can believe that. In my very humble estimation people are not so. They are, in the main, as I see it, weak and limited, exceedingly so, like Vaclav Melka or Mrs. Wscrinkuus, and to fill their humble brains with notions of an impossible supremacy, if it could be done, would be to send them forth to breast the ocean in a cockleshell. And, yet, here on my table, borrowed from the local library for purposes of idle or critical examination, is a silly book entitled "Take It!" —"It" meaning *"the world!"*; and another "It's Yours!"—the "It" in this case meaning that same great world! All you have to do is to decide so to do—and to try! Am I a fool to smile at this very stout doctrine, to doubt whether you can get more than four quarts out of any four-quart measure, if so much?

But to return to this same matter of right, truth, justice, mercy, so freely advertised in these days and so clearly defined, apparently, in every one's mind as open paths by which they may proceed. In the main, it seems to me that people are not concerned about right, or truth, or justice, or mercy, or duty, as abstract principles or working rules, nor do I believe that the average man knows clearly or even semi-clearly what is meant by the words. His only relation to them, so far as I can see, is that he finds them used in a certain reckless, thoughtless way to represent some method of adjustment by which he would like to think he is protected from assault or saved from misery, and so uses them himself. His concern for them as related to the other individual is that the other individual should not infringe on him, and I am now speaking of the common unsuccessful mass as well as of the successful.

Mrs. Wscrinkuus, poor woman, is stingy and slightly suspicious, although she goes to church Sundays and believes that Christ's Sermon on the Mount is the living truth. She does not want any one to be mean to her; she does not do anything mean to other people, largely because she has no particular taste or capacity in that direction. Supposing I should advise her to "Take It!" assure her that "It" was hers by right of capability! What would become of *right, truth, justice, mercy* in that case?

Or, once more, let us take Jacob Feilchenfeld and John Spitovesky, who care for no man beyond their trade and whose attitude toward right, truth, mercy, justice is as above. Suppose I should tell them to take "It," or assure them that "It" was theirs? Of what import would the message be? Vaclav Melka does favors only in return for favors. He does not like priests because they are always taking up collections. If you told him to take "It" he would proceed to take something away from the very good priests first of all. Everywhere I find the common man imbued with this feeling for self-protection and self-advancement. *Truth* is something that must be told to *him; justice* is what *he* deserves—although if it costs him nothing he will gladly see it extended to the other fellow.

But do not think for one moment because I say this that I think myself better or more deserving or wiser than any of these. As I said before, I do not understand life, although I like it; I may even say that I like this sharp, grasping scheme of things, and find that it works well. Plainly it produces all the fine spectacles I see. If it had not been for a certain hard, seeking ambition in Mr. Woolworth to get up and be superior to his fellows, where would his splendid tower have come from? It is only because I cannot understand why people cling so fatuitously to the idea that there is some fixed idyllic scheme or moral order handed down from on high, which is tender and charitable, punishes so-called evil and always rewards so-called good, that I write this. If it punishes evil, it is not all of the evil that I see. If it rewards good, then much of the good that I admire goes wholly unrewarded, on this earth at least.

But to return. The Catholics believe that Christ died on the Cross for them, and that unless the Buddhists, Shintoists, Mohammedans, et cetera, reform or find Christ they will be lost. Three hundred million Mohammedans believe quite otherwise. Two hundred and fifty million Buddhists believe something else. The Christian Scientists and Hicksites believe still differently. Then there are historians who doubt the authenticity of Christ (Gibbon; Vol. 1, Chapters 15, 16). Where is a moral order which puts a false interpretation on history as in the case of sectarian literature (lists furnished on application), or allows fetiches to flourish like the grass of the new year?

I will admit that in cases such as lying, stealing and the like there is always a so-called moral thing to do or say when these so-called moral principles or beatitudes are inveighed against. You have ridden on a street-car; pay your fare. You have received five dollars from a given man; return it. You have had endless favors from a given individual; do not malign him. Such are the obvious and commonplace things with which these great words are concerned; and in these prima facie cases these so-called principles work well enough.

But take a case where temperament or body-needs or appetites fly in the face of man-made order, where a great spirit-thirst stands out against a life-made conviction. Here is a man-made law, and here is dire necessity. On which side is Right? On which side God?

(1) A girl falls in love with a boy to whom the father takes an instant dislike. The father is not better than the lover, just different. The girl and boy are aflame (no chemical law of their invention, mind you), and when the father opposes them they wed secretly. Result, rage. A weak temperament on the part of the father (no invention of his own) causes him to drink. On sight, in liquor, he kills the youth. The law says he must be hung unless justified. A lie on the part of the girl defaming the lover-husband will save the father. On which side now do right, truth, justice, mercy stand?

(2) A man has a great trade idea. He sees where by combining fourteen companies he can reduce cost of manufacture and sell a very necessary product to the public at a reduced rate, the while he makes himself rich. In the matter of principle and procedure (right, truth, justice, etc.), since his competitors will not sell out, he is confronted by the following propositions: (a) forming a joint stock company and permitting them all to share in the profits; (b) giving them the idea, asking nothing, and allowing them to form a company of their own, so helping humanity; (c) making a secret combination with four or five and underselling the others and so compel them to sell or quit; (d) doing nothing, letting time and chance work and the public wait. Now it so happens that the second and fourth are the only things that can be done without opposition. He is a man of brains and ideals. What are his rights, duties, privileges? Where do justice, mercy, truth, fit in here, and how?

(3) A man's son has committed a crime. The man realizes that owing to deficiencies of his own he has never been able to give the boy a right training or a fair chance. The law demands that he give up his son, even though he loves him dearly and feels himself responsible. Where do right, justice, mercy

work here, and can they be made harmonious and consonant?

These are but three of fifty instances out of the current papers which I daily read. I have cited them to show how topsy-turvy the world seems to me, how impossible of a fixed explanation or rule. Scarcely any two individuals but will be at variance on these propositions. Yet the religionists, the moralists, the editorial writers preach a faith and an obvious line of duty which they label grandiosely "right" or "true," "just" or "merciful." My observation and experience lead me to believe that there is scarcely a so-called "sane," right, merciful, true, just, solution to anything. I know that many will cry in answer "Look at all this great world! Look at all the interesting things made, the beautiful things, the pleasures provided. Are not these the intelligent directive product of a superior governing being, who is kind and merciful into the bargain and who has our interests at heart? Can you doubt, when you observe the exact laws that govern in mathematics, chemistry, physics, that there is an intelligent, kindly ruling power, truthful, merciful, etc?" My answer is: I can and do, for these things can be used as readily against right, truth, justice, mercy, as we understand those things, as they can for or with them. If you don't believe this, and are anti-German or anti-Japanese, or anti-anything else, see how those or any other so-called inimical powers can use all these magnificent forces or arts in its behalf and against the powers of light and worth such as you understand and approve of. And when justice and mercy are tacked on as attributes of this intelligence there is no possible appeal to *human* reason.

"But only look," some one is sure to cry, "at some of the beautiful, wonderful, helpful things which Divine Providence, or Life, or Force, or Energy has provided now and here for man! Railroads; telegraphy; the telephone; theaters; gas; electricity; clothing of all sorts; newspapers; books; hotels;

stores; fire departments; hospitals; plumbing; the pleasures of love and sex; music." An admirable list, truly, and all provided by one struggling genius or another or by the slow, cataclysmic processes of nature: fires, deaths and painful births. Aside from the fact that all of these things can be and are used for *evil* as well as *good* purposes (trust oppression, enemy wars and the like), still it might as well be supplemented by such things as jails. detectives, penitentiaries, courts of law—good or evil things, as you choose to look at them. All of these things are good in the hands of good people, evil in the hands of the evil, and nature seems not to care which group uses them. A hospital will aid a scoundrel as readily as a good man, and vice versa.

Common dust swept into our atmosphere makes our beautiful sunsets and blue sky. Sidereal space, as we know it, is said to be one welter of strangely flowing streams of rock and dust, a wretched mass made attractive only by some vast compulsory coalition into a star. Stars clash and blaze, and the whole great complicated system seems one erosive, chaffering, bickering effort, with here and there a tendency to stillness and petrifaction. This world as we know it, the human race and the accompanying welter of animals and insects, do they not, aside from momentary phases of delight and beauty, often strike you as dull, aimless, cruel, useless? Are not the processes by which they are produced or those by which they live (the Chicago slaughter-houses, for instance), stark, relentless, brutal, shameful even?—life living on life, the preying of one on another, the compulsory aging of all, the hungers, thirsts, destroying losses and pains. . . .

But I was talking of Jersey City and my difficulty in adjusting myself to the life about me, thinking as I do. Yet such facts as I can gather only confound me the more. Take the daily papers which I have been reading to beguile my loneliness, and note that:

(1) Two old people who lived near me. after working hard for years to supply themselves with a competence, were ruined by the failure of a bank and were therefore forced to seek work. Not finding it, they were compelled to make a choice between subsisting on charity and dying. Desiring to be as agreeable to the world as possible and not to be a burden to it, they chose death by gas, locking the doors of their bare little home, stuffing paper and clothing into chinks and under doors and windows, and turning on the gas, seated side-by-side and hand-in-hand. Naturally the end came quickly enough, for Divine Mind has no objection to ordinary illuminating gas killing any one. It did not inform any one of their predicament. Impartial gas choked them as quickly as it would have lighted the room, and yet at the same time, according to the same papers, in this very same world——

(2) The sixteen-year-old son of a multi-millionaire real estate holder was left over fifty million dollars by his fond father, who did not know what else to do with it, the same son having not as yet exhibited any capacity for handling the money wisely or having done anything to deserve it save be the son of the aforesaid father.

(3) A somewhat bored group of Newport millionairesses give a dinner for the pet dogs of their equally wealthy friends, one particular dog or doggess being host or hostess.

(4) A Staten Island brewer worth twenty millions died of heart failure, induced by undue joy over the fact that he had been elected snare drummer of a shriners' lodge, after spending thousands upon thousands in organizing a band of his own and developing sufficient influence to cause a shriners' organization to tolerate him.

(5) A millionaire politician and horse-racer erected a fifteen-thousand-dollar monument to a horse.

(6) An uneducated darkey, trying to make his way North, climbed upon the carriage trucks of a Pullman attached to a

fast express and was swept North into a blizzard, where he was finally found dving of exhaustion, and did die—arms and legs frozen—a victim of an effort to better his condition.

Puzzle: locate Divine Mind, Light, Wisdom, Truth, Justice, Mercy in these items.

By these same papers, covering several months or more, I saw where:

(1) Several people died waiting in line on bundle day for bundles of cast-off clothing given by those who could not use the clothes any longer—not such people as you and I, perhaps, but those who were sick, or old, or weak.

(2) Mr. Ford, manufacturer of automobiles, was convinced that he could reform any criminal or bad character by giving him or her plenty of work to do at good wages and with the prospect of advancement; also that he was earning too much and wished to divide with his fellow man.

(3) August Belmont and J. P. Morgan, Jr., noting this item, concluded that they could not do anything for any one, intellectually, financially or otherwise.

(4) An attendant in an Odd Fellows Home, having tired of some old patients, chloroformed them all—a purely pagan event and not possible in an enlightened age and a Christian country.

(5) A priest, having murdered a girl and confessed to it, no way was found to electrocute him because of his cloth. Men whose services and aid he contemned insisted that he must be proved insane and not be electrocuted, though he did not agree with them.

(6) A young soldier and his bride, but one day married, walk out to buy furniture for their new home; a street fight in which three toughs assail each other with pistols breaks out and before they can take to cover a stray bullet instantly kills the soldier-husband. Subsequently the bride becomes morbid and goes insane.

(7) In nearly all the countries of the late great war a day of prayer for Divine intervention was indulged in, but prayer having been made and not answered the combatants proceeded to make more and worse war—Divine prohibition of combat, according to the Christian dogma, being no bar nor of any avail.

(8) A well-known Western financier and promoter of strong religious and moralistic leanings, having projected and built a well-known railroad and made it immensely prosperous by reducing the rates to the people of his region was thereupon set upon by other financiers who wished to secure his property for little or nothing, and being attacked by false charges brought by a suborned stockholder and his road thrown into the hands of a receiver by a compliant judge, was so injured financially thereby as never to be able to recover his property. And those who attacked him justified themselves on the ground that he was a "rate-cutter" and so a disturbing element—a disturber of the peace and profits of other railroads adjacent and elsewhere. His dying statement (years later) was that American history would yet justify him and that God governed for good, if one could wait long enough!

(9) One man was given one year for a cold, brutal manslaughter in New York, whereas a whole family of colored people in the South was strung up and riddled with bullets for so little as that one of them fought with a deputy sheriff; while a woman who had shot another woman through a window because of jealousy (aroused by her husband's assumed attentions to said woman) was acquitted and then went on the stage, the general sentiment being that "one could not electrocute a woman."

(10) The principal charities aid society of New York had spent and was spending one hundred and fifty thousand dollars per year on running expenses, and something over ninety thousand dollars in actual relief work, though it was explained

that the hundred and fifty thousand brought about much reference of worthy cases to other agencies and private charities, a thing which could not otherwise have been done.

(11) It is immoral, un-Christian and illegitimate to have a child without a husband, yet when six hundred thousand men are withdrawn from England to fight the Germans and twenty thousand virgins become war-brides it is proposed to legalize the children on the ground that it is nevertheless moral to preserve the nation from extinction.

(12) A doctor may advise against child-birth when that experience would endanger a woman or threaten her permanent disability, but if he gives information or furnishes contraceptal means which would prevent the trying situation he is guilty of a misdemeanor, subject to fine and the ruin of his career.

(13) The president of one of the largest street railway corporations in the world finds it wrong to fail to rise and give your seat to a woman, but right to run so few cars as to make available seats for only one-third of the traffic; wrong not to take extreme precaution in stepping off or on a car or crossing the tracks, but right to leave the cars without heat, the windows and floors dirty and the doors broken, making anger, delay and haste contribute to inattention and unfairness; wrong to read a newspaper wide open, to cross your legs or protrude your feet too far, thereby inconveniencing your fellow-passenger, but right to mulct the city, composed of these same passengers, of millions via stolen franchises, watered stock, avoided taxes, the refusal of transfers at principal intersections, to say nothing of the prevention of fair competition via the jitney bus and other means which would relieve traffic pressure, and all with no excuse save that the corporation desires the money; and a tame public endures it with a little ineffectual murmuring.

(14) A man has been found in a Western penitentiary

who had been there for twenty years and who had been sent there because of erroneous circumstantial evidence, the real offender having confessed on his death-bed.

(15) A certain landlord in New York compelled a certain family to move, because, not they, but some of their visitors, wore shabby, hence undesirable, clothes, thus lowering the social and material tone of the apartment house in question and causing their distant but still watchful fellow-tenants much distress of mind in being compelled to live in such an atmosphere. This was a Riverside Drive apartment.

But need I cite more, really?

It is because of these things that I sit in my hall-bedroom, a great panorama of beauty spread out before me, and in attempting to write of this thing, life, find myself confused. I do not know how to work right, truth, justice, mercy, etc., into these things, nor am I sure that life would be as fascinating without them, as driving or forceful. The scenes that I look upon here and everywhere are beautiful enough, sun, moon and stars swinging in their courses, seemingly mathematically and with great art or charm. I am wiling to assume that their courses are calculated and intelligent, but no more and no further. And the river at this moment is begemmed with thousands of lights—a truly artistic and poetic spectacle and one not to be gainsaid. By day it is gray, or blue, or green, wondrous shades by turns; by night a jewel world. Gulls wheel over it; tugs strain cheerily to and fro, emitting gorgeous plumes of smoke. Snows, rains, warmths, colds come in endless variety, the endless fillip which gives force and color to our days.

Still I am confused. For, on the one hand, here is Vaclav Melka, who does not care much for this alleged charm; nor John Spitovesky; nor Jacob Feilchenfeld; nor many, many others like them. On the other hand, myself and many others like me, sitting and meditating on it, are so spellbound that we have scarcely any thought wherewith to earn a living. Life seems to prove but one thing to me, and that is that the various statements concerning right, truth, justice, mercy are palaver merely, an earnest and necessitous attempt, perhaps, at balance and equation where all things are so very much unbalanced, paradoxical and contradictory—the small-change names for a thing or things of which we have not yet caught the meaning. History teaches me little save that nothing is really dependable or assured, but all inexplicable and all shot through with a great desire on the part of many to do or say something by which they may escape the unutterable confusion of time and the feebleness of earthly memory. Current action, it appears, demonstrates much the same thing. Kings and emperors have risen and gone. Generals and captains have warred and departed. Philosophers have dreamed, poets have written; and I, mussing around among religions, philosophies, fictions and facts can find nothing wherewith to solve my vaulting egoism, no light, and no way to be anything more than the humblest servitor.

Among so much that is tempestuous and glittering I merely occasionally scrub and make bright my room. I look out at the river flowing by now, after hundreds of millions of years of loneliness where there was nothing but silence and waste (past so much now that is vivid, colorful, human), and say to myself: Well, where there is so much order and love of order in every one and everywhere there must be some great elemental spirit holding for order of sorts, at any rate. Stars do not swing in given orbits for nothing surely, or at least I might have faith to that extent. But when I step out and encounter, as I daily do, lust and greed, plotting and trapping, and envy and all uncharitableness, including murder—all severely condemned by the social code, the Bible and a thousand wise saws and laws—and also see, as I daily do, vast schemes of chicane grinding the faces of the poor, and wars brutally involving the death of millions whose lives are precious to them because of the love of power on the part of some one or many, I am not so sure. Illusions hold too many; lust and greed, vast and bleary-eyed, dominate too many more. Ignorance, vast and almost unconquerable, hugs and licks its chains in reverence. Brute strength sits empurpled and laughs a throaty laugh.

Yet here is the great river—that is beautiful; and Mr. Woolworth's tower, a strange attempt on the part of man to seem more than he is; and a thousand other evidences of hopes and dreams, all too frail perhaps against the endless drag toward nothingness, but still lovely and comforting. And yet here also is Vaclav Melka, who wants to be a bath-rubber again! John Spitovesky, who doesn't care; Jacob Feilchenfeld, who never heard; and millions of others like them, and I—I think and grow confused, and earn nineteen-twenty a week or less—never more, apparently.

Come to think of it, is it not a wonder, holding such impossible views as I do, that I earn anything at all?

CHANGE

IF I were to preach any doctrine to the world it would be love of change, or at least lack of fear of it. From the Bible I would quote: "The older order changeth, giving place to the new," and from Nietzsche: "Learn to revalue your values." The most inartistic and discouraging phase of the visible scene, in so far as it relates to humanity, is its tendency to stratification, stagnation and rigidity. Yet from somewhere, fortunately, out of the demiurge there blows ever and anon a new breath, quite as though humanity were an instrument through which a force were calling for freshness and change. The old or unyielding die or crumble; the unwitting young arise to take their places. By this same thing which brings man into being is he ended before he becomes inelastic and unpliable. Indeed, Nature constantly replaces her handiwork, quite as in the case of the leaves on the trees, creating newer, greener, sappier things. This is just as true of religions, theories, arts and philosophies as it is of animals, races and individuals. Nothing is fixed. The most convincing and stable thing that you know may well bear inquiring scrutiny, even this law of change. Out of the well-springs of the deep what may not arise?

I often think how foolishly humanity opposes change at times and how steadily and uninterruptedly it flows in, altering the face of the world. With how many astounding changes has not life been visited—astounding only because life never seems to be prepared for the astounding. Our little earth minds, being only seventy years in duration and wise only by reason of the actual experience which can be crowded into that time, cannot but view as astounding those larger natural phenomena which in the endless duration of time come swiftly enough, however incalculably slow they may seem to us. "For a thousand years in thy sight are as but yesterday," a million years but a day in geologic time. But to a being whose duration is only seventy years, whose thinking period about forty, how remote they seem, even impossible! If one could live a thousand years the value of change in connection with many things would appear swiftly enough, and the seemingly astounding would become the natural and even the commonplace.

If one but observes the phenomena of geology and of biology one may see how ready Nature is to quit one form of effort for another, once its uselessness has become apparent, to drop a difficult tendency in one direction and pursue an easier one in another. Indeed, the theory of the pragmatist is seemingly well-emphasized at times by the disappearance of some large and presumably successful species for reasons of difficulty in connection with its sustenance, and the steady rise of some minor creature whose wants are simple and not difficult to satisfy. And it is not necessarily through æons and æons of time that those changes are accomplished but almost instanter, as when behemoth ended and the great auk puffed out. Man says to himself today, "I am the Lord of creation," but is he? A slight change in the chemistry of our atmosphere, so slight that it might be scarcely noticeable, a change in the odor of the air or the taste of the water, could soon end or debilitate him so as to make him of no import whatsoever. It might be unfavorable to man and favorable, let us say, to cats or spiders; then man, a sleepy stumbling creature, would be devoured by his hungry, pagan house pet and the theory of his domination disposed of. Remote? So was the rise of Christianity. If you do not believe this read history, or note what tragedies a slight trace of sewer gas can produce in your own household, how smoke ends a corps of firemen, how water, too much heat, too much cold, may destroy us all. And what star so humble that if it came near enough could not effect one or another of these changes?

Deep below deep lie the mysteries, and theories flourish like weeds in a garden—or let us call them flowers, for at times they are so artistic. Arts spring out of the mysteries, but the arts themselves grow stale if left to themselves. The thing that the individual should remember is that he is a part of this vast restlessness, uncertainty and opportunism. Life will have none of anything forever, neither Egypt nor Greece nor Rome nor England nor America; it will not have anything of one type of god, nor a fixed code of morals, nor a fixed conclusion as to what is art, nor a method of living. We build up rules wherewith life is to be governed, and behold!—some fine day the character of life itself changes and our rules are worthless.

Many of us now dream that there is such a thing as justice, but experience teaches us that it is an abstraction and that what we actually see is an occasional compromise struck in an eternal battle. Many believe that there is such a thing as truth, but, if there is, it is not within the consciousness of man, for he has not the knowledge wherewith to discern it. There is too much that he does not know to permit him to say what is truth. Likewise, virtue and honesty go by the boards as names merely, a system of weights and measures, balances struck between man and man. They are symbols of something which man would like to believe true and permanent. They represent a balance he would like to strike between extremes on either hand, but they are only important to him in his state here. Beyond him lie the deeps which may know them not. All we can know is that we cannot know.

Therefore, what I would most earnestly advocate, if it were of any importance so to do, would be love of change, for by change have come all the spectacles, all the charms and all the creature comforts of which our consciousness is aware. Life appears to be innately artistic in all that it attempts, so that we need not trouble ourselves about that; we can scarcely escape it. If there is a seeming love of order, of stratification, of fixity, in connection with many things, an equally unending force appears to be bent on change and variation, so that that something within us which tends to rigid duty and stratification spells suffering or disappointment for us in so far as we are unable to counteract it. The caution, sprung from somewhere, to keep an open mind is well-grounded in Nature's tendency to change. Not to cling too pathetically to a religion or a system of government or a theory of morals or a method of living, but to be ready to abandon at a moment's notice is the apparent teaching of the ages—to be able to step out free and willing to accept new and radically different conditions. This apparently is the ideal state for the human mind. Not that anything so much more perfect is in store (I, for one, do not believe that), but that a different thing is at hand, always, outside your door, around the corner, beyond the limits of the vision of even the philosopher and the thinker. To be always ready, if such a thing were possible, to meet the new and to know that it will be as valuable as the old—that is the great thing. But what vain advice! for the experiences, the capacities, the tendencies of man are not in his keeping. There is something controlling, of which we are a part and not a part; there is a mystery to which we belong yet which will not show to us its face. Only its impulses burst upon us from day to day and from century to century, making us weep from fear or regret, or faint with terror, or thrill wild with joy. Out of the deeps they come—the realms we do not know. What is Master? Who? What is He or It like? Only by the artistry and the terror and the peace and the change through which it works can we guess, and all names and fames and blames by which we qualify it are as nothing, save that they brighten the face of its one outstanding tendency, which we must accept whether we will or not —change.

SOME ASPECTS OF OUR NATIONAL CHARACTER

OUR most outstanding phases, of course, are youth, optimism and illusion. These run through everything we do, affect our judgments and passions, our theories of life. As children we should all have had our fill of these, and yet even at this late date and after the late war, which should have taught us much, it is difficult for any of us to overcome them. Still, no one can refuse to admire the youth and optimism of America, however much they may resent its illusion. There is always something so naïve about its method of procedure, so human and tolerant at times; so loutish, stubborn and ignorantly insistent at others, as when carpetbag government was forced on the South after the Civil War and Jefferson Davis detained in prison for years after the war was over.

Great men and great events, so I was told in my youth, went to the making of us. The dreams of justly dissatisfied and downtrodden souls elsewhere, so our histories read, impelled them to seek in a new land freedom from the tyrannies which had oppressed them abroad. Once here, they were prepared to fight and die in order that the vision which had led them forth might not end as an airy insubstantial nothing. For us (fatalistically, at any rate, if not really) Columbus sailed from Palos over the uncharted deep; Magellen rounded the Cape of Good Hope; and Vasco da Gama, Cape Horn; Balboa discovered the Pacific, Hendrick Hudson the Hudson; De Soto and Marquette the Mississippi. For us, especially (although before that, great sociologic, economic and moral dreamers had been at work), Locke, Paine, Von Humboldt,

Voltaire, Fourier, de Tocqueville, Rousseau thought and dreamed.

In our new land, fresh upon an unbroken soil, giant spirits swiftly arose to testify to the significance of these dreams—Washington, Jefferson, Franklin, Adams, Hamilton, intellectual and social enthusiasts all—who saw a vision, or seemed to, and dreamed tremendous dreams of the wonders to come to our nation and race, and because of it and through it to the world at large. We, more than any other nation, because ours was the youth and the strength, were to lift and maintain aloft the banner of intellectual and spiritual freedom. We were to do tremendous things, not for the human pocketbook but the human mind and soul. Our children and our children's children were to be free, progressive, fearless, mentally and spiritually alert, entirely loosened from the trammels and chains of superstition and the degradation of poverty and want.

Well, it is quite true that we have done some things: fought wars for our "rights"; freed the slaves (which, however, England did in her territories before we did and without bloodshed); "liberated" Cuba (to no exploitation since?); struggled with the Philippine and Mexican problems (to no final solution however); and then helped to crush the Kaiser without seeking gain for ourselves. However, it is also quite true that at no time in our history has this ideal been quite realized, even though in the hearts of a modest percentage of the population, as can be most safely asserted, this has been a dominant and moving ideal. Perhaps its realization is not within the possibilities of life. We are all slaves essentially, and there have as yet been no measures devised whereby strong and weak people will not be generated at one and the same time side by side. But it is useless to say to the average American that democracy is a dream and can never be realized. He will never believe it. Wars come and go. Strong men arise and plot and conquer and disappear. Weak men fail, and the poor are as much put upon here as anywhere and ignored and laughed at; but in spite of all these facts which endure in the face of every dream—of love, heaven, perfect happiness as well as perfect liberty—the American goes on dreaming his sweet dream, and will. Perhaps he already has all the democracy there will ever be, because he believes that he has it.

Millions of Americans born on this soil or arriving here from other lands believe thus. With them it was and perhaps still is a glowing and enlivening thought that whether they were or not they were supposed to be free. Their children and their children's children somehow are to be heirs to a magnificent and comforting land, one over which a wise and generous form of government, the fruit of the dreams and genius of their forefathers, their generosity and social aspiration, is to rule and ensure all the blessings for which they had hoped and fought.

Well and good. The thing has substance enough even now in the face of some setbacks and because of virgin soil and boundless untouched opportunities, unharassed by war or slavery, which offer to physical labor as well as to the imagination of those who come or who went before us, great opportunity. Their success hitherto has been written into our songs, our books, the public messages of our statesmen and patriots. Even to this day, many who lack even a shadow of the substance of these dreams are still dreaming, if not in their reality at least in their possibility and eventuality here. I in my youth was one of these. I saw in America what many others around me seemed to see: i. e., many if not all of the things for which our forefathers fought and bled: generous, protective and encouraging laws in all walks of life; an amazingly free and unterrified press; a warm, sympathetic and encouraging educational system reaching down to the poorest and humblest child and helping it to rise and better its station;

a real political referendum or ballot system by which all projected laws and movements for the betterment and control of the impulses and tendencies of the people were formulated and with their consent;—and these seemed real enough.

Well?

Well, I still think we have a modicum of these things. The pressure of the strong upon the weak is as yet not too grinding perhaps, and let us hope may never be, although it is daily becoming sharper. The poor are being put upon while being loudly told that they are not—fed on air and kind words, as it were. The powerful are learning that the poor, here as elsewhere, are either fools or, being poor, may not help themselves; a very dangerous state of mind to begin with, I think.

. . . .

Yes, in recent years a certain change has come over the spirit of our original dreams. Our bright morning sky has been overcast with something that was by no means foreseen by the charming and gracious idealists who framed our Constitution and, better yet, our ideals. America, ungracious as it may seem on the part of one who has prospered well enough in it, is neither so free nor so liberal as many imagined it would be. Our press, our school system, our laws, our political methods —do these today answer to the incisive aspiration which was characteristic, or at least was supposed to be characteristic, of the spirit of those who generated the American Republic?

Let us see.

The fact is that what is supposed to be and what is true of American history are two very different things. Because as a people we have instinctively craved some things and have written it into a Constitution that man is inalienably entitled to them, it does not follow that we have them; although most Americans, I am inclined to fear, think so. If I read American history aright, the men who drew up the Declaration of Independence and framed our Constitution were men who, like ourselves today, were in the grip of an ideal which had very little to do with their own condition or the actual working necessities and conditions of life as seen about them. Far from being democratic at that time America was quite the reverse, a most stratified and nobility-aping nation with feudal servants and thralls at the bottom and landed and all but titled proprietors at the top ("History of the Great American Fortunes," Myers). But those same leaders and many followers appear to have been in the grip of a time-spirit or movement which had its roots as far back in time as the thirteenth century, when Europe seemed to give new birth or breath to the pagan spirit and to revolt at the mummery and flummery of kings and the gorgeous paraphernalia of a religious idea run completely to seed. Hess and Bruno were but the foresteppers of Luther. Bacon, Locke, Voltaire, de Tocqueville, Rousseau and Paine, had much to do with the spirit of our American Constitution. Indeed, it is a question whether the latter six, and especially Rousseau with his "Social Contract," his dream of a new social arrangement in which the State should do so much more than it had ever before attempted to do for its constituent units, are not the makers of the Declaration of Independence. Yet nothing that Paine, Voltaire, Locke or Rousseau dreamed or believed concerning the essential capacity of man to govern himself is absolutely true. What is true is that autocracy or single-headed government without genius and a love of humanity is closely allied, or very likely to be, to tyranny; whereas democracy or multiple-headed rotation in control is likely to prove even more dangerous where it is merely dull. It has not even the advantage of being spectacular and interesting. Whether the individual, thus protected against tyranny, is likely to prove a greater and more useful engine or mechanism for the development of more and better thought, more beautiful dreams and ideals than the world ever had before, remains to be seen. Dominant

America, now in the saddle of the world, has an opportunity to prove this.

But does history provide a single analogy? Scarcely. The older nations were not built so much for the individual, that he might have life, liberty and the pursuit of happiness guaranteed him, as for the perpetuation and glory of the State itself, or the King thereof. This was true of Athens and Sparta as well as the Roman Republic, and more recently of Germany. It is very doubtful whether the modern republic is made any more for the humble, single individual than the old-time kingdom. Is not the modern trust-magnate or money-baron who taxes and drives him by his wage arrangements and food extortion as much of a King, or at least a medieval baron, as any such that ever lived? Take Rockefeller, for example. How different is he, or others like him—Morgan, for instance—to the Dons who in combination ruled Spain, laughing at its King, or the money-lords who direct the policy of England today, as did their equivalents in Russia and Germany before the late war?

The truth is that it is given to few, if any, individuals of a nation to understand it. By some it is assumed that the individual must rule. By others the mass. Neither is true. The mass at times must be pitted against the individual, and vice versa. But neither must disappear entirely. That would spell death or slumber. It is also a question whether any nation at any time ever collectively understands itself. Do not some portions of its units always misunderstand other portions? Take our part in the late great war. Sentimentally, a fair portion of America's integral units assumed that we entered the war to "free humanity from slavery" and "to make the world safe for democracy," a very large order; but, to quote one of President Wilson's later utterances, it was for a somewhat different purpose, namely, "the destruction of every arbitrary power anywhere that can separately and secretly and of single choice disturb the peace of the world." Well, that is not exactly the same as making it safe for democracy—but still—. The truth probably is that the nation, propelled by its instinct for self-preservation, entered the war to make America safe. It is not at all unlikely that sooner or later we should have gone to war with Germany had there been no European war. Germany was known to regard with avid eye many phases of this Western hemisphere, its resources, institutions, pretensions; so America very practically, however sentimental the reasons given may be, engaged herself on the side of four or five powers of the first rank (some long friendly, others not uniformly so) to protect her future interests.

From a practical point of view there were, and of course were sure to be, many who disagreed with the somewhat sentimental interpretation of all this. More than one person of authority at the time privately ventured the opinion that in giving so much to aid Europe something should have been done to secure for America its future integrity in the Western hemisphere. "In so far as Mexico, Canada, the West Indies and the Pacific are concerned," wrote one authority, "should not everything be done to further our interests there?" Canada, one would say, thinking of a nation that should be looking reasonably well after its own welfare, should be made at least sovereign—that is, independent of Great Britain—and compelled to enter into commercial and definite offensive and defensive alliances with us; the forts along our borders dismantled and all plans to oppose us at any future time set aside. Again, all of the West Indies, so it was argued, now controlled by European powers, should have been exacted or made independent under our protection so as not to fall into the hands of our enemies in the future. Should not, asked some, a halt have been called to European aggression in China, the open door insisted upon? . . . The seas should have been made absolutely neutral—policed by America, along with others.

A great, even dominant, merchant marine should have been built up. Why the expenditure of endless blood and treasure, with no definite strength added to the point of view—which the United States represents—the right of her ideas as well as those of other people to prosper and grow strong?

But witness what was actually done, where our chief interests lay: Belgium, a country that had never been a completely sovereign State with rights which were inalienable, but a State which was the product of the fears of Europe, commanding our sympathies as though it had been individual and free throughout history. It was torn from Holland by England and France only as recently as 1830. England and France chose its reigning house—the English Queen's uncle, who was speedily married to the daughter of the King of France. Yet with Ireland, India, Egypt, the Philippines, the Boer Republic and other violated lands and nationalities before us, the woes of this one country developed our greatest interest. Japan guaranteed the neutrality of Korea, but annexed it with the consent of the powers. England, before our very eyes, suppressed attempts at "self-determination by smaller nations of their rights" in Egypt, Ireland, India, the Boer Republic. Yet we thought nothing, or at least did nothing. Yet the Balkans, for some peculiar reason not easily to be explained, aroused another sentimental emotion in us. Although one would have said the interest of America in the question of what should become of Russia, Turkey and the Balkans was not direct, and from an old-time practical and political point of view never could be, yet America interfered there as elsewhere, laying down, or attempting to, a rule for the future organization of Europe (self-determination of nations!), and that without any referendum to the American voter, any definite constitutional inquiry as to what *he* thought of all this.

Yet the neglect of the latter, most important in a self-determining democracy or republic, one would suppose, was passed over as nothing, while it was assumed or preached by those in the lead, and in the face of much repressed grumbling, that we were engaged unquestionably with those who were nearest to and best for us intellectually, spiritually and in every other way, nations which would seek, or had invariably sought our welfare in the past. But history, of course, demonstrated that this was not true and that such alliances were only momentarily beneficial, if at all, and later were broken without so much as a by-your-leave or a farewell. But did this serve to alter the state of public feeling or illusion? By no means. In so far as England was concerned it appeared to strengthen it, although this was the first time she had ever been on our side (1776, 1812, 1865, 1896); (1897-8, the Boer War). In all those instances we were anything but pro-British. So again with France in 1788 and 1815, when we practically declared war on her in favor of England, although she had reason to expect our sympathy and aid. Our attitude toward Italy has varied, as it has toward Russia: now friendly, now the reverse. Taking into consideration the brevity of all international alliances one would have supposed that it would have been the imperative duty of American statesmen to make sure that in the course of a temporary alliance with European powers the best interests of the American nation would not have been imperiled, but being powerful and optimistic we assumed that our interests were safe enough, or, if not, that we could make them so, and let it go at that. But supposing we had not been so powerful? Would God, Justice, Mercy, Truth, Progress and a number of other things invoked during the great argument, have been on our side? All failure, some one has said, is due to but two things: weakness and error. Suppose we had been weak? Or foolish?

. . . .

A singular thing in connection with this same great war and the American people, their history, is the attitude of this nation toward the French, at this time and earlier. At the beginning of the war America—Christian America—was decidedly opposed to the French, on moral and intellectual grounds, their literature, their art, their stage, their vile tendencies to naturalism in thought and deed. Even before this, at the beginning of our history, the original Colonists, although of various nationalities—English, French, Dutch, Swedish, Spanish—were finally consolidated under English rule and a fairly systematic warfare waged against the French and the Indians, whom both the French and the English were employing by turns in their contest for supremacy. Yet later, at the time of the dispute between the English and the American Colonies, which ended in the Revolutionary War, French sympathy, due to ancient antipathy to England as well as the intense opposition to autocratic oppression in France, drew the Americans and the French together in a bond of sympathy. The French sent various Generals and Admirals (Rochambeau, Lafayette, Count d'Estaing, Count de Grasse) to help the Americans on land and sea. Yet in 1788-9, when France and Spain declared war on England, and especially later (after the French Revolution in 1789) when the French were struggling to maintain their democratic independence and England was seeking to put the Bourbon rulers back on the throne of France, do you believe that American sympathy was with the French? If you do, you don't know American history. Under the offensive and defensive agreement or treaty entered into between France and the Colonies in 1778, when the latter were struggling for their independence, it was confidently expected by the French that the Americans would help them against England, but nothing of the sort followed. When, in the belief that America must sympathize with France, "democratic" societies, after the French model, were organized throughout the States, and later Genet, the French Minister to America, attempted to fit our privateers on American soil and to establish admiralty ports for the condemnation of prizes, there was great opposition to this. Only read the history of that period (Burgess: "The Middle Period"; Babcock: "American Nationality"; Hart: "American History Told by Contemporaries"). America, according to this new attitude, was now to look out for itself, and in consonance with this in 1793 Washington issued his famous Neutrality Proclamation, leaving France to take care of herself. After the issuance of the Proclamation, Genet, still believing that American sympathy must be with France, appealed to the people and openly defied the Government. His recall followed, of course.

Then followed a very curious state of affairs. The French Revolutionists, angered by the official attitude of America, fell to attacking American shipping, looking upon it as a hostile power aiding England. American commissionaires, sent to adjust our relations with France, were ignored and representatives of the Revolutionists (or so it was claimed), using the initials "X Y Z," demanded tribute and a bribe. Hence the famous comment of William Pinckney, the American lawyer and statesman, who said "Millions for defense, but not one cent for tribute." And that against our late ally, France!

President Adams laid the correspondence before Congress, and the whole country was aroused. War with France was thought to be inevitable and (1798) Washington was reappointed Commander-in-Chief of the Army. Owing to the activity of French sympathizers in America and rabid criticisms in the newspapers of the Government's stand in this matter, the Federalists, who were then in power and who had no sympathy for France, secured the passage (1798) of the famous Alien and Sedition Laws. These laws gave the Government power to banish "foreigners" (meaning the French) from the country and to suppress obnoxious newspapers. Actual warfare with France went on upon the sea! But these laws, being against the then "fundamental ideas" of Americans in regard to free speech and the right of asylum to immigrants, were regarded by enough of the people as proving all the charges of tyranny urged against the Federalists, and at the next election (1800) they were defeated. In the meantime Virginia and Kentucky had resolved, owing to these same Alien and Sedition Laws, that a State might nullify a law of the United States. Congress, because of French attacks on our shipping, formulated the "Spoliation Claims," and it was not until Napoleon (1800), as First Consul of France, agreed to abandon the French Claim that America was still bound by the treaty of 1778 to aid her that these latter were abandoned and peace reached. In other words, we refused France aid in her most trying hour. Yet twelve years later, because of England's continuous attacks upon our ships and seamen, trying to prevent our dealing with France in any way, we went to war with her—only she did not quit until the victory over Napoleon removed the cause of her alleged grievances. One hundred years later, as we have just seen (1914-19), although opposition to France on moral grounds had been steadily growing in America, still in the contest with Germany all the refused sympathy and gratitude of 1800 was revived and France became once more the object of our tenderest solicitude. So much for national moods and gratitudes.

. . . .

Another curious phase of the late great war, as of all countries and wars perhaps, but one which illustrates the American temperament rather clearly, was the attitude of America to one and another phase of it, the psychologic flounderings and back somersaults, as it were, concerning one problem and another. For one thing, as we all perhaps remember, the preliminary internal contest was for peace at any price practically, and any one who suggested mobilizing a large army for self-defense (if nothing more) was, if not a traitor, something of an undesirable citizen. Mr. Wilson, if you will recall, was elected the second time on the slogan "He Kept Us Out of War"; also before we entered the war we were told what a blessing it was in one way, commercially at least. Later, as Germany appeared to be winning and America was actually threatened, the whole world had to be made "safe for democracy," an order so large that publicity was quietly refused it in all countries outside the United States. But that was the sweet milk fed to Americans. Later still, when it came to actually declaring war, although this is a republic and the people are supposed to have a voice in deciding that which they do, no willingness on the part of the authorities, executive or legislative, to refer the matter back to the people for a vote, was in evidence.

And once war was declared, the people were allowed or compelled to "take out" whatever opposition they might feel in private thought, not public or open opposition. It was openly admitted that a referendum might have prevented a declaration of war, yet afterwards public complaint was ruggedly suppressed—by the courts and officials, if not by the whole people, astounding farces by way of law being perpetrated. Still later on, when it came to "raising" troops, money and supplies (controlling food), volunteer service in the first of these fields was swiftly abandoned, and conscription, with all which that implied in the way of force and putting down opposition to it, free speech as well as free action, was used. "Public sentiment," as fostered by an administrative press bureau, to say nothing of much foreign propaganda, controlled or overawed the papers. Overawing sentences, such as forty years in the penitentiary, for circulating a pamphlet in opposition to the current will of the Government, were uniformly handed down in all parts of the nation by a judiciary whose independence, sanctity and what not were supposed to be the bulwark of American liberty. But at whose request?

By what authority? The necessity of strict and impartial justice?

I am not quarreling with the process; I am showing the thin line of difference between autocracy and democracy where necessity or passing opinion favors one course of conduct or another. Later on, when suggestions in regard to food-saving were rather freely ignored, the "suggestions" became not only suggestions but restrictions and, to quote the food administrator, "the restrictions will be voluntary, *but* any evasion will result in compulsory enforcement." Similarly in connection with bond-selling; the people were to lend and lend and lend because they loved their country, but (I am quoting a leading administrative organ) "the period has arrived (October, 1918) to discontinue wooing and soft-soaping. God help the man who is found with filled pockets if the war goes on because of a financial failure here."

And it was not alone in such matters where some independence or at least latitude might have been presupposed, but it extended to a press censorship and an intolerance of opposing opinion which compared rather favorably to darkest days of Russian autocracy. Although America is always naïve and "free," its innumerable blessings of tolerance and the like prated of, still there was but one *publicly endured* opinion in relation to the conduct of the war, and that was pro-war. Any other form of thought was rigidly put down, although in England and France one might say one's say with all but destructive freedom. One woman in New York was actually fined for saying that "Ireland was as good as England any day!" A booklet entitled "Shall Morgan Own the Earth?" and intended to show how the war was profiting some individuals, was first investigated by the Department of Justice and pronounced immune, then later the author was urged "as a patriotic duty" to change the title; still later, even under the milder title, it was refused the privilege of the mails by the Postoffice Department and the author warned that "to circulate it would subject you to ten years in prison. You know it violates the Espionage Law."

And to what astounding fol-de-rol in regard to the conduct of all wars in the future, if not in the past, were we not treated! There were to be no more brutal wars of any kind anywhere. Ever! Oddly enough, the horrors of the Civil War, especially the part of the Northern soldiers in it, were entirely forgotten; also the "water cure" and "Hell Roaring Jake Smith" of the Philippine campaign were forgotten—those natives, for instance, who were stood up in rows and shot down one after another by an officer with a revolver or who had water poured down their throats and into their noses until they died of strangulation, because they could not, or did not choose to, reveal that which possibly they did not even know. Nations as well as individuals have short memories. Before we entered the war it really looked as though a great war must necessarily be fought with tooth-brushes, so great was the opposition to brutality. Later we were never to fight any more wars at all, or if we did it was all to be ended by one war. A little later one of our greatest agonies was that we could not visit on the enemy something much more terrible than they were visiting on us—national annihilation, no less. We could not live in peace with autocracy—although, forsooth, we could live in peace with the Japanese, the Chinese, the Imperial Russian Government before it fell, England in India, England in Egypt—anything and everything, indeed, save with a nation that did not fight as we did. Never again were the erring nations to be restored to their old place in the world. Between chortles over an immense trade increase, a finally united railway system, new and better methods of food control, intensive agriculture, lessons in self-denial and thought, still, and idiotic as it may seem, the war was an unmixed evil; the Germans were all wrong. "The passage of a thousand years will not obliterate the memory of Germany's crime. She will get her good name back when Judas does." (I am quoting from the Cincinnati Enquirer of March, 1918.) And this in the face of the above-recited blessings pointed out in this very paper! What are you to say for such a ragbag point of view, a national intelligence that can blow hot and cold with the same breath?

Actually, it looked for a time as though America were suffering from pernicious mental anemia. Its whole original significance as a forward-pushing, clear-thinking nation appeared to have been clouded over, and, not unlike the bee and the coral insect which apparently serve only one or two purposes in life—the one to gather honey and pollenize the flowers, the other to build a coral island—that it had been invented by Nature to devise and manufacture machinery which it should never have the courage or brains to apply to the limits of their possibilities. It was as though the Germans and the English and the Japanese, seeing the peculiar gifts and mental limitations of the American, were to be permitted to use his gifts, quite as we use the stored labor of the bee or the coral insect, and leave him to go on moiling in his brainless mechanistic way. For the average American, who could so easily invent a flying machine, a submarine, a range-finder for guns, a revolving turret, a steel-protected battleship, a steamboat, and what not, was being urged to believe, at first, that he had no heart for their use and that he was "too proud to fight" or lacked the courage to face the horrible grinding necessities of life; later that he was the greatest fighter of all. Only, having proved that, he was still to believe that he was here only to save the world, never by any chance to further his own interests. His great inventions were to be put aside like toys or sold to others or reserved for moral purposes only.

For note, up to the hour of sheer tragic compulsion, everything was, and no doubt still is, to the average American, a matter of morality, and morality, take note, in the limited sense in which he understood and appreciated morals up to that time. You might invent a battleship wherewith to defend yourself and kill other people, but if you used it for any but a Christian or moral purpose, or the enemy who was non-Christian got it (and used it) it was terrible, shameful, a moral crime, not to be blotted out by a thousand years of expiation. To an American, a machine, however deadly in intention, or its method of slaying, was not to be used unless some distinctly moral end was to be achieved by it. And he was to judge as to the moral end involved. But, to his horror, he was finding and did find that the savage and the pagan could get hold of his machine gun or his flying machine, or submarine, or his battleship, or chemic invention of any kind, and turn it on him without any moral compunction whatsoever—and to his still further Christian horror it worked just as well for the savage or the pagan as it did for him. Nature, or God, did not prevent the submarine from discharging a torpedo at an unarmed merchantman any more than it aided the firing of one from a Christian submarine at a pagan battleship. In short, Nature seemed to be without Christianity or Christian morals, and this shocked the American terribly. He found that he had to lay aside, for the time being anyhow, his fine-spun theories and fight in any way that he could, and he proceeded to do so. Whereupon, he won. But to the American, nevertheless, and in spite of all this, Nature was and is still strictly moral. She has fixed, definite and Christian ways by which she works. Whenever the good American by any chance discovers that Nature is betraying him in any way, not working according to the code as handed down at Sinai, or the Mount in Palestine, he is horror-stricken! What! Nature not working according to the Ten Commandments? The weak do not inherit the earth? "Thou shalt not kill" not a universal law? "Thou shalt not steal or commit adultery" not chemic or psychic truth running through all nature? Who says so? Where is our God who told us these things? Why does he not act in our behalf? Why does he not confound the enemy in his blasphemies, destroy him, for flouting these fundamental religious truths?

But behold, God does not, or did not act until the Americans, bestirring themselves and laying aside their theorizing, proceeded to fight as do the heathen. Then and then only, with the moral and exegetic rust rubbed off and the good American, standing up vital and dangerous, did the tide turn. Up to that hour the tide was indifferently going against him. The heathen, noting his mood, had picked up the American's subtle inventions where he laid them down—fine, powerful, complete but immoral instruments—and had used them for "immoral" purposes. And the machines and the schemes of the American, moral though he thought they were, worked just as well for the unmoral heathen as for himself. To his pathetic horror and utter Christian decay he found that if he was to succeed at all he must not only invent subtle and deadly things, but apply them in the same spirit in which he invented them or other people would—horrific Nature, working through other non-Christian nations quite as effectively as it worked through good Christian Americans. In other words, Nature was not Christian, not moral, in the sense that a race or an organized society working to protect its selfish internal arrangements and comforts may be, and no amount of energetic spouting on this score helped him in the least. Nature, or God, or what you will, showed that it cared no whit, not a snap of her or his fingers, what becomes of man or an American with his theories, religious or otherwise, unless he was able to protect himself. A man or a nation had to have wealth and power to survive, and if the Germans had had more power they would have survived, methods or means to the contrary notwithstanding. Ten thousand pagan shrines did not save Rome from the pacifist destruction which Christianity involved. Ten million Christian churches spouting peace and non-warlike ways could not and did not save America or any other country from a nation which put its faith in war and the ruthless forces of Nature herself. Only greater war on our part could do that, and did.

. . . .

But let us consider some of America's other equally potent and definite moods or opinions in regard to some other things: the negro for one. By the year 1700 slavery, which up to that time had been more or less a matter of individual preference or taste, there being no general Colonial agreement in regard to it, had become an economic institution in Colonial life. A legalized status of Indian, white and negro servants had preceded slavery in almost all, if not all, the English-maintained colonies; but apparently it paid to make them slaves, and they were so made in spite of the legal fact that they were not. Later the difference in the industries of the several States made slavery more desirable in some States than in others, and then the natural boundary lines of the slave territory began to develop. Georgia and South Carolina especially were clamoring for slave-labor on the tobacco, cotton and rice plantations; whereas in the North it was found to be an unsatisfactory system, and so there was early developed in those Colonies a sentiment against a negro population and the institution of slavery in general. It cannot be said that this was due entirely to the economic disadvantage of keeping slaves in the North—there always existed some opposition to slavery in the minds of individuals—but would it have been effective if slave labor had been profitable—as profitable, say, as it was in the South? Jefferson, for instance, wrote a denunciation of slavery into his draft of the Declaration of Independence, but later, owing to its probable effect on slave-holding Colonies, erased it. And negroes were freely lynched and burned in New York City in 1712 and 1741 because they were suspected of a desire to rebel against slavery. A public slave-market was established in New York City as early as 1709!

Yet to hear the average Christian American of today or earlier talk of slavery and its horrors and the great war fought to free the negro, you might assume that he liked him. Far from it. Although a Northern Congress (March 2d, 1867) attempted to impose universal manhood suffrage on the South and (1875) passed a law forbidding discrimination against negroes in inns, public conveyances, theaters and other places, aimed principally at the South, still the negro has never been accepted in the spirit of these laws either in the North or South. In any residence neighborhood anywhere in America, when the black man begins to come in the whites move out. Excellent as he may be, and I have known many who were wholly admirable, he is not even wanted in the same churches or schools. And the feeling, instead of growing less, becomes stronger. Almost daily he is burned alive somewhere in America, and for all but indifferent crimes. America may have fought and bled for his physical freedom, but she does not want him about; and when, as in 1917 in East St. Louis, employers attempted to use him to break a strike, he was murdered (117 of him in that instance), his homes burned, his wives and children driven out of the region; and in the far South, where one of him has even so much as insulted a deputy sheriff, he has been done to death, he and his entire family. Yet the American has no plan for the negro—his threatening future here. He merely allows the question to go begging, trusting to luck, no doubt. Puzzle: does the American citizen want the negro, or doesn't he?

. . . .

Take once more the matter of the American and the idle,

greedy or predatory rich, as you please, and their attitude toward America, all being citizens of the same land. Because a Colonial American once wrote it down in our Declaration of Independence that men are created free and equal, that they are, and *of right* ought to be, entitled to life, liberty and the pursuit of happiness at the hands of their fellow-citizens and the world, the American ever since has been amazed and troubled by the curious human or chemic contradictions of and oppositions to this, not only in others but himself. Struggling along trying to be free and happy he finds that he is constantly interfered with by others who are doing the same thing, and that, Declaration of Independence or no Declaration of Independence, the curious fact remains that the strong, the ruthless, the shrewd get along as well here as they do anywhere and that they are constantly developing ways and means of undermining him and foreshortening his peace and happiness in favor of their own.

Thus, in illustration: (1) A Federal judge (1919) ruled that although Congress (1918) had forbidden any one to compel children of ten or more years of age to labor in cotton mills, still it was unconstitutional for Congress so to forbid and those who wished could so employ children. Result, hundreds of thousands of children returned to eleven hours per day factory labor.

(2) A New Jersey judge, one Gumere by name, ruled (1900) that a child's life, lost in an accident on a railroad or other public conveyance, was not worth more than one dollar, the child not being as yet a source of profit to its parents.

(3) An Ohio circuit judge (William H. Taft, afterwards President of the United States) ruled (1893) that quitting work without the consent of the employer was a criminal offense on the part of an employee.

(4) The Federal Supreme Court ruled (1908) that arbitration in labor disputes is unconstitutional, therefore something

which an employer may not even enter upon with his employees.

(5) The Oregon Supreme Court decided (1903) that a citizen might be legally held in duress (jailed) for one month without trial—this in the face of explicit prohibition on the part of the American Constitution.

(6) The Massachusetts Supreme Court held in one dispute (1906) that where conditions are unsatisfactory there is no remedy open to labor save by individual and personal suit; union or combined action being illegal or unconstitutional.

(7) Four magnates, two of them controlling the production and two the distribution of milk for and in New York City, decided (January 10, 1919) that since they could not agree as to how the profits of the sale of milk in New York City were to be divided among them, New York was to have no milk until they could agree. Time of city without milk, one month.

(8) One Barnet Baff, wholesale chicken merchant in New York City, was murdered because he would not enter upon a scheme with other chicken-wholesalers to fix prices and extort a higher profit from the public. Secondary executors, but not primary instigators or murderers, were caught and electrocuted.

(9) In Lachnor vs. New York (198 U. S. 45) a majority of the judges of the New York Court of Appeals held unconstitutional a law limiting the hours of labor of bakers, many of whom (women) were forced to toil twelve hours daily in cellars to earn wages barely sufficient to keep them alive. The Court held that this law was void because it interfered with freedom of contract.

(10) In Ives vs. South Buffalo Ry. Co. (94 N. E. R. 431), a case in which a railroad employee, crippled for life while at work and without "contributory negligence," sued for recompense, the New York Court of Appeals unanimously decided

that the law under which the suit was brought was unconstitutional. The judges admitted the injustice, since the man was helpless, but held the Constitution responsible.

. . . One might thus go forward for pages. I merely cite these in order to present a few definite instances. The truth is that while the average American imagines he is better looked after and more free here than he would be elsewhere, it is more a matter of thought than anything else. As to his daily earning and living capacity, while it is true that he gets more pay he also pays more for what he buys. A rising scale of wages has so regularly been accompanied by a lowering of the purchasing power of the dollar that he has not been much comforted by higher wages. In fact, the National Department of Labor (February, 1919), after studying family budgets in various cities of the country, announced that the then exorbitant cost of necessities bore heaviest on incomes of one thousand dollars or *less,* although five per cent of the population controlled ninety-five per cent of the wealth of the nation. And one should further note the rising Protection policy of a hundred years, under which the trusts flourished without any notable increase of wages to the local consumer, and the local consumer paid uniformly higher prices than those paid by foreigners for the same grade of goods, often the very same goods made here and shipped abroad. This protection explains the American multi-millionaire; also the American beggar and his slum. It also explains the profiteer. If the average American has had a little more of food and clothes than the men of some other countries, he has also been confronted by the very irritating spectacle of thousands upon thousands who have so much more than he has or can get. He has been made to appear as poor as any churchmouse anywhere, and, worst of all, his woes get but small attention from those who, financially able to control his only medium of expression, the newspapers, insist upon telling him that he is well and happy. If any one should doubt this, let him consult, for one thing, the report of the Federal Trade Commission appointed by Congress (Report handed down June, 1918), wherein it was charged and proved that large exactions and safe profiteering permitted more than one giant concern to double, treble, even quintuple, its capitalization and still earn from 100 to 227 per cent in one instance. Coal, valued at five cents a ton in the ground, was being sold for twenty-two dollars a ton in New York—not over two hundred and fifty miles away. Milk was shoved up rapidly from seven to seventeen-and-one-half cents a quart, and with no interference on the part of any one and no effort to pool the wasteful competition and duplication of systems which, on the other hand, were offered as an excuse for the necessity of the more than 100 per cent increase. Wheat, potatoes, meat, oil, sugar rose in proportion. There was no corresponding increase in the wages, save to unionized labor (which was the only form of labor in a position to demand a just share, and which constituted but ten per cent of all employed). And these had to indulge in three hundred and sixty-seven strikes in the first three years of the war to effect even so much as a twenty per cent increase. (I am quoting figures furnished by the United States Bureau of Labor.) When complaint was made, one enthusiastic retort on the part of a corporation press was that the natural law of supply and demand must be allowed to work, that interference with exhorbitant prices meant curtailment of production at the source. The poor producer, robbed of his just right to high prices under a strenuous demand, would become discouraged and quit! On the other hand, the producer was constantly complaining that he was getting little more than before, while the rapidly increasing cost of labor was cited as proving the need of a from 100 to a 1000 per cent increase on everything—shoes, clothes, food, rent.

That is all simple and interesting enough when one accepts

human nature for what it is: a thing of rough balances and equations only or a catch-as-catch-can struggle in which the strong or the shrewd survive and the weak go under. But when, in the same land in which these things occur, the air is full of a huge hubbub over the extreme merits of democracy, and when at the same time any one who says anything against profiteering or intimates that democracy as such may be subject to at least some of the faults of autocracy is looked upon as an enemy, if not an enemy alien, it becomes slightly anachronistic, to say the least.

. . . .

It is also a matter of pride with most of us, frequently expressed in disparagement of our European contemporaries, that we are a nation of workers. To hold a position in any American community, so the thought runs, a man must have a job. We do not conceal our contempt for the chap who fails to go down to an office or a business every day. Often, of course, our ostentatious *workers* do go down but do very little work. Still, somehow it is felt by the public at large that every man owes it to the community or the nation to put in from six to ten hours outside of the residential district doing something, if no more than twiddling his thumbs. Hence the huge commuting armies oscillating to and fro, between home and office or factory. And yet can it be said that American commercial activity is so immensely more profitable than that of any other nation? Or even as much so? During the late great war it was actually proved that both Germany and England had shrewder and more profitable business schemes and methods. The German plan for national co-operative buying was one. Again, the superior efficiency of the Germans and even the English was one of the facts which burst like a flash of lightning out of a clear sky upon the astonished American, the instantaneous skill with which all national resources—food, clothing, transportation, man-power—were mobilized and put at the services of the nation, the relative cheapness of it all, the efficiency with which it was maneuvered once it was in the hands of the Government. Yet the American business man as well as the American executive, while English and French Commissionaires were instructing our factory masters and "Captains of Industry," had been bustling down to his desk each day, his telephone to his ear, or racing from one directors' meeting to another—and the result to America was the largest war debt per capita for time of service in the war and number of men involved of any nation in the world, not even excepting Russia. Question: Is the American business man as efficient as we think he is? As honest? As patriotic? Is he?

. . . .

Another curiosity of American character is, or was before the war, its adoration of all things foreign. Everything abroad was, if it is not now, excellent, priceless, beyond all praise or blame; whereas anything native, or even occidental, was more or less worthless or inconsiderable—even such things as the Andes and Amazon, as contrasted with the Alps and the Nile; Brazil and Argentina, Mexico and the Canadian snows were as nothing compared to Belgium or Turkey, the Riviera, Asia, Africa. One cannot help smiling a little at times at the grand manner with which the only moderately equipped foreigner, intellectually or otherwise, has been permitted to walk abroad in America and either sniff at or patronize all with which he comes in contact as though it were nothing. And the pathetic desire of the American to live up to what foreigners expected of him—even the waiters of France or the middle class or gentry of England. And as for the English lord, the French or Italian count, the Austrian or even German baron, the Spanish grandee, the Russian prince or Turkish pasha—it is folly to deny that he was—may be even yet, for all one knows—overcome by his attentions. To the American they were inherently better, in some strange sense, more versed in the ways of that great world which he longed to explore. Let a restaurant advertise a French cuisine or cook; a tailor say he is English; a beauty-parlor or dressmaker that it or she or he is of Paris; a writer or artist that he is of French, Russian, Italian, English extraction—creak goes the American knee and instanter your native American is down on his marrowbones, his eyes rolled heavenward. Of Paris! Of London! Of Rome! Of St. Petersburg! Of Vienna! Ah! How many American fortunes have been re-banked in Europe to the order of the thinnest of noble pretensions! What millions have not been expended in an all but useless effort to take on the color and surface veneer of European manners and culture! To this day a foreign make of car, watch, cloth, is inherently better than that of any American manufacture. Formerly foreign plays practically excluded the American product—and rightly enough, in my judgment. We have been "raised" on the foreign book, the foreign picture, the foreign object of art. The Swiss, French or Austrian Alps—how for a hundred years at least have they not outrivaled everything America has to offer!

And well enough, perhaps, since as yet America has no intellectual atmosphere, no native art force wherewith to present its claim, even to itself. A drab, and in places narrowly ignorant, people, imagining that it is religious, moral, conservative—a thousand things that really it is not. Since it is mental capacity that makes a country interesting to itself and others, perhaps it is the drab attitude of the American toward what he has and is which makes his land so uninteresting to himself and others. Give him a different mental attitude, more perspective, "punch," daring in regard to life itself, and America would soon take on a luster not outrivaled by that of any other land.

. . . .

Let us contemplate in this connection another and, in so far as this essay is concerned, final phase of the American mind—for I have elsewhere dealt with moral narrowness—and that is his serious and, were it not so pathetic and at times tragic, one might say, amusing, faith in the ballot and what it will or can accomplish for him. Always, always he is voting for some one—a mayor or a State legislator every year; a congressman every two years, a senator every four or six; a governor every two and a President every four years—and he is under the illusion that thereby, by his vote, his choice of a candidate, he is running the Government and maintaining his so-called liberties. The futility of his vote in the late great war might have taught him something, if only he were to be taught. To this day he has not discovered that, in the main, he is merely voting for individuals thrust upon him by interests and forces over which he has no control, never has had, and apparently never can have, and the election or defeat of whom does not depend upon him or the individuals about whom he is so excited. Mayors, governors, state legislators, congressmen, senators, and even judges and presidents, come and go, but the powerful interests at the top remain; and however much the former may be imbued with a desire to do something for the rank and file, the latter are there to revise or repress their emotions or opinions, and the ordinary voter finds himself about where he was before—of small force or weight in the vast welter of American politics. In short, keen money-masters at the top long since learned that a bare majority of votes anywhere, in or out of congress or a state legislature, is sufficient to confer rule and that, apart from convincing the intellect by sound argument, there were many, many ways of bending the representatives of the people to their will. If this is not true, how is it that five per cent of them have ninety-five per cent of the wealth and the other ninety-five only five?

Those who have made a study of the history of the American judiciary have stood in amaze before the evidence that non elective branches of the Government could so consistently, so openly and so contemptuously undo the work of the elective branches (The Dred Scott decision; the first nullification of the income tax; to cite only two). In what American city would an outside corporation desiring real facilities or privileges not deem itself lunatic not to see the individual local boss, who holds no office of any kind but who is nevertheless the last authority and can tell the local mayor and the local council, often the local governor, what and how? And to whom does the local boss bow—the local governor or national president? Not at all. He makes them, or helps. He bows to but one force: money, the great national monied interests, and none other. It is only when the financial powers at the top fall out among themselves that the least of benefits accrue to the people. It is always so, and has always been so. Equation—equation. The monied individual against the mass; the mass against the monied individual.

In what American city or state, pray, would a popular vote for any franchise or improvement, however needful, be of any avail unless the consent of the financial oligarchs at the top (in Wall Street principally) were first obtained? So much is this a commonplace that even the voters themselves would laugh at the suggestion of any power lying in them to obtain any such thing. Before the Government temporarily took over the railroads during the period of the great war, Lucius Tuttle (a mere single illustration, this), president of the Boston & Maine Railroad, controlled the political life of Maine, New Hampshire and Vermont and lifted up or cast down, at his personal whim, members of legislatures, governors, and United States senators. This is a matter of record, not of rumor. The quondam Senator Chandler of New Hampshire, one of the foremost senators of the nation of his day, was thrown out of office on orders from Mr. Tuttle for the most inconsequential exhibition of independence. And Mr. Tuttle took his orders from Charles S. Mellen, president of the New York, New Haven & Hartford Railroad; Mr. Mellen took his orders from J. Pierpont Morgan, the elder, financial master of Wall Street. And Mr. Morgan took his orders—from whom? God?

Is it not a commonplace of fact, recorded in every newspaper file in America as well as every history worthy the name, that the Goulds, Hills, Harrimans, Rockefellers, Vanderbilts and such great banking houses as Kuhn, Loeb & Company, absolutely ruled—via agents, attorneys, lobbyists, paid legislators, governors and the like—the politics of the states through which their roads passed? The little minnow voters running here and there in schools might amuse themselves as they would by voting for this, that or the other unimportant thing—a mayor, say, or a governor or a president—but let any vital question appear, something affecting the purse or privileges of the money-lords, and the votes of the voters were cast out or miscounted, their elected representatives suborned and made false to their oaths and pledges, the judiciary ruled as the money interests dictated, the newspapers made to cloud the issue with specious or false arguments, and even presidents and parties faced about, leaving the dreaming, ambitious, hopeful voter to dream on or to seek his so-called constitutional rights in some other vain or ridiculous way. Money has always ruled America, and apparently always will. As well ask five cents to contend with five billion dollars as to ask an ordinary voter or business man of minor import to maintain or obtain his so-called rights, privileges, hopes, dreams via the ballot, or any other way. Even decent consideration for him or his affairs from those above him financially has not in the main been granted. He has been whipped and harried by the very rich as they chose; and still, because he has the ballot and can go to the polls every once in so often and cast it—and at such times as he is not whimpering over his defeats—he imagines he rules!

• • • • • • •

The truth is that America has not as yet had an intelligence or a culture worthy the name. It has no visible intellectual purpose, unless it be that of getting money. What little so-called culture we have had, if we have had any, has been borrowed from abroad—principally England, which itself has needed to be revivified along the lines of true culture; for it, too, as to its written and spoken professions at least, has become puritan, pharisaic, religious and never has been democratic. If you want to see America illustrated rather clearly as to its cultural, or lack of cultural, results contemplate the American millionaire. He had, if he has not now, the prevailing idea that money is power; he worshiped and slaved for it in the hope that it would make him wonderful in the eyes of all men.

But consider the pathetic result. He got it. A great war crisis arrived. He wished to be useful with his great (and purely imaginary) power, to do some significant thing which would help the world or at least his country in its hour of stress. Had he the mental or spiritual equipment to see or even feel what was needed? Or was he but one of that immense class of American men and women who discovered in this crisis that business somehow failed to fulfill their spiritual needs and reached out from it, only to find themselves lost in a maze of wider relationships for which they had no technique? Ford organized a peace ship! He, with a little load of editors, journalists, preachers and what not, going to Europe to "call the men out of the trenches by Christmas!" (1915). And the wise American papers, especially in our Middle and Far West, full of his praises, and the probability of success! It could be done! And that, in the face of an amazing and subtle racial movement and propaganda, with war and conquest as its under-stones, organizing in Germany since the year 1813. The rest contented themselves with making more money. So much for one American business giant's success, and his intellectual grasp on life!

. . . .

Take yet another phase in conclusion. At the beginning of the great world war we were constantly hearing talk of "the obligations laid upon us," "our duty to civilization," the necessity for "making the world safe for democracy," when, as a matter of fact and according to our chief spokesman's own admission it was not until between the third and fourth year of the war that we began to realize the true program or purpose of the enemy and that some such enthusiasm as was at first called for might be necessary! We talked of the time having come for us "to play our part among the societies of the world" —and then sent a Root and a Francis (corporation lawyers and agents both, and long since discredited by the American people themselves) to argue with the representatives of a torn and war-worn people seeking a new and better form of social and political life. In the war itself it was apparently assumed that "men, money and ships" (the old American idea of quantity, you see, not ideas or wits wherewith to match the deepest schemes of our adversaries as well as our friends) was the point. But life or international politics and relations or diplomacy is something more than that. It may, and did, require nothing less than a mobilization of new characteristics and unique forces on the part of the pacifistic and religious-minded American. It actually compelled him to open his brains to the fact that life is more dark and mysterious than he had supposed, more forceful and terrible and cruel than his petty little pacifistic and puritanic dreams would previously have permitted him to believe. A door was unlocked, a window opened, and looking out or in on the deeps of Nature he saw—dimly enough even then, it must be admitted—what he has not even yet digested; that Nature has no strict and God-given rules, that nothing is really fixed; anything may arise, and that within the bounds of an unknown arc of equation anything may happen—anything.

But it took a world horror to crack the armor of smug, ignorant self-sufficiency which has covered the average American from crown to sole.

And has he learned? Does life really mean any more to him than it did before? I wonder. As some one else has brilliantly said:

"The fierce, rudimentary mass mind of America, like that of some inchoate, primeval monster, relentlessly concentrated in the appetite of the moment, knows nothing as yet apparently of its own vast, inert, almost nerveless body encrusted with parasites. One looks out to-day over the immense vista of our society, stretching westward in a succession of dreary steppes, and one realizes what it means to possess no cultural initiative or tradition, filling in the interstices of energy and maintaining a steady current of life over and above the ebb and flow of individual necessity or animal appetite or purpose." Money, money, money. To build, build, build, in order to make more money, to make a show, to be better than thou—financially only. It is told of the quondam Russell Sage that he kept near him in his office a strongbox containing $78,000,000 in what he called "gilt-edge" securities, the which, whenever he wished to prove how wonderful he was and how great his life had been, he brought forth and exclaimed: "There—there isn't a man in America who can show that many first-class stocks and bonds! Not one!"

And there wasn't, perhaps.

But what of it?

He died, and not knowing what to do with it (splendid testimony to the American financial intellect), left it all to his wife; who, old and ignorant herself and not knowing what to do with it, but fearing its senseless distribution, left it, after various benefactions to sectarian schools and much influence brought to bear, to the Russell Sage Foundation. And the Russell Sage Foundation, not knowing exactly what to do with it, has been "investigating," and re-investigating and re-re-investigating ever since, this, that and the other, with a view to finding out what it should do with it, what one thing, if any, to help. And what great thing, if any, has the Russell Sage Foundation done?

Well, America, in its own peculiar and interesting way, may find itself intellectually. As an old char-woman who worked for me remarked, "I'm not so dumb than I look." So, possibly and probably, America.

To be sure, a new country must at first borrow its culture from somewhere. One does not come by such a thing instanter and out of a silk hat. Still here is a nation now three hundred years old; it has one hundred and twenty millions of people, if not more; it has as great, and in their way forceful, cities as exist anywhere on the globe; its architecture is already most imposing and fast attaining a splendor hitherto never equaled by any land; a far better and more satisfying mechanical equipment is here than in any nation elsewhere. We have, in so far as material facilities are concerned, more and better opportunities for genuine culture than are now available to the mass anywhere. Then, why are we so bent, I should like to know, upon more money, and, when not that, upon idealistically misinterpreting life? The few genuine thinkers that America has thus far produced are taboo: Poe, Whitman, Twain. Only in one field, finance—not in war, politics, the arts and sheer intellect—do our essential individuals compare favorably with those of other lands. In the main we are too idealistic or illusioned in all but our material affairs. But why all the delusion *in re* the ordinary intellectual facts of life? No single nation has more of wealth, courage, industry, or more impressive varieties of scenery, be it of mountains, lakes, valleys, the coast. We should be, and for all I know are (although the signs are not numerous), at the opening of an era of art and letters such as the world in none of its great periods has surpassed. Yet in spite of all this, and in so far as the mass and its ostensible leaders are concerned, we are intellectually dull and unperceiving in regard to all the basic facts of life. All men are still honest, kind and true (or should be) in America; all women pure as driven snow (or should be) in America. The Sermon on the Mount is our real Constitution; the Ten Commandments our only laws. We all do justly, think kindly, and it is only bad men from the world without, strangers and evil-thinkers, who come from heaven knows where—for our intellectual and spiritual cosmogony does not admit them—to cause us trouble.

America in its own good time may come to a great end. And again it may not. It may be—who knows?—a mere money machine, a honey-gatherer like the bee, a material welter like Rome, without the slightest vision as to what to do or how to act once it has its great store. Other and shrewder nations, far less able financially or physically, may yet lead the giant by the hand, pull him around by the nose. He may be psychologically the same as the wealthy heir to whom life's pains and doubts are and remain unknown, who, being pulled in upon expensive pleasures or the ventures of others and given a superficial reason, is cheerfully willing to pay the bill and depart.

Well, if so be, so be. Who can help it? Nature, if not man, has a way however, if not wisdom. In the course of time She disposes of nations and their dreams, as well as man and his, by rotting them and their material splendors back into primal chemical substances and forces and forgetting them. Rome has gone; Greece has gone; and many, many another. But speaking for a nation that wishes to stand forth mentally significant among the peoples of the earth, that wishes to lead or at least be among those that lead, must not thought—intelligent, artistic, accurate vision—be among its primary characteristics? And is it not possible that as with individuals so with nations—where the power to think is lacking failure follows? Sometimes, and in view of the careers of various nations past and still present, one is hounded by the thought that as with individuals so with nations; some are born fools, live fools, and die fools. And may not America perchance be one such?

One hopes not.

But—

THE DREAM

SCENE: *The vicinity of 115th Street and Broadway, New York City, on a warm, lowery May night. Time, 11.15.*

Approach along Broadway from 116th Street George Paul Syphers, Professor of Chemistry; Forbes Mitchell, Professor of Philosophy; Abner Barrett, Professor of Physics. Syphers is medium in height, slim, fiery, black-whiskered, barbered to perfection. He is loquacious and demonstrative. Mitchell is attenuated, humped, gray. He is quite old. Barrett is fifty, blonde, bald, heavy, silent.

SYPHERS

(As they reach the corner.) Well, I turn off here. That was an interesting discussion we had, eh? The fact is, Mitchell, as I told you the other day, I have passed out of my old materialistic point of view to a certain extent—not entirely—but now I see more order in things than I once did—a necessary if mechanistic order. It seems more or less inescapable to me, doesn't it to you?

MITCHELL

(Doubtfully) Well, yes, I might say—only—of course——

BARRETT

(Dogmatically.) I do not see how any one can doubt law. Everything obeys law of one kind and another.

SYPHERS

Quite so! Quite so! Law, of course. Everything obeys a law or laws of one kind and another. Nevertheless, there are so many confusing contradictions. Laws seem to conflict at times, don't you think, even in chemical and sidereal space. You don't deny that, do you?

BARRETT

Still, more knowledge might prove them to be anything but contradictory.

SYPHERS

Well, I admit that, too. Only I was merely suggesting that I see more definite order than I once did. A few years ago I could see nothing but disorder, chaos, the inexplicable clashing of forces. Of late I am not so sure. This matter of orthogenesis now; it appeals to me very much as demonstrating an intellectual if not a spiritual order, some great controlling force somewhere. I seem to see a definite tendency to order in things. Life has certainly built itself up through the ages in a very intelligent way indeed, don't you think?

BARRETT

(*Loftily.*) Ye-es, of course, only there have been many errors and conflicts there too—sudden stoppage of plans in various directions.

MITCHELL

True, as I was about to point out.

SYPHERS

(*Almost unconscious of interruption.*) I admit that. I admit that. What I am getting at is this: all life, as we know it, is based on the cell—cell origination, cell multiplication, cell arrangement. That is an old story. Now here is something which is my own idea—it's a mere theory, of course—that the whole thing may have been originated, somehow, somewhere else, worked out beforehand, as it were, in the brain of something or somebody and is now being orthogenetically or chemically directed from somewhere, being thrown on a screen, as it were, like a moving-picture, and we mere dot pictures, mere cell-built-up pictures, like the movies, only we are telegraphed or telautographed from somewhere else, like those dot pictures that are now made electrically, built up dot by dot, millions of them coming rapidly by wireless or wire and being thrown on a screen of some kind—ether, the elements—you know what I mean. You have seen the telautograph pictures I mean, of course?

BARRETT

Yes, of course. Very ingenious. Very ingenious. But how do you prove the origination of the cell in the fashion that you want?

MITCHELL

(Aside.) A rather slow movie, I should say, considering the length of time it has taken to build it up.

SYPHERS

Well, in this way—it has its drawbacks, of course; you remember the experiments of that Irish scientist Burke, don't you? He generated what he called a radiobe—a single cell in a plasm culture which he had hermetically sealed and which he kept under the influence of radium. I do not recall the exact facts of the case at the moment, and I do not believe that his deductions have since been accepted, but that is neither here nor there. That idea of his illustrates mine very well. If we could prove that one cell, one radiobe, had been or could be originated or generated by an outside influence of this kind—radium, if you wish, in a plasm of that kind—we would have to admit that the whole thing might be built up in some such fashion. Why, you could base a new philosophy on that, Mitchell. One radiobe generated in a plasm culture under radium or something else, some autogenetic force manifesting itself through a thing like radium, and there you are. After that you would have to grant the possibility of millions and billions of cells coming in that fashion, whole nations constructed of cells, as they have been.

MITCHELL

My dear Syphers!

BARRETT

There was some hitch in that experiment, however. The chain wasn't quite complete.

SYPHERS

I know—I know. I grant you that. All I'm insisting on is that if one cell, one radiobe, say, can be generated by a synthesis of energy, why not millions? And if millions, why not billions, the whole human family, in short, since we are a synthesis of cells—this whole visible scene in all its details? I know it sounds wild, but *(to Mitchell)* I have heard you yourself say that you thought it might be possible that we were all a part of some invisible psychic body, force body, in the mechanism of which we function in some way, just as the cells do in ours.

MITCHELL

(Much flattered.) Yes, I have said as much.

SYPHERS

Well, then, why may not my theory be true?

BARRETT

May? May? Of course it may. But how are you going to prove it? I myself have suggested that Mitchell's larger psychic body, as he calls it, may be nothing more than a fetus, a secondary creature being built in the womb of a still larger organism, but what of it? All of us, everything that we see here, may be nothing more than parts of organs that are being constructed in some huge womb. This so-called higher psychic body may not even be complete yet, not ready to be born in its realm. But how do we know? There's nothing to prove it.

SYPHERS

Just the same, if I had a few hundred thousand dollars I would enlarge my laboratory and pursue this subject. I believe that something may be discovered. I believe that I could prove it in the course of time. Why, snow crystals, tree and flower forms, everything, gives us a hint, sometimes instantaneously.

Why do snow crystals assume almost instantaneously and out of nothing their beautiful forms? The controlling impulse is certainly artistic, isn't it, and outside of anything we know? *(He notes that he is pressing the matter too far and boring his two friends.)* Well, good night. Glad to see you two at the meeting to-night. It was interesting, wasn't it?

BARRETT

Very. *(To himself.)* He's a terrible bore.

MITCHELL

Delightful. *(To himself.)* I'm glad he's done. *(They bow and depart.)*

SYPHERS

Dolts! Fogies! That's always the way, dull and cautious.

BARRETT

(As they walk up the street.) An ingenious theory, but dangerously speculative. He ought to read Stromeyer on "Impulse."

MITCHELL

I often wonder about his work and just how sound he is.

SYPHERS reaches his own door and goes up the steps, unlocks it and mounts the inside stairs to his room. He lights the gas in a chamber which is half library and half bedroom.)

SYPHERS

(Seating himself and gazing about dreamily.) A great idea. I'm sure of it. Along this line is coming a scientific revolution. If I had enough radium and stromium, why—but they cost so much. *(He yawns.)* Life is really a dream. We are all an emanation, a shadow, a moving picture cast on a screen of ether. I'm sure of it. *(He gazes about, yawns again, and begins to undress.)*

A TELEGRAPH INSTRUMENT

(At 110th Street Station.) Tick—tick-tick——tick-tick-tick—tick-tick——tick—tick-tick-tick-tick-tick——

TELEGRAPH OPERATOR

There goes that blamed machine again *(begins to write)* "Professor George Paul Syphers, 621 West 115th Street, New York City. Your uncle, Edward Fillmore, died at eleven to-night. By the terms of his will you are the sole heir to the bulk of his fortune, three hundred thousand dollars. Come at once. A. J. Larywind, Counsellor," (*Aside.*) I wish someone would leave me three thousand cents. *(To a waiting messenger.)* Here, Patsy. Take this up to 115th Street.

PATSY LAFERTY

(Cock-eyed, overgrown, contentious.) Sure, it's just de night to keep busy. It's goin' to rain, an' it's me late watch. Oh, well, dere's nuttin' like bein' poor an' honest. *(He seizes a black cotton umbrella almost as large as himself and goes out.)*

SYPHERS

(Crawling into his bed.) The curious thing is: why should any dominant force outside this seeming life wish to create it—the smallness, the pettiness, the suffering? I must write a book about that. Here I am—*(he suddenly bethinks him of opening a window and gets out. Looking out)*. It's going to rain, I do believe. *(He returns and stretches himself to rest.)* There, it's thundering already.

PATSY LAFERTY

(Trudging solemnly up Broadway.) It's funny, dese mokes wot git messages at one in de mornin'. I'll lay a even bet I don't git nuttin', neider. If you'd come wit a million dollars after twelve o'clock dere's guys wot'd git sore.

SYPHERS

(Dozing, but still continuing his speculations hazily.) I must try to find the psychic impulse which originates and directs the cell. That is the great thing. We're all shadows, I say, shadows—adumbrations—impalpable nothings—rumors

—dreams. *(He turns on his side.)* If our ills become too great we might be able to wake up or drive them away by thinking of this. It may be that that's what we do when we die—wake up. But that's Christian Science, isn't it? Bah! *(He snores slightly.)*

PATSY LAFERTY

(Arriving at the door and closing his umbrella.) A fine night, dis. An' he won't be in. Dat's my luck. *(He rings the bell.)*

SYPHERS

(Beginning to dream.) Radiobes! Radiobes! Flying radiobes as big as houses—monsters—*(He stirs. As he does so the ringing of the bell, the rising wind and the thunder and lightning, which rapidly become violent, identify themselves in some weird way with his thoughts. He is on a large plain now over which a battle is being fought. The flashes of lightning and bellows of thunder gradually identify themselves in his mind with some impending disaster, vague and yet oppressive. He begins to cerebrate in an imaginative, illogical way. A sense of something ominous pervades him, a feeling of great change. Then the rat-a-tat-tat of machine guns begins and armed figures running and fighting appear in the distance.)*

SYPHERS

(Who once saw military service.) War! And fighting men! *(It begins to rain.)* That is a machine gun. Now I am in real danger. How did I come here, anyhow? *(He moves a hand, thinking he is hurrying to cover.)*

PATSY LAFERTY

(Standing at the door, ringing the bell and shifting from one foot to the other.) Wot a swell night! Wot a swell night! Now it's startin' to pour an' I'll have to stand here aw'ile, I guess. Holy Cripes, dem drops is as big as marbles! *(He pushes the bell again.)*

THE PROFESSOR

(Hearing the whirr of the buzzer in his dreams and taking it for the rush of artillery and men.) Ah, the horror of war! What was I thinking?—ah, yes! If one had some method of waking up. *(He mingles the dream notions of his waking philosophy with the figures of his dream.)* Then there would be no more war, no horrors. It is entirely possible, now that we know this existence of ours is a dream. I may be dreaming now—who knows? If so, I could wake up and all my ills would vanish—or would they? *(As the thunder and lightning increase.)* How horrible this is! *(The dream sky lights up as if with red fire.)*

PATSY LAFERTY

T-r-r-r! T-r-r-r-r! T-r-r-r-r-r! Wot's de matter wit dis bell? W'y don't de guy answer?

THE PROFESSOR

(Dreaming and looking about him in apprehension.) War! War! How terrible! How did I come here? How does there happen to be war? Those are fighting men over there! They are killing each other! Horrors! But the great thing is to escape. That fire is dreadful. It means death. *(He struggles to put himself in motion and grunts in his sleep.)*

PATSY LAFERTY

(Ringing again.) Well, dis is some sleeper, all right. Or else dere ain't nobody home. I'll kick, I will. *(He kicks.)* Come to! I ain't supposed to stand here all night. *(Kicks and knocks are without result.)*

SYPHERS

(Still dreaming heavily.) And here comes a file of soldiers—I hear them tramping—a great company. Merciful heavens, they see me! *(He begins to run. As he does so the file of dream soldiers begin to run also.)*

THE FILE OF DREAM SOLDIERS

Halt!

THE PROFESSOR

(Breaking into a heavy sweat.) Great God! I haven't a place to hide! Oh, Lord, what shall I do? *(He turns, and in his dream he imagines a deserted stone hut set in a grove of thick tall trees, which seems to offer shelter. He runs towards the hut.)* As I live, here is a stone hut among thick trees! I'll hide in it. Perhaps they won't see me. *(He dashes wildly in, slamming a heavy door behind him.)*

A SCORE OF DREAM SOLDIERS

(Hurrying after him and knocking with their musket butts on the door.) Knock! Knock! Knock!

PATSY LAFERTY

(At the door.) Knock! Knock! Knock! Gee, wot a night! Dese raindrops look like spits. An' dat lightning! Dat last one looked like a telegraph pole standin' straight in de air!

SYPHERS

(Cowering in a corner.) Oh, Lord! My life is worth nothing! Here I lie hiding in an empty stone hut, and those men at the door want my life. What is life? A dream! A dream!—but, oh, such a precious dream! I would not want to disappear—not yet! No, no! I would not want to wake up. I don't want to die—not yet. Not yet! *(As he lies there cowering, all the coruscations and thunder of a great battle afflict him; cannon, machine guns, human cries, commands. He cowers lower, and yet in spite of the thickness of the walls which seem to protect him he can see through them to the surrounding trees to where the dream soldiers await him—tall men in red coats and towering shakos—and beyond them again to the battlefield, red with flame and gore. As he stares, the men in the shakos glare at him.)*

FIRST DREAM SOLDIER

(Pointing at him and speaking to another.) We'll easily

get him out of there. Can't you see him lying there, close by the wall? *(To the other soldiers.)* Bring a battering ram. *(A soldier starts off.)* No, bring a cannon. We'll blow him out. *(A second soldier goes.)* He thinks we can't get him, but we can. *(Other soldiers draw near. They move in the curious, indefinite way common to figures in dreams. Nothing is clear, and yet there is a sense of impending disaster. The Professor studies the nature of his predicament with a sense of horror.)*

THE PROFESSOR

(Lying on the floor, close to the wall.) Ah, if I could only escape! I was thinking a while ago that life was a shadow of something else, an adumbration, a thing built up point by point like the dots of a telautographed picture. Now if that were so I could get out of here. It would be a dream. I could wake. I could cry "Avaunt!" I could stir and it would all disappear and become as nothing. But here! Here—*(he pauses and stares. A company of dream soldiers on horseback gallop up and swing a cannon into position.)*

THE CAPTAIN OF THE DREAM SOLDIERS

(Dramatically.) Position! *(They unhook the horses and man the guns.)* Load! *(A shell is put in.)* Fire! *(It belches flame and smoke. A great hole is torn in the wall of the hut.)*

PATSY LAFERTY

(At the door.) Gee, dat las' crack was a boid! If he kin sleep troo dat he soitenly won't hear me—or maybe he ain't home. Well, I might as well stand here. I can't go back in dis. *(He decides to make himself comfortable in the doorway.)*

THE PROFESSOR

(Imagining he is crying.) Help! Help! Oh, save me! Save me! *(He realizes that he emits no sound, and groans.)*

FIRST DREAM OFFICER

Once, more, men! Another shell here! *(Another is put in.)* Fire!

THE CANNON

Poof! Boom! *(Another great hole is torn in the wall.)*

PATSY LAFERTY

(As a second electric crash occurs.) I don't know wedder I'd better stay here. I don't wanna get killed. *(He walks about uneasily.)*

THE PROFESSOR

(Heavily and desperately.) I am lost! I know it. Oh, if my idea were only true! What if all this turmoil and agony were a figment of the mind merely, a cell or dot picture? Here I am in this hut; these soldiers are about to destroy me. If I could just cry "Avaunt!" "Disappear!"—or if I could know that I am not real, and disappear myself. I wonder if I might not try it? *(He jumps to his feet.)*

A FLASH OF LIGHTNING

Click—Sssssss!

A CLAP OF REAL THUNDER

Boom————!

THE PROFESSOR

(To the dream soldiers, defiantly.) I defy you! Do your worst! You're not real! I'm not real! This whole thing is a dream! I'm a dream, or I'm dreaming! I defy you!

FIRST DREAM SOLDIER

(Drawing near with a rifle.) Is that so? You defy me, do you? I'll show you whether I'm real or not. *(He takes deliberate aim.)*

SECOND DREAM SOLDIER

Yes, kill him. That's the way!

THE PROFESSOR

(Lifting his hand.) Wait a moment! Don't! I—I'm not sure!

FIRST DREAM SOLDIER

But I will, just the same. You say I'm not real? I'll show you whether I am or not! *(He fires.)* How does that feel?

THE PROFESSOR

(Who has twisted himself about until he has one hand under him in a most painful position.) Oh, God, I'm shot! And now I'll die! This whole scene, real or not real, will pass away and I will never know—or will I? And yet once I was a man, and it was good to be alive. Oh! Oh! Oh! *(He weeps and sinks down. A powerful clap of thunder half arouses him. The knocking of Patsy Laferty becomes dimly audible, a cross between the clatter of musketry and a knock. He stares at the soldiers, some of whom seem already to be growing thin and wavering.)* Dying! Alas! I'm dying! Never will I see this wonderful world any more! *(He partially wakes.)* Or will I? What's this—I'm not dying, after all! They're not real! I'm only dreaming. How astonishing! *(To the dream soldiers, defiantly.)* You're not real, after all. You're mere shadows, thin air. I'm dying, but you're not real. This house isn't real. It couldn't have holes in it if it were, or at least I couldn't have seen through it in the first place if it hadn't. You're shadows, tissues of nothing, a mere fancy of the brain. Oh, wonderful!

FIRST DREAM OFFICER

(Standing by the cannon.) Are we? Well, you're a fool! Wait! You may be waking into another state, but you'll be dead to this one. But we won't. Ha! Ha! We'll still be here, alive. *(To the second dream soldier.)* He thinks he's not real. He thinks we're not real. He thinks he's not going to die, but wake up into something else! Ha! Ha! *(They look at each other in a strange, fading, unreal way.)* When he passes out of this won't he be dead to this, though?

THE PROFESSOR

(Amazedly.) What is this? Am I dying, or waking up? Which is it? Are there various worlds, one within another?

Are those soldiers really real? Great heavens! How strange! I am waking up, and yet this world in which I am is real enough. I died there. I certainly did, or I am dying there. *(The house begins to dissolve like smoke; the trees can be seen through the bodies of the soldiers.)*

PATSY LAFERTY

(At the door.) I'll give dis guy one more spin an' den I'll quit. I ain't gonna stand here all night, rain or no rain. Clump! Clump! Clump! *(He kicks with his heel at the same time that he rings.)*

THE PROFESSOR

(Bounding out of bed.) Oh, blessed heaven! What is that? I'm not dead, after all! I am really alive! It was a dream, all of it. How glad I am to be awake! *(He reaches for his trousers.)* But those soldiers! They argued with me about it! They did! They made fun of me! Isn't that amazing! This dream is a call to me to seek out this mystery. If ever I get money enough to do it that is certainly what I will do. I shall devote all my life to solving this mystery. If only I could find somebody who would endow a laboratory for this purpose. *(He pauses and stares, as the bell whirrs.)* Yes, yes! I'm coming! *(He bustles downstairs, turning up the light as he goes.)*

PATSY LAFERTY

(Irritably, as the door is opened.) Syphers?

THE PROFESSOR

Yes.

PATSY LAFERTY

Tellygram. Sign here. *(He produces about a half inch of pencil and holds up a signature blank. The Professor signs. Absentmindedly he tears open the message, but while doing so turns and closes the door. Patsy Lafferty stares at it disconsolately.)*

THE PROFESSOR

(Reading.) A miracle! $300,000! Just what I need for that laboratory! It's a sign! The dream is a portent, a call! My poor dear, good uncle! What moved him to leave me that? Now I know the dream was an omen. And yet—*(thinking of a certain maiden he has been courting)*—should I really do that? Three hundred thousand are three hundred thousand, and where would I ever get that much again? *(He hesitates mentally.)* We could live beautifully on that. I'm not so sure. Perhaps I could get some one else to furnish that money. *(He starts upstairs.)* But that poor boy! I forgot to give him a penny, and it's storming. *(Returns and reopens the door, looks up and down the street, and comes back.)* Dear, dear, dear! I should have given him a dime, anyhow—bringing such a fortunate message. But I must think about this laboratory, though, and this money. I must not act too hastily or inadvisedly. Three hundred thousand are three hundred thousand, and——*(He goes upstairs again solemnly.)*

PATSY LAFERTY

(One block south, staring at the sidewalk.) Wot did I say? Wot did I say? Dey never comes across wit nuttin' after twelve—nuttin'. Not if you handed dem a million.

THE AMERICAN FINANCIER

THE long line of American financiers, beginning with Stephen Girard (1750-1831), and extending via Astor, the Vanderbilts, Goulds, J. P. Morgan and F. W. Woolworth to Henry Ford of the present time, suggests nothing so much as a procession of thrifty and, in the main, cat-like animals weaving a devious way amid intricacies of law and public opinion and theories as to morals, duty, charity and the like, until finally one is led to conclude that, by and large, the financial type is the coldest, the most selfish, and the most useful of all living phenomena. Plainly it is a highly specialized machine for the accomplishment of some end which Nature has in view. Often humorless, shark-like, avid, yet among the greatest constructive forces imaginable; absolutely opposed to democracy in practice, yet as useful an implement for its accomplishment as for autocracy; either ignorant or contemptuous of ethical niceties as related to thine and mine, yet a stickler for all that concerns mine; moral and immoral sexually—both types abound; narrow to all but an infinitesimal line in nearly all that relates to the humanities as applied to individuals; wise and generous in the matter of large, even universal benefactions, yet guilty of the meanest subterfuge where their own interests are concerned; and seeking always to perpetuate their own fame. In other words, typical men and women of an avid pagan world (vide Hetty Green, Russell Sage), yet surrounded by religious and ethical abstrusities for which they care little and of which they understand less.

Such might be called the pathology of the genus financier, not only in America, but everywhere.

In regard to our American specimens it is more or less anachronistic to speak of them as purely American in character, although, in a way, they are. The organizing and financial type of mind—American, European or any other—is really little different from that of all preceding countries and ages. Yet financial manipulation, in the extended modern sense, is comparatively new. It dates from the industrial revolution in England in the eighteenth century. There was a time when the organizing type of mind, comparable to our modern examples, was engaged in other things: money-lending and exchange principally. The machinery for finance in the modern sense was lacking. You might have found a J. P. Morgan, a J. D. Rockefeller, or a Russell Sage as Keeper of the Exchequer and Supervisor of the Grain Stores of, say, Egypt or Assyria, or Adviser to the King, whether he ruled in Babylon, Persia or elsewhere. One cannot help thinking what an excellent type of Keeper of the Exchequer, Vizier or High Priest our own John D. Rockefeller would have made. The robes! The sanctity!

As we come forward in history to the end of the Roman Empire and the beginning of that mental darkness known as the Middle Ages, when all intelligence, financial and other, seems to have been completely swept away, we find the purely financial and organizing type but slowly developing. Joseph (he of the coat of many colors), fabled Crœsus, who ruled in Asia Minor, and Lepidus and Mæcenas, friends of triumvirs, emperors and poets, are excellent examples of the ancient financial type. Their like is not to be found until after the revival of banking and trade in the fifteenth century. And if you look back you will see that to-day, in another way, we have been repeating in Wall Street (or were until a few years ago), the type of man who occasionally sat as Emperor over all the Romans. If you are inclined to doubt this you might, if the opportunity offered, examine the collection of portrait busts of Roman Emperors of the highly executive and financial type

(Hadrian, Trajanus, Titus, Caracalla and the rest) in the Vatican, the Musee del la Terme and the British Museum. Hadrian, for instance, was as much like the late Commodore Vanderbilt, side whiskers and all, as one man might be to another; and Trajanus greatly resembled the late Mark Hanna, whose name somehow suggests that of a Roman. Any one of ten or fifteen portrait busts of ancient Roman Emperors might almost be mistaken for Armour, Morgan, Gould, Sage, Crocker, Stanford, Hearst. For example, compare Russell Sage to Julius Cæsar; or Wm. H. Vanderbilt to Augustus Cæsar. Indeed, if you were to examine some of the major operations of the successful Roman Emperors you would find that their power to maintain their positions with the Prætorian Guard and the Patrician Class (which was really the Roman world, so far as they were concerned) was largely financial and organizing in the same peculiar spirit in which we find those qualities operating to-day.

It is not until the fourteenth, fifteenth and sixteenth centuries in Italy, Flanders and north Germany that one encounters financial types very like those with which we have been very recently dealing. Italy of the Renaissance found a most interesting specimen of this type of mind in Cosimo I. of the Medici —"Pater Patriæ," as he was called—who was little more than a very active Vanderbilt I. of his day. The family first conducted a successful pill business, then Cosimo engaged in the banking business. Being a financier he secured control of nearly all the financial channels of Italy, France, Greece, a portion of Egypt, and the Lowlands. It is charged that he brought about the death of one or two enemies in Florence, not because he disliked them, but because he thought they were dangerous to his interests, and once he came very near to being gibbeted himself. He was a patron of the arts, not so much because he was emotionally and poetically enthusiastic about art as because, as at present, it was a distinguished thing to be. The trick of currying favor via art patronage is old. His descendants, having less of his force and more of the refinement which invariably follows wealth, did more for art and less for trade, and so while we see the Medici family identified with the most brilliant period of Italian art we also see it slowly sinking into financial and political insignificance. That it finally degenerated and passed out is no reflection on the significance of Cosimo, his primary import. Although the coldest and most financial of them all, he was also the best.

This was equally true of Louis XIV of France and Frederick the Great of Germany, organizing and financial types both, although monarchs by birth.

England has had its full share of the type in the officers and directors of its famous East India Company (Warren Hastings, for one) and their efforts to monopolize and exploit the Indian Empire, as well as in the very excellent Rothschild, who flourished at the time of the Battle of Waterloo and who stood behind a tree to view the battle in order that he might decide for himself which side was going to win and so get to London and the stock-market first. There he spread the report that England had lost so that the already trembling stocks of the nation might tumble and he be able to buy them for a song. When he had gathered in all the shares he could carry he gave out the correct news of the victory and reaped his harvest. Dishonest? As you choose to look at such things. But when has high finance been honest, or let us say, considerate of the interests of others? The financial history of this particular individual is so selfishly single-minded as to be almost ridiculous, suggesting a power which invents man for one purpose and no other, as generals, saints and the like are invented.

In America, the history of our financiers is so full of thievery and selfishness as to appear comic were it not for the mass misery which so many of their deeds involved. Stephen

Girard, for instance, stole his employers' ship at the outbreak of the American Revolution (pretending it had been sunk, of course), and with the proceeds opened a wine and cider business in Philadelphia. John Jacob Astor drugged the Indians with fire-water and bought their furs for a song, as well as bribed Government agents to permit him so to do. J. P. Morgan senior at the outbreak of the Civil War sold the Government five hundred of its own condemned rifles for twenty-two dollars each, after having but the moment before bought them *from* the Government for three dollars and fifty cents each, and that with money borrowed on the strength of the proposed contract. (History of the Great American Fortunes, Myers, Vol. II., page 172.) Cornelius Vanderbilt blackmailed the United States Steamship Company, plying between New York and California, in the amount of nearly $500,000 a year by threatening to operate a rival line. (Ibid. Vol. II., pp. 120-121.) Jay Gould robbed the various States through which his railroad ran and drove some of his rivals to suicide. Russell Sage robbed the city of Troy of a railroad and bribed the Minnesota and other State Legislatures. (Ibid. Vol II., pp. 12-16.) The record is too long to be more than mentioned here; those interested should read Myers' remarkable work, in which the crimes as well as genius of our long line of money kings are described in full.

That the world has always been troubled with the huge financial innovator and the self-seeker is of course a commonplace; the objection to him has been, as a rule, that he has too few human traits. Like the astronomer, the mathematician, the philosopher and the historian, his thoughts are more or less remote from the concerns of the ordinary individual, although his dealings are with him. To do anything which is to be of benefit to the individual it requires the mind that sees the individual en masse rather than in particular. Indeed, the thing that has always confronted the individual of ability since the beginning, aside from his own inner driving emotions, ambitions and needs, is this same organized need of the mass as represented in constitutions, governments, declarations, which in order to advantage himself he must flatter, satisfy or exploit—but which he must meet in some way or fail. And only when the organized sense of the mass becomes sufficiently intelligent for it to act in concert is it possible to sweep away or even curb the individual. For the individual and the mass are interdependent facts, and the one cannot escape the other, try as each may.

But never, apparently, previous to the French Revolution, which was a revolt against centralized and hereditary constructive craft and ingenuity, had it occurred to the world, or rather the mass, to rout these individuals and make pariahs of them, although the world in recent days has developed an especial aptitude for it, one must admit. England, which is not so much a democracy as an ordered hierarchy of powers, largely financial in character, has never felt called upon to drive these gentlemen from their positions or quarrel with them for the often singular and fantastic manner in which they have achieved their success, or the indifference they may have displayed toward the millions below them. The gentlemen at the top may or may not have intentionally done anything for the peasants at the bottom in the past, but until very recent days they have not been asked to relinquish their control of the machinery. Yet now the world presents another angle to this proposition: the organizer and financier is being suspected and harried everywhere. Only in America, the home of anti-financial legislation, the multi-millionaire is apparently becoming safer than ever and more powerful. Yet to the economist, the historian, the student of politics, it is already a truism that economic reforms are not and never have been permanent; also that no one, however self-interested, ever succeeds wholly in working for himself.

He must do something for the mass if he is to do anything for himself. It is a condition of life, not a theory.

The trouble in America, in so far as this type of mind is or was concerned, is or was this: that when it appeared it came rather speedily and roughly into contact with the pen-written notion or ideal embodied in our American Declaration that all men are born free and equal, and that they are possessed of certain inalienable rights, among which of course are those of life, liberty and the pursuit of happiness. And these latter were not supposed to be interfered with by financiers or organizers seeking power. Yet the race has always been, and will so remain, of course, to the swift, the battle to the strong; chemical and physical laws not being easily upset by fiats of government. Time and chance still continue to operate as before, sometimes to destroy the strong, sometimes to destroy the weak. The best that can be said for the theories laid down in the American Declaration is that they do more credit to the hearts of those who penned them than to their heads. Yet that these sentiments so expressed should have moved to bring about a conflict between the American individual and the American mass might well have been foreseen, although curiously it has not yet done so. Other countries without any Declaration are far more alive to their inalienable (so-called) rights than is America, if one may judge by recent developments in Russia and elsewhere. All good things may be and, no doubt, are gifts, but they are not conferred by governments, any more than death and disaster can be prevented by governments. Sometimes innate strength and fortuitous circumstances help some of us, yet this merely illustrates once more the truism that nature "plays favorites" and that many are vastly better equipped than others.

A great voice, for instance, is a gift, and cannot be acquired at any school or for any price; the beauty of a woman, however modest or staggering, is a gift and cannot be purchased or even manufactured (amazing as that may seem in the face of all the drug companies), although ugliness, apparently, can almost be wished on a person, so lavish is life with its disfavors. The ability to paint a great picture, to design a great building, to lead an army, to organize a government, to construct a philosophy, to dream a religion, is a gift and cannot be added to any one by taking thought, however quickly it may be taken away. Neither can the possessors of these be reduced to the level of those who have nothing to offer, no ideas, no dreams. Christ said one really significant thing, "Who by taking thought can add a cubit to his stature?" If He had followed the logic of that statement He would never have delivered the Sermon on the Mount or the Beatitudes and would not now be so popular, but apparently He was genius enough to be illogical.

What has confronted the American organizing genius, now known as a captain of industry, a multi-millionaire, a financier and the like, has been—aside from a mass need for this, that and the other and his desire to supply it in order that he might improve his own condition, strengthen his own individuality, etc.—this same pen-written theory about all men being free and equal. Free they might be to begin with, one might hear him saying to himself—to a very limited extent, anyhow—but equal to himself, however much they might be equal one to another, never. It became his business, therefore, as he soon found and as he afterwards phrased it, to "drive a horse and wagon through the Constitution," or indeed any other law that might be devised to stop him and his dreams. I do not believe that any financial genius, American or other, anywhere or at any time, ever stopped to consider that there was such a thing as law or a Declaration of Independence or a Constitution when he began; or, if he did, it was as something to be evaded or overcome. To the aggressive organizing mind life is and always has been a free and practically uncharted sea. It finds itself blazing with an impulse to get some one new thing done; it conceives some great scheme, is inspired with some great enthusiasm for something; and thereafter all else is as nothing. Being strong and magnetic and enthusiastic, it rushes in where it is generally assumed angels fear to tread and seizes upon all which it deems may aid it in its dreams. The average man is of as little significance to such a temperament as a stalk of grain to a reaper. Any ideal other than its own is likely to be looked upon as an impediment. But always, of course, there exists the tramping mass of lesser individuals who have been going to school and church and there learning (in America at least) all the religious and copy-book maxims, which argue that the world was made for the individual and that he was born free and equal, each as good as any other and each called upon to aid the other; and these begrudge, and always have and always will, these great giants their power. They often fight them and sometimes beat them.

But they are not to be wholly undone by them at any time, anywhere. Like the Lilliputians, the mass as often succeeds in binding Gulliver with their threads as Gulliver succeeds in tearing through their petty stays. The twain are ever being born side by side in nature; the giant and the pygmy, the shark and the bluefish, the whale and the minnow. "Look," cry the minnows to their fellows, "this whale imagines he is better, wiser, greater, than we! He moves in larger ways, disturbs our great sea, taking his choice of the realms and pleasures of life. Why should this be? Are we not as good as he? And yet he does all these things which we cannot; he breaks the law which governs the average minnow, whereas we cannot. Therefore he must be evil. We will seize and bind him and so end his privileges, if not him." Immediately and always, at this point, there arises an intermediate figure or group, the sophisticated "advocates of the people," "tribunes of the people," individuals less powerful than the giants, though shrewder than the pygmies, their employers, many of whom are sincere enough in their conviction of unselfishness; others self-seekers and charlatans purely, yet each and every one crying that he will deliver the mass from its bondage, and actually attempting, or pretending, to adjust the impossible demands of the people with the almost impossible individualism of the egoist. But, honest or dishonest as they may be, the mass is never made quite free; the financiers or individuals are never wholly curbed. Both merely proceed to develop new issues and new battlefields.

Personally I believe that most of us would prefer that the mass should not sweep away the individual, for each of us would prefer to be somebody in however small a way rather than mere unrecognizable cogs in a machine or bees in a bee-hive. At best, we are little more than that; even our greatest individuals, individual as they may seem. They, too, are but minute factors in the total machinery, little able to forefend against disaster or the ultimate nothingness that swallows them. But one thing is sure: the individual in the course of the development of his dreams and ambitions does scheme out and construct or bring into organic operation functions which are valuable to mass prosperity, and on that score there is scarcely any fault to be found with him.

The thing that might seriously concern a thinking American would be whether the American financial type, as contrasted with those of other lands and times, is more or less admirable. Greece had Crœsus; Rome, Lepidus, Hadrian; Italy, Lorenzo, the money-gathering Popes; France, Louis XIV, the Baron de Hirsch; England, the first Rothschild, the late Cecil Rhodes, Harmsworth, Strathcona; Japan, Shibusawa.

While it may be admitted that the organizing types developed in America have not had any too great charm or virtue (Astor I., Vanderbilt I., Gould, Sage, Harriman, Morgan), still they appear to compare favorably with most ancients and moderns. If they have done less for the arts, as many seem to think, socially, or at least economically, they have done as much if not more than their predecessors. Astor I. may have begrudged a washerwoman fifty cents, dunned his tenants for rent, debauched the Indians, but he opened up the most remote portions of America and laid the way for roads and railroads. The first Vanderbilt was no doubt a brutal, cruel and savage man, but he had the vision which made a transcontinental railroad possible. His greed and vanity made it possible. As much might be said for Gould, Russell Sage and Harriman, though the picture of Sage keeping apples in his desk to avoid buying lunches for his friends or well-wishers and using his old plug hats for umbrella stands in order to get a little more wear out of them could not be of much interest to the mass except in a Dickensian sense. Unless one accepts the subtleties of Nature as one finds them, sees in all an inexplicable and yet biologic or universally constructive plan, and in these riant and lawless individuals a scheme of hers to achieve something quickly, there is nothing very admirable or even explicable about the dark goings to and fro of such types as the late J. P. Morgan, H. H. Rogers, Thomas F. Ryan, William C. Whitney, or any of a score of other large fortune-builders so recently in control of stupendous matters here and elsewhere. They are not explicable save as motivating forces in the hands or will of higher powers—good, bad or indifferent. Seen at close range they are more suggestive of sharks and we of sniveling blucfish, and it is plainly to our best interests either to keep out of their way or unite firmly to oppose them in whatever way we can, unless we choose to be promptly eaten.

Yet are they any worse than their prototypes anywhere? The worst that can be said for the American is that as yet no one of him has been able to rival Lorenzo the Magnificent or Louis XIV to gather and use in any marked way, supposing there has been anything of importance to use, the significant artistic personalities and materials (American or general) of his time after the fashion, say, of a Lorenzo, a Hadrian or a Can Grande. Perhaps he has had few opportunities, no Michelangelos to countenance or foster, no Raphaels or Leonardos to attach to his court or entourage. Again it may be urged that he has never been in any position to organize or dictate, being by no means in any free or superior position in a democracy such as this. The best he has been able to do apparently is to buy, although of course the power to patronize nobly and generously has to a certain extent been within his range. Still, a stranger to our rich and powerful land might (I do not say he would) be struck by the abject poverty of a Poe or a Whitman, scarcely knowing which way to turn for means, as contrasted with the enormous affluence of so many financial geniuses. Why, one such might ask, should either a writer or poet of the transcendent merit of either of these have lacked a financial sponsor? And why, the same inquiring mind might ask, was there no Mæcenas to befriend the late George Inness, Harris Merton Lyon, or MacDowell, the musician? But in other ways—via libraries, gifts to art museums, schools and universities—he would have to admit that the American multimillionaire has done quite as well as the others; only, in so far as I can see, he has in the main lacked the insight to connect his gifts with an impulse toward the truest art values and realms of mental freedom and refinement. Too often, as in the case of our universities, his gifts have been far too subtly identified, aside from purely technical progress, with mental retrogression, or at least the perpetuation of religious and moralistic dogma not compatible with the truest mental development. At the same time the retort might be that it has never been a part of the organizing ability of any money genius anywhere to plan for true mental progress. It may not be necessary. Life may be taking care of that "on its own," as the phrase runs.

However that may be, one cannot help thinking how interesting it would have been if in New York or elsewhere any one of the above-mentioned men had in his day troubled to gather about him in some private court a representative group of intellectual and artistic personalities, for the sole purpose of testifying to his interest in that side of life, if nothing more. After all, the living individual is worth something, and any one of our financiers might have done what no American of wealth, as far as I know, has as yet done: invested some of his boundless wealth in personality. Or he might have endowed a wholly independent magazine or newspaper or theatre, of which there is at present not one, or a school of special learning free from dogmatic interference, or a publishing house, or a university which should have been a true university and not one devoted to the economic or social or religious theories or moods of any particular period. The strangest lack or flaw in the American organizing financial temperament, in so far as I can see, is or has been, hitherto, its inability to see either character or significance in anything save movements which tend to further the most material financial aims: railroads, butcher-companies, electricity, gas, typewriter and other purely mechanical or material organizations. Yet possibly, up to the present time, the land has only needed things of this kind. And perhaps the next generation will make amends. Who knows? Thus far there has been little if any tendency to invest in anything save such art or art forms as have been heralded by time.

To this day, ancient Asiatic, Egyptian and European art forms continue to pour in on us in a brilliant phantasmagoric stream, until we threaten, or did, to drain the world of its treasures. Our private mansions groan with the antiquated skill of Asia and other continents, but of these other matters, or the cultivation or preservation of a single living personality, not a word. It is possible to go forth and raise any reasonable or even unreasonable sum for any number of useless or surplus charitable organizations or hospitals or churches, whereas if it were a question of cash for a truly civilizing movement of some kind, or a personality, the obstacles would prove well nigh insurmountable. Some of the trashiest homes I have ever had the misery of beholding have been those of men of tremendous wealth and alleged refinement, stuffed to overflowing with bogus furniture and art. Yet, when all is said and done, are they to blame? Are they not specialized machines sent here for a purpose? And should one expect more? Verily we have our reward in their practical achievements. . . . Yet, also, when one looks at them one cannot help remembering that Walt Whitman lived in a back street in Camden and depended upon a friendly admirer to bring him a fish for his supper; that Poe lived in a hut in the woods, unable to achieve or afford a more suitable abode. I am not quarreling; I cite these as interesting facts.

. . . .

An interviewer once questioning me in regard to the significance of the American financial type (it was just after I had published "The Financier"), raised the question as to whether the American financial type, then so abundant and powerful, had ethically the right to be as it was or do as it was doing, seeing that it was being and doing about as it pleased. My answer was, and I still see no reason for changing it, that, in spite of all the so-called laws and prophets, there is apparently in Nature no such thing as the right to do or the right not to do, if you reach the place where the significance of the social chain in which you find yourself is not satisfactory. The murderer has under the written law no right to murder anybody. It is perfectly plain that he has the right if he is willing to pay the penalty, or if he can evade it. Conscience, this thing called conscience to which people repeatedly appeal, is, as I have pointed out elsewhere, little more than a built-up net of social acceptances and agreements in regard to society or the agreed state of facts in which we all find ourselves when we arrive here; in other words all the things which we wish to do and be, or avoid. It is not anything save an inherent condition of balance in Nature which desires and achieves a very rough equation, but nothing which works exact justice to any individual anywhere. The so-called "still, small voice," ever present at one's inner or spiritual ear, is, if it is anything at all, a sense of self-preservation and conditional desire for equation or peace —stillness, rest, lack of friction.

It is true that the individual may not always agree with the ethics of his time, or that he may smack of anything but sweetness and light, may even seem a little gross or terrible; but if he prove essential, as he nearly always does, his revolt against the commonplace fixity, rigidity and the like of the slower-moving man cannot be looked upon as either wholly evil or in vain. Indeed, if he did no more than throw a new light on this strange phantasmagory called existence, then, ethics or no ethics, he would have been worth while and it would make no essential difference whether he agreed with passing theories or not. Apparently the world, or let us say the race, is moving along in some curious way to possibly a larger, more widespread condition of complexity and articulation, part with part (variety in unity, unity in variety), and a self-sensating intellectual perception and appreciation of the same. Who knows? But beyond that, what? Is man better, purer, more spiritual, more generous than ever he was? Do any of the savages or animals lack any of the emotional or charitable traits which we possess? Observe the wolf with its young; the cat; the dog; the lion. Are not all swayed by conditioning laws of subsistence and which they obey, but nothing more? True, they kill to eat, to preserve themselves. Has man ever done less—or more?

Any naturalistic philosopher can, of course, trace all the steps for you, how it is that you have come to be seemingly so different, although he cannot tell you why or where you are going. My own guess would be that we, or rather the race, is going on to a greater individuality, plus a greater weakness as to its component and clinging atoms, providing it does not suffer an endless dark age of mass control or total extinction in some form or other. Nietzsche appeared preaching individuality, greater individuality for everybody who could achieve it, and to a certain extent he was right. Greater individuality than the world has yet seen will certainly be achieved by some. Schopenhauer, before him, announced that only failure for the individual was possible, and to a certain extent he was right also. The two saw the over-soul from different angles. Again, Marx, the humanitarian, appeared preaching solidarity for the mass and mass control, and his work will probably result in greater material battles between the individual and the mass than any yet witnessed. If one stands with the individualists, as one may well do, and believes that there are no laws created by mass conditions and necessities which the individual should not be allowed to break for the subsequent good of the mass, and also that the mass only moves forward because of the services of the exceptional individual, then one will be compelled to agree with Nietzsche that it is folly not to wish that the significant individual will always appear and will always do what his instincts tell him to do. On the other hand if one feels, as so many of the less well-equipped do, that in the long run and in the plan of Nature itself the individual is nothing, the type all, and that mass conditions favoring the production of many of the best type are most important, then the airs and dreams of the individual in regard to his personal satisfaction and satiation will not seem so important, the general welfare of each individual of the mass more important than anything else. And this will mean that always the special individual, the genius of any kind, will be curbed and restrained if not actually pushed into the background. And, in the main, life proves this nearly all the time. Attempts at world domination on the part of one individual and another have proved failures, as witness Darius, Alexander, Hannibal, Napoleon, the Kaiser.

Yet theories and doxies wear thin with the course of time, and the "still, small voice" of one age is not the "still, small voice" of the next, strange as it may seem. At best, all we have is the individual, not always financial, by any means, or artistic, but one who has dreamed out something: music, a picture, poetry, a machine, a railroad, an empire—anything, in short, that man as race or nation can use or rejoice in. If to have a Woolworth Building, a transcontinental railroad, a Panama Canal, a flying machine, to say nothing of literature and art, means that we must endure a man who is dull, greedy, vain, ridiculous in many ways or even an advocate of every conceivable vice in order to twist his brain into some strange phantasmagorical tendency, the result of which will be some one of these things, there are many who would enthusiastically say, "Then let us have him along with all his lacks or vices, in order that this other may be." If it is a question of having a Villon or not, provided we cannot have him without having a thief at the same time, then the same or another group would cry, "Let us have the thief and the poem concerning the 'Snows of Yesterday.' " For my part I am convinced that so-called vice and crime and destruction and so-called evil are as fully a part of the universal creative process as are all the so-called virtues, and do as much good—providing, as they do, for one thing, the religionist and the moralist with their reasons for existing. At best, ethics and religion are but one face of a shield which is essentially irreligious and unethical as to its other face, or the first would not exist.

For myself, then, I cannot say that personally or socially the

American or any other financier, as I have investigated him, is not as satisfactory as may be, all things considered. Artistically thus far he is not much to survey, but a giant or a Titan he certainly has been. As for the majority of them, they were by no means presentable or even acceptable socially, but what would you? They were, in the main, too ignorant, too insistent on their own views, too self-hypnotized by their own dreams of self-advancement and dominance. A leader of polite society anywhere, for instance, might not be willing to welcome a Russell Sage, a Jay Gould, or a John W. Gates or his wife, or indeed any other American financial type thus far known, and this solely on the ground of expediency or social or artistic fitness or unfitness for the lighter forms of living, but that in itself proves nothing. It could truthfully be said, on the other hand, that it would scarcely be possible to admit the average society man to the threatening precincts of radical energy or thought in any form. One thing is sure: the individual cannot wholly understand the mass, nor the mass the individual. Both have their significance, their place, but if one were to say of either that it or he alone had claim to significance as a helpful factor in life, or as dramatic or artistic material, or as a spectacle, one would be greatly mistaken. Both have. All have.

THE TOIL OF THE LABORER

A TRILOGY

I.

"The ears to hear! The beauty
Of life is unceasingly calling.
The eyes to see! Its glory
Is ever unfolding anew!"

THE toil of the laborer is artless. There is in it neither form, nor color, nor tone. For months I have been working as only workingmen work, and in the dreary round of the hours it has come to me that the thing which is wearisome and disheartening about it is that it is utterly devoid of art. In the construction of a building, for instance, whereat we labored for three long months, I discovered that with each day's labor I was in contact only with that which was formless and colorless and toneless. Huge, misshapen, disheartening piles of brick; commonplace, indifferent and colorless masses of stone, wood, iron, sand, cement; bone and sinew of what was to be, but in themselves devoid of all that could appeal to the eye or touch the heart, and scattered about in such an aimless way as to bring to the mind nothing but a wearying sense of disorder. This disorder, however, as soon became clear to me, was not apparent in a definite way to all those who worked amidst it. These mixers of mortar and carriers of brick toiled in the grime and dust without seeming to realize that it was a wretched condition, hard, grim and, so far as the sum of their individual lives was concerned, but meagerly profitable. Carpenters, masons and iron-workers went sturdily about their labors, but the artless and unlovely nature of their work was over it all, and despite their seeming unconsciousness to it one felt the drag of its absence, their eagerness to get away, their innate yearning to be where things were not in the making, the urge to be out in the larger and more perfect world where form and color and tone do abound.

For, after all, in the main, things do stand complete, as we see them. The hills have their enduring roundness, the trees their perpetual forms. Landscapes and skylines are not torn and scraped as in the vicinity of some (comparatively) minute constructive labor. Nature is nearly always cunningly pleasing to the eye on the surface, whatever may go on below, whereas the average constructive processes are so often discordant, broken, disordered.

Seeing this, and not being able in my own consciousness to explain why, my heart was sad and I wondered why life should be thus grimly organized; why formlessness in the parts of the thing to be formed; why tonelessness in that which when laboriously organized would be all tone; why colorlessness in that which in the end would enliven the heart with color and dance before the eye a perfect thing.

In the progress of the work, however, it was given me to see that, in the production of all things here, there is at bottom this very formlessness innate. For to organize and perfect one thing we must take from and destroy another; and in doing that we fly in the face of that which we most desire: order and harmony. Therefore, if we would have that which the inexplicable urge for something new and more beautiful commands, we must apparently steel our hearts against the old and destroy it, although, having committed the offense of destruction, we must repay or balance by the labor of construction.

It is not given to all of us to follow the ramifications of

Nature's planning nor to see wherein justice or the seeming injustice lies. Most of those about me—average short-reasoning creatures—took their labor drearily enough and were not able to see in any definite inspiriting way the approaching beauty of that which their hands were building. It did not concern them. Many of them came and labored but a little while, doing but a minute portion of that which was to be the whole, seeing only the mass and chaos of it without ever obtaining one glimpse of the loveliness which was to be.

But when the labor had been completed, when the mortar had been mixed and the brick and stone removed from their uneven masses and set in order, when the wounds of the earth had been smoothed over, the scattered débris removed and the grass allowed to grow, when in the light of the restful evening there rose, in this instance, high in the air a perfect tower, buttressed, arched and pinnacled, with here a window reflecting the golden Western glow and there a pillar standing out in delicate relief against the perfect background of the sky, the meaning of the chaos came home. Here it was: color, form, tone, beauty. The labor of the excavator, the toil of the iron-worker, the irritating beats of the carpenters' hammers, the mess and disorder of the field of action, had all blended together finally and made this perfect thing—only they were no longer a part of it. To most of them it was all but meaningless. Having labored on but portions of it they could scarcely conceive it as a whole.

And yet as I looked my heart rose up, and I, for one, was thankful to have been in part a worker, to have worked a little, to have wearied a little, to have sighed a little, that so lovely a thing might be.

II.

The toil of the laborer is thoughtless. There is in it neither conception nor initiative nor the development of that which is new. Though the hands labor and the body bend, the heart is not in it. It is all a weariness and a travail of the flesh, and the profit is unseen.

In a certain factory, not far from the heart of the city of New York, I worked as a laborer. My duty was to carry shavings and lumber and to sweep the floor. All day, from the blowing of the whistle at seven in the morning to its welcome blast at six at night, my body was busy bending and lifting in the effort to keep the floor clean of shavings and supplying a half-dozen machines with lumber. The slow, unchanging, imperative nature of the work, the fact that I went on whether one man came or another one stayed away, the dreary persistence with which it was necessary to repeat the same motion day after day, week after week, month after month, year after year, was, to the thinking and restless mind, maddening.

In this factory at the time there ruled a foreman well fitted to the scheme of things. He was a strange, egotistic, vainglorious soul, with a mind so set up by the fact that he had been foreman of this little shop that there was no living with him. He was arbitrary; his word was law. With an air that might have become a tragedian, he walked about his domain and glared upon each and all, meditating upon his exalted position. Every word was either a command or a reproof, and in times of excitement or depression, such as naturally flow from the hurry or the lack of work, he was always about, venting his humor or wrath, as his mood dictated.

This situation, coupled with the meager wages, the enormous wealth of the corporation which controlled it all, the utter indifference of those who sat at the top to those who worked at the bottom, was a difficult thing to endure. It was so very apparent to any one who thought that the work of those at the bottom was entirely without point save as a means of subsistence. To lift and carry, to move along given lines and within certain limits—this was the sum and substance of wisdom required, and it mattered little who did it. Some small personal characteristics figured in, such as whether a man was naturally quick or slow, good-humored or ill-humored and the like, but the main point was to do the work as conceived, planned, initiated and developed by some one above. And this could be acquired until it was not a matter of thought but of rote. What you thought or how you felt was not involved.

One of its pathetic aspects was that it was involved with the maintenance of a condition which was not necessarily beneficial or worthy of approval. So many of the owners, for whom these thousands upon thousands of individuals labored, were mere idlers in society, social loafers, daily bulletined as the chief factors in a dozen trivial amusements, and as wholly unconscious of this under-condition which made for their situation and pleasure as if it did not exist at all. For every motion and bending here, some one else was deriving the privilege not to move or bend there. It was as if some untoward power were momentarily taking something from each of these and giving it to some one who did not even know whence it came.

And the saddest part of it was that these toilers, born for the most part to a condition and with brains unsuited to anything much better, were still not so dull that they could not see, and that rather plainly, how scurvily Nature was using them, with what a vast, contemptuous indifference. It was little to Her whether they lived or died, did poorly or well. Most of them were mere machines who had acquired the little they knew by observing others, who, if they were capable of thinking at all, were restricted by the nature of their labor in utilizing thought, and yet they could see so plainly that those above them did very little or nothing, and received much, so much more. It was one of those situations in which labor, a mere round of motions, took the place of thought and left them weary and disinterested at the close of the day, not fit to originate a thought if it had been possible or necessary.

And yet, after a time, it occurred to me that it was not, perhaps, so much the thoughtlessness of it that was so wretched as that any human being, toiling to his full capacity, should not receive more of the legitimate profits of his labor. These men, ignorant and, in a way, valueless without direction, were nevertheless useful creatures and, in this sense if no other, were deserving of a far more reasonable share of the profit which their efforts created. That it should not be so, that despite their willing or non-willing they should be driven early and late to create a surplus which was not directly applied to the pressing needs of society as a whole, but to the frittering amusements of the few, not much better in the main than themselves, seemed hard.

And yet sometimes when I looked out upon the world as it glimmered before my windows—when I saw, as it so chanced, the waters of the river flowing by, the splendid boats riding at anchor or steaming peacefully past, and the wonder of the hills and hollows, all set suggestively before the eyes—it came to me that, perhaps, in spite of the seeming injustice involved in this situation, variety was as essential to happiness as so-called justice or equation, and that the very inequalities I was bemoaning were the things which I was admiring in Nature. To blot out the light and the shadows, to remove the hills and dales, to take away the far reaches which spread between luxury and want, idleness and toil—might not these be the things which after all would rob life of much of its value and charm? Might they not?

But as I turned again to the weariness of my labor and saw once more the routine, the comparative slavery, the drag of almost endless hours, I could not help wishing for each that there might be some better solution than this necessity for variety—that perhaps the heights and hollows need not after all be so vast. To survey a mountain, to view a desert—was not this the privilege of but a few? And might not the true beauty of life exist in the way-places where are neither heights nor depths but only a tender and appealing undulation? I wondered, and still do, for in spite of endless personal inconvenience I have never been able to believe that an unbreakable dead level of equality should maintain, that none should suffer overmuch, that none should want to the extreme. And yet at this time, in this place, the less varied seemed the all-to-be-desired. That it was not to be found in so starkly diversified a world as here offers did not lessen the pain of the labor or the value of the ideal in the least. To work, to wait, to hope, to pray for some such change—how important these loomed in the hour of weariness! And yet the charm that hope cast over effort was as though the difference had already in part been bridged and that the realization of the ideal was almost at hand.

III.

The toil of the laborer is without mercy, its grim insistence unrequited by anything save the meager wages wherewith it is paid. There is no true beauty in it, no tenderness. There is no thought of anything save what muscle and the strength of the individual can be made to yield. More than this, the sum of what is accomplished passes almost entirely into other hands. There is no provision made for those who will be as tattered remnants when the things for which they labored have been accomplished.

For several months I worked with the laborers for a great railroad. It was the kind of labor that falls to the lot of every man who is unskilled and whose sense of honesty or compulsion or duty or need commands that he labor. Those with whom I worked were employed to carry lumber, load brick, shovel earth and mix mortar. The work was requited at the rate of fifteen cents an hour, and nothing more than this was allowed for overtime. We worked nine or ten hours a day, as the light permitted. There was no rest for those here employed save in a form of subterfuge, which was as wearisome as the toil itself to one not accustomed to it by long years of practice. To be sure one might delay in the carrying of anything; it was possible to be deliberate, to hang first on one foot and then the other; there was a way of resting on one's pick before lifting it; but the gain was scarcely worth the pains. At the close of the day the sum of idleness thus secured would not be sufficient to produce a restful feeling, and the knowledge that a watchful foreman was well aware of the spirit of your labor was not conducive to comfort.

We were under a foreman whose conception of life was that it meant toil, and who himself was perfectly equipped physically to meet it. He did not stop to parley or temper the necessities with tenderness but shouted and cursed his commands, the fulfilling of which was as much of a burden on his mind as upon our bodies. Work there was in plenty, vast quantities of labor extending into the weeks and years, and the only thought which the conclusion of one hard day's toil could bring was that there was another exactly like it tomorrow. It had no end for the individual save in arbitrary cessation on his part, the ending of his pay, or in disintegration and death. And need drove so many to continue day after day, without rhyme or reason in so far as the individual was concerned.

I could not help pondering over this from time to time, wondering at the lust of the controlling powers at the top for money and place, the fierceness of Nature in placing such an impulse in them, the fierceness of the temper of our immediate masters (general managers, superintendents, foremen and the like), the persistence of their frowns, the manner in which, when anything was delayed or the work went wrong, they visited the blame upon the heads of those beneath them, the urge and blame finally falling with sharp effect upon the carriers and serfs at the bottom. Life did not seem to require or justify it, I often thought. The rewards achieved by those at the bottom at least were too inconsiderable. The enormous and almost useless surplus of this great corporation flowering out into exotic social forms at the top was proof that it was an unjust exaction. A man should be a man in spite of the orders of his superiors. Mercy and tenderness should qualify our every deed. . . . So it looked from the bottom.

And then one day I was made a foreman.

I was determined that I, as foreman, would hold persistently, through whatever wearinesses might come, to this earlier creed of courtesy and consideration. I told myself that I would do better than these others. There should be no harshness in my tone. I would not swear. A moderate effort would be demanded of my men, but nothing more. So much for good intentions.

In this new capacity I found that my duties were of a different nature from those of my former. Here, instead of running at the beck and call of another, I had men running for me. I had from a dozen to fifteen men under me, as the work varied, and my principal duty was to see that they did not shirk.

I accepted this with a light heart. It seemed easy enough, something which could be accomplished in the most gracious spirit. All I had to do was to take my position beside my gang, humming a tune, and to watch (as I thought) their progress with a gentle and merry heart.

How speedy and how sad was my disillusionment!

Before one day was gone I was made to feel that the pressure which was on me from above must be transferred to those who were below, regardless. There were orders to be complied with, periods to be observed, standards of quality to be maintained in certain kinds of work, which my men did not always understand. Nor did an explanation or a simple request always result in understanding or ready willingness to comply. They were often tired, a night's rest not always apparently repairing the weariness of the day before. None were so dull that they could not see that many reaped where they had not sown, took joy in that for which they had never paid, while others like themselves sweated under a load which they had never willed to carry. Dark looks, dark moods, dark wishes were as common as ever, yet if my own position or my superior's good will were worth anything to me I could not allow them to fall below their quota of toil. It was necessary to achieve a given result, or resign, and at every turn there were rules, rules, rules.

How hard I tried to adjust my new relationship to the ideal which had previously been mine, and at the same time comply with the rules of the company, I will not say. For a time I did manage to keep a cheerful attitude and to speak gently. I tried to overlook the indifference and subterfuge which I knew they were practicing and which before, in part at least, had seemed justifiable but which must also in part be overcome, if life were to go on at all. For Nature, as I had come to see, had established these inequalities, the smallness of mind in some, the strength and vision in others. Who was I to set about establishing exact justice or equation, where I had not created? Or how or where? Or I might smile and smile and urge with pleasant compliments, but how did that justify or make amends? And although for a time it seemed as though I might succeed in avoiding all difficulty, still the memory of my own recent feelings was too fresh not to influence me deeply.

Then came a day when the pressure of work to be done was

so much greater than it had been before that the usual subterfuge of the men became an irritation to me. They were painfully and exasperatingly slow, if not without reason, and the pressure on me from above was heavy also. A heavy rain had washed the earth into a long trench which we had been excavating. It was necessary to hurry the reopening of this in order not to delay other work. Concrete had to be prepared, a large foundation set by a given date. We were under urgent surveillance from our superiors and could but follow out their orders or resign.

In this situation I confess that I did not do much parleying with my sense of equation or justice. Although I knew these men to be in the main underpaid and overworked, and in so far as the corporation was concerned mere machines to be pushed to the limit of their capacity and discharged when no longer useful, still I stood beside them and ordered and commanded, urging first one and then the other with shouts and gruff words, until at last they were as wrought up and as harried by me as they had been by any one of whom I had previously complained. They were driven, harassed *by me,* until one, irritated by the anachronism of it all, no doubt, my previous enthusiasm for better conditions, turned on me with: "Yes—hurry! Hurry! You didn't work so hard yourself, though!"

I paused in my ordering and walked aside a little space to consider. How true was the thing he said! I had not worked so. It had been a constant complaint with me, in my own mind at least, that so much insistence and heartless driving had never been justified by the reward offered, that the men were entitled to more than they received for the grudging toil they gave. And here was I outdoing these drivers who to me had seemed most brutal!

For that day then, and for many others, I tried to discover just how it was that I had drifted into so rough and exacting an attitude. Did I not know now, as well as before, that the corporation for which we were all working was enormously rich? Had I not more evidence than before that the men were overworked and underpaid, my own demands proving it? Could I not see in the orders given me that there was no consideration for them, but only the thing to be accomplished at the least possible expense?

I acknowledged freely that this was absolutely true, and yet I now pleaded with myself that I saw no way to remedy it and that if I did not fulfill the company's orders some one else would. The work had to be done. There was no way of permitting these men to shirk and take their time, without noticeably delaying the work. If the corporation was to be run, its present efficiency maintained and the public served, it would of course have to be done at a profit which would induce men of initiative and skill at the top to serve; otherwise no man would undertake the matter, and there would be no labor at all for any of these men at the bottom. For Nature apparently went on the theory of great reward for those who could or would originate and conduct in a large way, little for those who could not; and these at the bottom did not and apparently could not originate. Their reasoning powers were not as yet sufficiently developed for that. They were, by reason of their mental equipment, hewers of wood and drawers of water.

After a time I felt that I could no longer go on without making a definite choice: I must serve them or their masters wholeheartedly. The retort of the laborer had proved too great a shock, and it was long before I recovered my exterior equanimity, and never again my internal peace, here. Plainly I was not one called by nature to this task. Reason as I would, the two elements of capital and labor, exacting strength and helpless weakness, would not adjust themselves within my consciousness save in some such rough way as I here saw operating, and so because of my natural sympathy for these underlings I was forced in spite of myself to choose sides. Either I must relinquish my former attitude of sympathy for the men and opposition to the indifference of the company, or I must side with them. There could be no middle ground, and until I should choose my conscience would give me no peace.

It was after a particularly hard day's work and because of some special conditions that I managed finally to reach a decision, which, however much it may have benefited me, helped them in no least way. We had been mixing concrete and, a touch of my old cynical uncertainty dominating me, I had been driving them all the day long, urging one to shovel faster, calling to another to bring the wheelbarrows of stone almost before they were needed, sending this one for water and that one for cement, until the men were running about like ants. About four o'clock of this long day it began to rain. It had been gray and lowery all day but now the moisture descended in a fine drizzle and we were compelled to work or leave unfinished the batch of concrete we were just beginning. In a sullen mood, because of my own dreary part in this, I stood and held them to their task, not caring much what became of them or myself either, until at last the work was completed. At dusk, damp and dreary, I took my lunch-box and tramped doggedly along the tracks toward the depot, comforted by one thought only: that the day was over and I myself was free.

It was at that hour when the traffic outward from the great city assumes its most imposing aspect. Along this magnificent highway of steel were speeding the trains of one of the wealthiest corporations in the world. Limiteds were passing, their splendid interiors aglow with half a hundred lights. Seemingly more prosperous citizens than we were reclining there in comfort. Others were gazing out idly. The dining cars of various trains were set with silver and white linen.

As I paused near the station to turn my eye on this truly appealing scene and to gather its significance as contrasted with that which I had just left, there passed by, going in my direction, the little procession of Italians over whom I ruled, bearing with them the tools with which they had been laboring. There was Philip, whom I had often noted as I stood beside the trench in which he was working, his body all twisted and bent from long years of unremitting toil; there was Angelo, old and leathern in feature, whose one boast was that he had never missed a day's work in seventeen years; there was Matteo, thin, spare, worn-looking, whose eye was alight with a kindly humor and whose willingness to work I had never been able to question; there were John and Collarbrace (as we called one Calabrian), Mussolin and Jimmie, all trudging patiently onward like cattle, the day of their labor having brought forth nothing but a night of weariness.

And as I stood there looking at them I could not help contrasting the weariness of their labor with this (one of many, many), flowers which it, or labor like it, had produced at the top. Here was this immense corporation with its magnificent equipment, its palatial depots, its comfortable trains speeding onward bearing their burdens of the comfortable (?) and the more fortunate (?), and here at the very bottom were these humble trudgers making their way homeward in the night and the rain. And as I thought of the meagerness of their wages, the manner in which I had driven them, and the profitless luxury, in so far as they were concerned, to which their labor trended, I resolved that I, for one, would have nothing more to do with it.

Not to drive where I could not ease, not to urge where I

could not repay, not to be a tool in the hands of their indifferent masters who could not or would not interest themselves in them, was something, even though my ceasing could not relieve them of their toil.

PERSONALITY

IN the last analysis personality appears to be a sense of power resting on a feeling of capability or wisdom and usefulness, and hence a right to be; or this may be reversed for some and it be said to be a sense of capability or usefulness which springs from inherent wisdom and power. At best it is inexplicable to the individual himself. He does not know from whence it comes, why he has it, why he of all people should have it and so many other billions not, why his thoughts should be large where those of others are so small, his cunning or subtlety great where those of so many others are obviously less. If he has in addition any charm of character, being thus endowed, he will be courteous, considerate, merciful; but it by no means follows that he must so have or be. That would not explain an Attila, an Alaric, a Can Grande or a Torquemada.

"Why should I be born with a great mind," a Cæsar, a Shakespeare, a Hannibal or a Leonardo might well have asked of himself, "whereas so many have little ones? Why is my frail bark speeded by winds of destiny or chance over favorable seas to power, where so many are beached or foundered en route? Did I make myself? Did I foreknow all?" Where so profound an egoist, even with a minute brain, to claim so much?

The truth is all good things are gifts, a voice, strength of body, vigor of mind, vision, the power to lead, as in war, any art, beauty, charm. This is not to say that these things may not be technically improved, and are, but this is the business with which mediocrity is chiefly concerning itself. I know that the world, where it lacks the strength to think on the subject, thinks differently, but this is mere nonsense and without import.

The man of personality or destiny realizes the guidance, enmity or favor of not necessarily higher, we will say, but different powers. (I am not for saints, guardian *angels,* Buddhas, Christs, perfect gods all.) He realizes all too keenly the element of chance, luck, unpropitious as well as propitious hours. Sometimes, in spite of himself and to his wonder, he notes that his affairs prosper. "There is a tide—" At other times (and who has not realized this?), try as he will, he had better lay aside all effort and disappear. Fortune will have none of him. The furies hover over his path. Harpies beset him. Go where he will, there will be elements to annoy him, if no more than an ill wind to blow his cap away or to cast dust into his eyes. He, above all others, knows that time and chance happen to all men.

But it is so easy to cite the old-time virtues of honesty, stability, truthfulness, fair-dealing, etc., as proving character, its value, and the power of any one, however weak or defective, personally to achieve it. But always, in spite of the advocates of simple and normal and moral things as proving in themselves genius and worth, there is something more—magnetism, for instance, a thing not necessarily or solely a part of these other so-called virtues, and strength, assurance, courage, generous or the reverse. These are not things of ethical import necessarily, but they make for success just the same. Observe that youth admires color, flare, pugnacity, brute courage and daring; middle age, knowledge of sorts, aggressiveness, endurance, success; old age, wisdom, generosity, humility, etc. How many of the former are ethical? In the quiet halls of learning or reflection certain of the tabulated virtues may be extolled, but to whom does the world pay attention, to whom has it paid attention? Darius, Artaxerxes, Alexander,

Cæsar, Hannibal, Attila, Alaric, Peter the Hermit, Napoleon, the Kaiser; possessing what of all these virtues? Cæsar kind, patient, honest, truthful? Napoleon the same? Antony the same? Attila the same? Not even the popes, the preachers, the founders of religion were so. Always craft, force, diplomacy; but little of the sacrificial media so extolled and commended to the rank and file in order to keep them at rest.

It is significant of the intellectual development of America, if not of other countries, that we hear less these days of *character,* that something or somewhat which we were all supposed to have, or at least develop for ourselves or make (!) à la Washington, Lincoln, Grant, etc., who in most American schoolbook essays and college addresses were and still are supposed to have *made* their skill, endurance, resourcefulness, etc.; and more of that other thing which we call personality and which for a long time apparently we were not supposed to have, that unexplainable, inescapable something with which we come and in which even here in America we are now beginning to believe. Yes, we are beginning to suspect that there are certain things which some of us cannot do, however much we may wish or try to. Also that ability in many realms and forms comes without volition on our part, fate and circumstance causing it to blaze for us whether we will or no. After many volumes of another kind of mush, this is at last becoming rather apparent. There is less talk now of being Napoleons all, adding inches to our stature by taking thought (lifting ourselves by our boot-straps, in other words), and more of plain effort according to our especially inherited abilities or capacities. It is a sad truth for most men, more especially for most Americans, when they discover it, but it is nevertheless an economic and helpful one. Men do better once they realize their genuine limitations and cease reaching for the moon. For so very long, here in America at least, we have been fed on something so very different: our inalienable ability to do anything and everything equally well.

One wonders at times whether the light is really breaking. Can it be that we are getting ready to admit that we are not Cæsars each and all, held back by our own idleness and indifference? One begins to rub one's eyes. I have often wondered why it is that the word "common," in its sense of being plentiful and therefore indifferent, has not struck home to the many of us for what it is: an expression of contempt; and that "uncommon," "extraordinary," denote approbation. Why, if this is not true, should everything that is common be held so lightly of the mass, whereas that which is special or individual, inherited or no, is of such intense interest to it? For example, the individual skill or personal traits of the actor, painter, writer, sculptor, the exceptionally talented in any field?

The truth is that the average man, dull as he is, realizes quite well that a creature who has little or nothing that is different from millions of his kind is of small import here or anywhere. There is no especial demand for what he has to offer. If he wishes to stand out above his fellows he must bring something new, and this he cannot provide by mere wishing or thinking. There is something more than that—inherent capacity, a something which he cannot create for himself, try as he may. He also knows that Nature sends bubbling up from her inexhaustible springs an infinitude of creatures who are of small import, because they have no inherent power wherewith to develop very special characteristics, or better yet individual impulses—in other words, personality. They cannot, and are not asked to, create them after they arrive here. They must have them to begin with, or they are not important, cannot make their way easily. And again, it is obviously quite right that a creature with qualities except those of the species should have to confine its claim to an existence entirely within the limits of the species, and live a life conditioned by them. If Nature wishes one to rise above the conditions wherewith he finds himself surrounded at birth She usually provides him with the equipment for so doing during gestation, or before, and in addition accidental and most opportune circumstances invariably aid him. He is the heir of most propitious conditions. Vide Cæsar, Napoleon, Shakespeare, Luther, Lincoln, even Goethe. Yet, it is impossible, I presume, to convince the mass that this is true. It would be too discouraging.

Again, it is a common fallacy among the ignorant that no lower animal possesses more than the generic characteristics of its species—such-and-such powers, such-and-such limitations, such-and-such instincts,—although this of course is not true. There are weak and strong animals of the same species, more cunning and less, more ferocious and less, better-natured and less, just as there are among men. (If you do not believe this study cats and dogs, the historic wolf of Cevennes in France.) Indeed in many intellectual circles, so-called, it is still claimed for man that he is the only one to possess individual character. But this is not true, as the "Origin of Species" plainly shows. Sometimes I think that man, take him by and large, presents less differences than some of the individuals of species of the so-called lower animals. He is supposed to reason more, but does he? It seems to me that the average cat reasons quite as well as the average plumber or grocer, if not better. Give a good pagan tomcat a man's body and sensory capacity, and how long do you suppose he would remain a plumber? The truth is that man, somewhat confused at present in his response to those chemic instincts which appear originally to have guided him, has been all but done for mentally by vain isms and theories. At times these same appear to be able, and quite completely, to do for him mentally, as does cancer and tuberculosis for him physically—vide Christianity, Mohammedanism, Shintoism, etc. On the other hand, the animal has no such handicap, let us say, as Catholicism, Shintoism, or what Mohammed or Buddha or Zoroaster said. It has just life and its own bare wits or chemical responses wherewith to do, no restraining and deadening rules. Hence it has very marked personality at times, and makes its way exceedingly well and without restraint or deadening aid of community or mass governmental advice. This is true of snakes, birds, fishes, monkeys and all other creatures *lower,* so-called, than man.

In most men, individual character, that thing which is supposedly so superior to lower animals, comes to very little. They run in schools, join secret orders or churches, vegetate, label themselves in a dull way democrats, republicans, socialists, and strive in all ways to make themselves as like others (those within their immediate ken) as possible. My father, for instance (peace to his spirit!), wished to prepare himself by self-abnegation, prayers and good works here on earth to fit himself for an entirely mythical heaven, to be a standardized angel—wings, harp, robes and all—such as he saw in the "saint pictures" in the various Catholic churches which he attended from time to time. These were the only representations of the future life with which he was familiar, hence he accepted them as true! Indeed as a rule the average or ordinary man (fortunately there is no exact average) cannot think or see beyond his quite immediate environment and binding rules, his neighborhood, his church, what somebody else says or thinks.

A plumber wants to be exactly like the next successful plumber he sees; a grocer, the same; an undertaker, the same. Most rich men would like to live in a house like that of all the other rich men they know. Show them the very different house of a rich man in Spain, in Egypt, in India, in Japan—it would never, never do. It is not like that which they know. Their thoughts and desires, like their faces, are those of the species to which they belong. In the main, they are of a trivial, commonplace character, as unimportant as a bean or a pea. Like animals of so limited a mentality as the duck and the penguin, if you know one you know all. You might almost say that they have come to their end spiritually. Nothing can be done for them. Some more vigorous active thing—i. e., the thinking, restless, dissatisfied individual—must come along to rebel and push them aside. If ever the surface of the commonplace is to be disturbed the individual moved by some inherited or bestowed impulse must do it: Luther, Galileo, Keppler, Newton, Columbus.

Anything that is strong, special, different must, as a matter of course and by its very nature, stand alone in the world where so many things are not strong, special, different. That which places one being over another and sets differences between man and man is not alone intellect or knowledge, as some would have us believe (Schopenhauer, for one), but these plus, other things being equal, the vital energy to apply them or the hypnotic power of attracting attention to them—in other words, personality. It is that peculiar quality or ability which makes a way for our plans, desires, dreams. Cunning, which is by no means knowledge in the sense in which we use that word, nor intellect of a high order perhaps (although it may well be), still may play a magnificent share in personality and contribute to its triumph. No truer book than Machiavelli's "The Prince," although it earned him the distinction of equaling the devil, was ever written, although the necessary gift of hypnotic personality was by no means sufficiently insisted upon. Was not one of the amazing qualities of Julius Cæsar, as of Hannibal, Napoleon and, indeed, most of the outstanding figures of history, cunning? The average man, realizing his own limitations, does not like to believe it, but it is none the less true. Did Alexander the Great, for instance, lack it? Or Lincoln? On the other hand, mere strength without cunning is so little. Contrast the tiger and the Norman horse or an elephant. Which of the three is truly superior? Which one commands your innate respect?

Whatever else you do, believe nothing in regard to the individual's ability to develop an especial and remarkable capacity, unless it is already inherent in him at birth. Nature works in no other way. Another thing, life cannot do without brains, however much disassociated from beatific virtues these may be; for these are a gift and can no more be created here than you can add to your height by taking thought. What life does is to develop and train especial inherent capacities—an eye, a hand, a taste, a smell perhaps; but the instinct and the ability to foreknow, to appreciate, understand—these things are not taught in schools. Schools labor with them to improve, polish, give them a special turn or bent; little more and little less.

A COUNSEL TO PERFECTION

BRIEF as are the sensations of success, victory, happiness, etc., yet these are things of actually some duration and as such can be looked forward to and back upon with pleasure, which in itself is a kind of reward for living. Love is real, a kinetic vibration of great comfort and a reward, as well as are the gratifications which arise from a sense of wealth or power or any hunger satiated. All these may be exceedingly brief and do fade, but however brief and however quickly faded they endure for at least a minute fraction of time and are therefore, and legitimately so, the basis of much human hope, ambition, delight, as well as despair and all the other contraries which might otherwise be inexplicable. The pathetic thing in connection with them all is that they are so plainly baits as well as rewards, that they do prove man to be the victim or evoluted mechanism if not tool of some higher, perhaps scheming force by no means essentially friendly to, if it is even conscious of, him, and that an enduring state of pleasure for anything is not contemplated by Nature as an essential portion of the career of man; also that it may be by no means concerned as to whether or no man, its tool, achieves any moments of triumph or satiation.

Looking at most lives—the defeated, the hungry, the poorly equipped mentally and physically, the homely, those seized on in childhood by the strong and shrewd and made to serve pointless and wretched purposes entirely alien to their lives—I should say that Nature does not care and that distinctly for them life may not be worth its pains. On the other hand, where crass chance lifts a given organism to great power or builds it with such care that it is an almost perfect and delicately responsive machine, life may well be and no doubt is worth all its costs. Many organisms, by accident of dullness or non-responsiveness of a higher sort, come off with less pain, and Nature, either accidentally or intentionally, builds most of these. They are machines well suited to the rough grind of material and psychic forces, and may be said to strike such a neat equation with the circumstances of life that they achieve a kind of sensory comfort or satiation and so do well enough. Again, dulling religion or illusions of one type and another, fatuitous hopes far beyond the pale of possibility, sensory response of a comfortable character to this earthly scene as a spectacle, or depleted nervous energy or force which reduces many to the point where nervous or sensory response is lacking, eases many to the place where it may be said that if they do not enjoy keenly they at least do not suffer keenly.

But is man happy? Is his game worth the candle? The sophisticated reply that the fear of death proves that life is worth while, since all are so eager to avoid it. But this is worse than no answer for it predicates either no life at all, which is certainly no recommendation, or that there may be worse things *there* than those which befall man *here*—certainly no proof of a keen joy in this.

The essential tragedy of life, then, and the thing which makes it painful to consider, is this: that once man is raised above the non-cerebrating and automatic sensory responsiveness of the beast he becomes conscious of the rather obvious fact that he is either an intelligently or an accidentally evoluted mechanism or minute tool in the hands of something so much more significant than himself that he is as nothing; and again, that to this force or intelligence above him his little earthly schemes bear about as much relationship as do those of an office boy bent on becoming a baseball pitcher to those of the

Standard Oil Company or the German Emperor bent on world dominion. And again—and this is the darkest thought of all—it, our personal Creator, assumed by the religionists at least to be so careful of our individual welfare, may be little more than the veriest tyro in so far as the larger and largest creative forces or impulses in the universe are concerned. Manifesting little or no interest in us, no more perhaps than is needful to its own welfare, it may be as little to the powers above it as are we to it. For who can guess whether the thing or power which makes man is the ultimate power or guiding force in so spacious a thing as the universe? Already our chemists and physicists are inclined to doubt it. Its impulses, humors, appetites and methods, as manifest in man, are by no means of so glorious or illuminating a character as to inspire admiration, even in its machine: man. Plainly its methods and actions bespeak as much of the lowest as of the highest that we know, and this is as much evidenced by the thoughts, aspirations, tastes or habits, chemically compulsory or no, of man, its product, and through whom it seemingly expresses itself, as by its methods and procedure in other ways, fumbling efforts and failures of all kinds. For man in his capacity as chemist, physicist, fumbling philosopher, didactic or synchronetic poet, experimentator or agnostic is scarcely a fit creature for one to contemplate as the highest product of a so-called supreme intelligence or God, or Good, however well he might look as the product of a minor and so seeking hieratic power. For if God, or Good, as so many have already pointed out, can do no better than produce the quarreling, eating, seeking, spewing thing we know as man—and that is the chief concern of His intelligence—!!!

We will assume that you have read at least a simple work on astronomy or chemistry or physics. If so, could you possibly believe that the present intelligence of man, or even any conceivable progress which he can make in his present limited form and with his present equipment of senses, would be of sufficient force to gather either the meaning or sensory impact of spaces, distances, weights, relationships which at present, except in the most minute and fragmentary way, are entirely beyond him? Consider the meaninglessness of numbers to you, of great weights, distances. I for one would be the last to cast a shadow upon man's dreams or pride, but when one investigates even the little we are permitted to know—the darkness, the inexplicable confusion, the non-reason in all the things we think, believe, hope for—it would, at the least, suggest that æons must elapse and man himself change radically and develop powers (which, if they are his at all at present, are in embryo) before he could begin to conceive of the significance of even the smallest of the forces which he seems to use but which in reality use him.

All the great things, the creative impulses and substances such as produce even the most minute forms of life which at present we can see, are entirely outside the range of his limited group of senses. He does not know, for instance, where heat or cold begin or end; what shades lie beyond the outer edges of the spectrum; what are the limits or the immediate beyond of sound, light, weight, space, etc. His weak senses plus his devised instrumental aids offer him no real help. They merely multiply his difficulties. Something has invented an eye, an ear, an olfactory nerve, the ganglia of the fingertips, the central cerebral cortex and so-called reason, all of which appear to be nothing more than assembled and synchronized reactions to other and unknown stimuli, wherewith it is possible now for man to apprehend only minute portions of the immense energies and substances blowing about him. Yet with all these aids and the evidences of the mechanism of the universe outside him which they yield, still man, attacking special bits and portions, finds it quite impossible to suggest the reason for anything. He lacks the equipment and power, which even the thing which made him may not have, of creating such finer perceptive organs as might aid him. At present and at best apparently he is allowed only to invent some things—such, for instance, as are or may be useful to the propagation and rearing of man in the matter of numbers, not brains. His Creator apparently is either unable or unwilling to endow him with such equipment as might make for great knowledge. Tremendous psychic opportunities appear and go by, as when a duller and more ignorant Rome conquers a sensitive and highly perceptive and meditative Greece. Owing to his minor equipment, ignorance and vain beliefs flourish, and he stumbles from one vain illusion and delusion to another—to achieve what? Something, possibly, which his Creator can use. Or so it would seem.

But it is not this phase alone which is troublesome. One might and does get along well enough knowing but a minute portion of that which, it would seem, our immediate Creator must plainly know concerning the processes by which we arrive, depart and function during our little stay here, but to a seeking intelligence there is inescapable tragedy in the plain implication, written large over everything, that to the accidental Creator of man the largest intelligence of whatsoever bent or character among him is of no more importance to the ruling force than the veriest gnat or leaf. It, whatever it is that makes man and the animal, manufactures intelligences as though they were buttons or pins, and though it create from time to time an Anaximander, a Plato, an Alexander, a Socrates, a Keppler, a Newton, a Leonardo or any other titanic brain, yet to it the least ditch-digger or wastrel is as important. The mass is everything, the individual nothing. With the greatest nonchalance or blundering inconsequence it strikes down a Hertz, a Raphael, a Curie, a Spinoza, a Schubert, a Keats. Seventy years is the allotted span for all, great or small, an average amount of strength, the same stomach and blood capacity. Though an individual had seemingly the most important ideas under consideration, great schemes wherewith to benefit or further the so-called progress of man (the especial care, as we learn, of his Maker), still this is of no least importance to his Creator. It is invariably on, on, out of the way, as though the Creator had most carefully arranged not to take advice from any one He made, or as though a blind process were at work which could not. If the former, one might say small blame to one so powerful. Presuming Him even moderately intelligent, how unimportant His little mannikins must be to the ultimate scheme of things, the giant forces through which He manifests Himself and which grind, helplessly create, helplessly control! Imagine taking advice from a loaf of bread you had accidentally evolved, or listening to the protests or advice of a ginger-snap of your own creating!

Nevertheless if it were possible in the face of the driving forces which seem wholly to manipulate him to reach man and by a suggestion aid him, it would be that in the face of so much confusion he no longer wastes time on theories wholly unrelated to himself or his own material welfare, his essential necessities here, but rather that he see to it first of all, and clearly, that his life here is something which is to be lived here and now to the utmost, in the best form for all—during seventy years, if not longer—here, and not elsewhere, and that some reasonable and concentrated effort be made to make it livable for man here and now instead of elsewhere, however glittering or picturesque that elsewhere may be, thin romance that it is. For is it not high time that we all realized how essential it is to make life worth while for all here, knowing as we now do that man is not a pet in Nature and that if he makes anything of himself and his social as well as his mental state here it must be with the full understanding that he can expect but little if any aid from Nature or the forces directing him, certainly none that would tend to ultimately enlarge his own mental clarity and supremacy. To this end therefore it would seem advisable that man as a whole throw over as swiftly as possible all his old-time religious and moral conceptions, his restraining conventions, taboos and the like, and re-examine for himself the data concerning which, accidentally or otherwise, he now finds himself capable of cerebrating and according to which he is now supposed to regulate his life. It may not be true that he should limit himself as his present theories and ethics suggest. And furthermore, his greatest problem being that of living longer, of being stronger, happier, not so much the butt and jest of chance or the willful or indifferent moods of the surrounding and stronger forces in Nature, that he devote himself entirely to solving those problems.

Elsewhere I have indicated a possibly broader moral conception which may be of value to this end. One of the greatest achievements, of course, would be to rid the human mind of all vain illusion concerning things spiritual, to get it to see, if it were possible, that man is not necessarily an enduring spiritual creature endowed—for who can know?—with an enduring and progressive soul, but rather that he is an implement or tool in the hands of something else which is creating or using him as, for example, the vine does the leaf, yet which itself may be of no great import in Nature.

If, by any process of investigation, and as now seems possible, it could be proved that man's Creator is no universal lord by any means but a blind fumbling force, it should be possible for man to do one of two things: either ally himself strictly with such impulses and instincts as he can detect as coming from this lesser and plainly more immediate Creator —many of them plainly non-moral enough, as we may see by like impulses in him, and so aid this Creator to discover Himself; or, now that he has a foothold here and appears to be a fairly self-perpetuating machine, to endeavor to reveal to himself and for himself the secret of self-creation and perpetuation and so become the equal of the force or forces now using him. But to that end he would need to rid himself of the delusion that anything in life should be accepted in blind faith and without question as permanent. One of the oldest of the Hebraic sayings is "My son, get wisdom, get understanding," and a later saw declares "Knowledge is power," and so it is. Adam, in the fable of the genesis of man, was condemned not so much for eating of the Fruit of the Tree of Knowledge as for the fact that "in the day ye eat thereof your eyes shall be opened and ye shall be as gods, knowing good and evil." And Prometheus (forethought), the other "God" who is supposed to have created man out of earth and water and who for man's benefit "stole fire from heaven in a hollow tube" and taught him all the useful arts, was punished for this by Zeus, the supreme "God," by being chained to a rock and having his liver daily torn by an eagle—certainly a most significant fable, for he was trying to make something of man, or rather teaching man to help himself, and this the Supreme Ruler of the Universe did not want, probably for the same reason that the Hebraic "God" wanted Adam to remain a dull machine or clod.

But the Greek fable is far more hopeful and significant than is the Hebraic one, for, in the former, strength (Hercules) subsequently slew the eagle and released Prometheus, or forethought, thus allowing him to aid man; while in Genesis man is condemned, slave-like and forever after, to "eat his bread in the sweat of his face," a very sharp commentary on the nature of his Maker as the ancients conceived him. What is implied by both fables is that man is a waif or accident in Nature, not intentionally endowed with wisdom or the power to get it, and that Nature (Zeus, Jehovah, anything you will) markedly objects to his obtaining any "lest he become as one of us" and "put forth his hand and take also of the Tree of Life and eat and live forever."

In view of this one might ask, Is life worth living? Is there any use? Perhaps there would be if man, accidentally evoluted or not, but coming at last, by accident or not, to the place where he finds himself able to reason upon the processes which have brought him thus far, could seize upon the constructive processes and so begin a creative, constructive career of his own which would redound to his own benefit and comfort and none other. Only there is no least evidence as to that yet, i. e., that it is possible. In so far as one may judge by chemistry and physics man appears to be in the grip of a blind force or process which cannot help itself and from which man can derive no power to help himself save by accident or peradventure. Even now, for all one can know, he may be sinking into a blind, unreasoning mush instead of evoluting further, so many are the theories which counsel him to believe in some vague, aimless peace hereafter and which he so readily accepts. The important thing for him to do, supposing that he could, would be to avoid henceforth all destroying notions of this character and to think of himself rather as a waif, an unloved orphan in space, who must nevertheless and by his own effort make his own pathetic way in the world. Or, if that is too harsh, then to think of himself as part and parcel (leaf and vine) of some hard-pressed Creator, a sun, a group of chemic forces synthetized into an individual somewhat like himself, not a Supreme God, by any means, but a kind of local manufacturer or well-meaning Prometheus who is trying to make something out of man and Himself at the same time, being in or of man, or man in Him ("I am in the Father; the Father is in me"), but who in turn and so through him, man, is being assailed by larger or rival forces and cannot always make His way as well as He might wish. Hence, He needs the consideration and even help of man, the atomic force of which

He is composed. That being the case, the burden of life might possibly come to seem less hard.

But, aside from such an hypothesis, thought offers but small comfort to the thinker viewing the drift of fact as one must. For see how painfully and often most sadly our scientists and philosophers dig at this riddle of existence and how slowly, if at all, we are really fitting ourselves for the giant task, these greater and greater contests with Nature, which must come if man is to come to anything. Even individual self-preservation via chemistry, physics, mathematics, economics, sociology, philosophy, astronomy, botany, biology, and what not, is a slow and difficult process. On every hand are destructive forces that beset us, and we have apparently only ourselves to look to that we be not so persistently tortured. All religions and theories of Divine aid to the contrary, man has been and is now compelled to battle hourly and momentarily for his "right" (how pale is that word!) to live and grow, let alone think—against heat, cold, destructive rivals and enemies of all kinds, destructive insects, savage animals, savage men, droughts, storms, dissensions, diseases, death—whereas he in turn has sought and does now seek to help himself via farmers, butchers, inventors, scientists, doctors, seeking to wrest from forces apparently alien to the one which prospers him, if there is such an one, some of the powers which apparently they hold in such vast abundance and which might even contain the secret of eternal life. Who knows? Indeed, surveying what has befallen him throughout the ages, I should suggest to man that he accept as true the fabled statement made by "God" in Genesis iii. 14:19, and seek persistently and without too much reverence for some method of solving his own difficulties. He should reject vain theory, especially that which relates to a mythical reward hereafter, and cling only to those methods and forms of procedure which give promise or hope of a larger reward here, tending to strengthen his capacity for living here and now. Such a theory or belief, however antagonistic to current religious theories, would at least tend to make man less depressed and indifferent to his state here and more conscious of the fact that if he is to extract any joy out of his span he must think and plan to make things better not only for himself but for others, since joy for himself depends upon his joy in others and they in him. Indeed, it would give him more zest for the game here if he did. By that last I am not arguing with the moralists for all their shabby, little pinchbeck repressions, the idea that the less you do and know the better you are; but rather that the more you do and know the better off you are, physically and mentally, and the more you make your state or form of government do and let you know the better.

How soon would not such an attitude—not on the part of all, for one cannot hope for that, but of even a moderate minority—make for a more vivid, aggressive, fascinating world! How soon might not the now seemingly sealed doors open, unsolvable (so-called) riddles end as solved, man acquire new reasoning faculties, senses and powers, and finally stand forth a creative force himself, a genuine creator on his own account, able not only to fend and forefend against many of his present disasters here but to give new powers and thought, and even creative force, to things which now crawl meekly at the feet of man? Who knows? Is not courage better than fear? a healthy, if skeptical, seeking better than blind, dull acceptance of anything or nothing, as the case may be? I, for one, think so, and, for my part, would prefer to be a seeking Prometheus chained to a rock and my liver gnawed daily by the eagle of an irritated and jealous higher power than a crawling worm or whimpering slave praying for some endless Nirvana, or a minute part in an endless legion of cherubim harping the glory of something which had plainly sought neither my peace nor my signficance but only my painful, unimportant and even worthless service.

NEUROTIC AMERICA AND THE SEX IMPULSE

I SOMETIMES think that a calm and exhaustive study of the American temperament in relation to sex and its various manifestations would result in the scientific conclusion that this country, taken as a whole, is as much a victim of a deep-seated neurosis relating to this impulse as any, the most morbid of those who appeal to psycho-analysis for treatment. The profound and even convulsive interest in any case involving a sex crime or delusion (Thaw, Leo Frank, Billy Brown, Carlisle Harris, Nan Patterson, Durant; or any negro rape case in the South); the ridiculous and quite neurotic interest displayed by grown men and women, to say nothing of children, in the exploits of so-called "cuties"—the "Spring Blossoms," "June Elfs," "Violet Dawns" of the movies—the perennial and astonishingly profitable (in so far as a certain class of theatrical management is concerned) interest of the male and even female American in the utterly mechanical and standardized beauty chorus shows with their (presumably) seventeen-year-old maids in bathing, bedroom-bath and other forms of abbreviated attire! Are not these points in evidence? In the matter of the latter, no story is necessary; just erotic color, music, dancing evolutions and double-meant (I almost said "mint") jokes, and the thing is done.

Again, look at any American city where morality or religion, or both, presumably have full sway (and in what American city are they not supposed to be dominant?), and what do you find? The most desirable locations in the best portions of the city, outside of the trade centers, given over to the leading churches and the newspapers, which preach a lofty code of ethics and morals which they themselves find difficult if not impossible to practice; while elsewhere the local bookstores and picture shops and bill-boards are crowded with a class of literature and illustration, or so-called "art," which to read or view, according to the adjacent churches and newspapers, would result in the loss of your immortal soul as well as your local standing. And yet these same are displayed, sold and read plentifully and with avidity, for the very good reason, no doubt, that they satisfy a craving and a thirst not otherwise open to satiation. In any town of any size, what pictures are not displayed and sold: "September Morn," "Youth," "Purity," "Innocence," "Yes," "Waiting," and the like, disguised as little as the law will permit. Again, where will you not find a swarm of sex magazines labeled "breezy," "snappy" and the like, the kind that any sex-suppressed neurotic might well crave, and all received with the profoundest gratitude and widest distribution? Where in America, any more than abroad (barring countries of Asia, Africa and the South Pacific, where sex-suppression is not the order of the day) does one lack for pornographic nudes or privately circulated writings of the most lurid character? Are the art or book or drug stores of the small towns free of them? Is it not true that you can still buy almost everywhere, "Three Weeks," "Life's Shop Window," "The Yoke," and other such classics, whereas those admirable volumes of life and satire "The Decameron," "Droll Stories," "The Confessions," Cellini, are only to be discovered, and that by chance and peradventure and "against the law," on the dark and musty shelves of some out-of-the-way old book store, and these consumed by the intelligensia and the sex-satisfied only, and with an upward mouth-curl of amusement at the innate humors of passion? The hobble-skirt, the tango dance, the Hula-Hula or Hawaiian melodies—what did each in its day indicate? Plays like "Everywoman," "Experience," "The Girl from Rector's," "Parlor, Bedroom and Bath"—what did they suggest?

Not so very long since, I stopped for a little while in a town of a hundred thousand population in the South. It was moral, religious, conventional—in other words, American. It might as well, however, have been in New England, the Northwest, the Southwest, the Middle West, for any difference to be discovered in its moral texture. In this home of chivalry, courtesy, purity and the like, erected originally on the backs of driven slaves, a number of its most interesting points of vantage were as usual occupied by the churches, as impressive and prosperous as those anywhere. It had only one theater of consequence, and that open only two nights a week, if so often. Its poorer classes were entertained by three or four moving-picture establishments ("Passed by the National Board of Censors"); but the well-to-do also attended these, for they had no other place to go for amusement. Yet, in the face of the highly censored "movies," theater and bookstores and the absence of houses of ill-repute (all suppressed), there were two or three "first-class" hotels, all with their Thès Dansantes, cabaret suppers and the like, of the character of which I propose to speak later. The most exclusive bookstore was so very moral that it would not carry any books not approved by the "Watch and Ward" and "Library Protection" association, nor would the vine-covered library in the best section, although at any time you might have gone to the principal dry-goods store and by a roundabout process secured nearly all that you desired.

While I was in this city a twelve-year-old boy was arrested at one of the railroad stations about two hundred yards from the principal beach for appearing in a two-piece bathing suit. It was not asserted in the prosecution which followed (which was vigorously defended by his father) that a twelve-year-old boy in a two-piece bathing suit was immoral, but a man in a one-piece one or a girl in any kind at all would be, and to avoid the possible vitiation of public purity which might thus follow the boy was arrested. He was discharged with a warning—but even so. You can see how high the virtue at this city should be.

Yet, at the same time, in this same city, were the three aforementioned hotels with their Thès Dansantes, roof gardens, cabaret grills, this, that and the other, and in these might have been seen, any late afternoon or evening, winter and summer, such a collection of sex-struck infants and elders as would be worth the same price of admission anywhere. The clothes! The wondrous shoes and gaudy purses, the subdued and yet moving and suggestive combination of colors! The efforts to flagellate the already too harried imagination with a promise of delights which the local morality squad, I fear, would never permit to be realized. You could pay as much in either of these places for a pot of tea and three little thin slices of toast as you could anywhere in the world. In their efforts to provide you with a superior (sex) atmosphere they made it possible for you so to do.

Wrong? Not a bit. I am not describing it for that purpose; nor am I quarreling with human nature for expressing its inmost desires, being what it is: avid, alluring, secret, hungry. I am smiling at the anachronistic spirit of the same community which would arrest the boy in the bathing suit, prohibit "near beer," snip every even weakly suggestive passage out of a "movie," "run" any indecent play ("Hedda Gabler," let us say, or "The Wild Duck," since it could not understand them) out of town. No copies of "The Song of Songs," Rousseau's "Confessions," "The Decameron," or the unexpurgated "Arabian Nights." Never, never, never! Yet look at these same hotels, these girls and youths clinging to each other in the suggestive dances! The movements, the sinuous, almost savage, abandon, the love-looks, the whispers! And the automobiles lined up along distant country roadsides in the dark later—although not a single house of assignation or prostitution was tolerated within the city limits. One had to secure a Ford and employ the open woods and fields instead. And in the basement next to the barbershop in each hotel was one or more "manicure booths," curtained confessionals or recessionals, into which one might retire with a manicure maid to have one's fingers done. Owing to the dashing quality of these maids the business was large.

For myself, I do not know what the psychic or spiritual or creative significance of these impulses of the sexes may be, unless, in truth, within equational limits they are moral or at least essential, and so to be cherished as a good instead of an evil; but one thing is certain: their appearance in this florid public form and in the center of a vice-cured city would indicate that either the attitude of the nation is wrong or that we have in our midst a host of neurotic or sex-struck degenerates who ought to be eliminated from the body civic in a very radical manner. But are they neurotic? Or is it the nation that is wrong, and these but the neurotic symptoms of its error? Certainly, nowhere outside of America and especially in such a vice-taboo realm as this, I fancy, are the terrors of sex excess, the degradation and disease following sex libertinage, more enthusiastically or more glowingly pointed out as the psychic or spiritual aftermath or heavenly punishment of these "sins"; and, yet, for all the length of time these horrors have been "known" or insisted upon or pointed out, and regardless of whether they are really true or not, is there any marked diminution of the so-called sex evil in America? Has the denying of drink or prophylactics to the American sailor or soldier cured him of his interest in sex? Will it? The world apparently, or that part of it expressed by, in or through the sexes, is as avid and seeking as ever. We know, or some of us do, that the chemistry by which we and the sex impulse are compounded is above the knowledge or volition of man, although its object in so far as human moods and passions are concerned, is plain enough. But in America we are not willing, if we do know, to admit it. Our increasing numerical presence here should be evidence enough of its force, but we waive that in favor of our theories in regard to the inherently moral and Christian home—even the complete suppression of sex! That a balance or equation between excess and license and inane, mollusc-like passivism in regard to sex and its expression is all that is ever struck in Nature, is plain enough to those who think; but that an American in authority in state or church should admit it! Life, apparently, is never exact in anything, and the desirability of having it so is of course open to question. But still——

Yet, to me, the impulses we are trying to suppress are, this side of excess, perfectly normal, while the thing we think we want is an infantile conception of life and its processes, unsuited to thinking men and women. Our conviction is apparently that sexuality is essentially wrong and debasing, and yet we do not really think so, as our intense national interest in every phase of sex proves. We are afraid to face ourselves honestly and openly in anything, neurotically so, and that is what makes the American intellect so utterly contemptible and negligible at times. What is nearer the truth is that our attitude is to be psychoanalytically traced in various ways to the strangely exaggerated (neurotic, I think) conceptions of the part sex or its over-emphasis plays in life due to repression, which have followed upon impossible religious theories brought from abroad (Quaker, Methodist, Puritan, Mennonite, Catholic), and our reaction to them. These have developed that repressive social and biologic ignorance regarding sex characteristic of so many American families, offspring of these sects even when they are no longer of them. The conviction that sex is debasing, dominant at least at this time in nearly every American mind, I believe, is to be traced so often to these earlier experiences, particularly with regard to parents and their views. The average American child—and I suppose England is not much better, judging by their novels and morals—is permitted to base its ideals of life and social relations, especially sex relations, on this earlier pretense on the part of parents that sex does not exist—for them at least.

So it is that we find adult boys and girls pretending, even to themselves, that they do not know what sex is and the manner in which children come into existence, and preachers and pretending thinkers speaking and writing as though sex were not an all but dominant force in life. And instead of viewing this inconceivably dull attitude as something that needs modification and bringing ourselves to the realization that there is nothing inherently disgraceful about having sexual desire, or at least knowledge of it, and of eventually gratifying it, we allow ourselves to be kept in tow of crack-brained religionists and ethic mongers who insist on painting our very normal natures as abnormal and so developing national neuroses and psychoses which make us ridiculous, not only to ourselves but to every other nation. It has even succeeded in twisting our judgments in regard to politics and economics. For without a rational conception of the part, and the very normal part, sex plays in life, how can there be sanity in these other things? One cannot be wrong as to one vital point in life and right as to all others. We continue to assert, as a nation and as individuals, that everything sexual is wrong, while at the same time having sexual feelings and impulses which we can scarcely disguise even to ourselves and which we satisfy or over-compensate for in ways too ridiculous to mention (a Billy Sunday revival, for instance; a White Slave Crusade in which our papers blaze with sickening criticism; an insane, an impossible pursuit of money or vice, due to the repression of every other normal instinct). Truly, a goose nailed to the floor by its feet and stuffed daily to produce an enlarged and salable liver, could be no more ridiculous or pathetic than the average American debarred from every avenue of intelligence or effort save that which relates to money.

It is a bit curious, one cannot help remarking, that the widespread fame and weight of such sincere and eminent investigators as Kraft-Ebbing, Ellis, Freud and his host of followers, with all the profoundly moving evidence of the pathos of sex-repression which they offer, has not had more influence upon our national, if not the world's international, mind. The sorrows revealed! The grisly prison doors unlocked by the patient and brilliantly revealing researches of Freud alone! The old sorrows dragged from the depths of the repressed subconscious and at last permitted to come forth into the light, where the fortuitous and yet crushing weight of earthly illusion and error may be noted! And yet they have not apparently as yet enlightened or broadened us.

At this point I would like to present a citation from the writings of one of our leading neurologists and psychoanalysts (H. W. Frink) in regard to the type of patient (neurotic) pouring in upon him from all parts of America. "My own experience," he writes ("Morbid Fears and Compulsions," page 224), "is that the sexual factor comes to expression in every analysis at once, usually within the first two or three visits, and I am sure that for this result no special technique or dexterities are required; about all that is necessary being to let the patient talk. To the question, Why is the sexual factor dominant in every neurosis? I shall not attempt to make any detailed reply. The answer is perhaps to be sought in the direction indicated by Meyer ("Discussion of Some Fundamental Issues in Freud's Psychoanalysis," State Hospital Bulletin, Vol. II, No. 4, 1910), when he says: 'No experience or part of our life is as much disfigured by convention as the sex feelings and ambitions.' That is to say, if we had other impulses which throughout the whole life of the individual were so consistently and unremittingly warped, cramped and deformed in every conceivable and unnatural manner (as they are in America) and they had the same strength to rebel against such treatment as have the sex impulses, *then* we might have neuroses in which they and not the sex factor played the dominant role."

For my own part, I cannot understand why it is that the human mind, and more especially the American or Anglo-Saxon mind, unless it is regulated by biogenetic forces over which it has no control but which have full control over it, functions so dully in regard to sex and its import. One would assume, from the average religious or social conception of the time, that the sole function of sex in all its ramifications is the production of more children, to live, work and die according to the prescribed routine of the dullest Christian formula. But, unquestionably, sex means much more than that. While it is true that some of the minor professors of psychoanalysis are offering what they are pleased to term the "sublimation of the holophilic (or sex) impulse" into more "useful," or, at any rate, more agreeable fields of effort via suppression or restraint, this in my judgment is little more than a sop, and an obvious one, to the moralists. What is actually true is that via sex gratification—or perhaps better, its ardent and often defeated pursuit—comes most of all that is most distinguished in art, letters and our social economy and progress generally. It may be and usually is "displaced," "referred," "transferred," "substituted by," "identified with" desires for wealth, preferment, distinction and what not, but underneath each and every one of such successes must primarily be written a deep and abiding craving for women, or some one woman, in whom the sex desires of any one person for the time being is centered. "Love" or "lust" (and the one is but an intellectual sublimation of the other) moves the seeker in every field of effort. It is the desire to enthrone and enhance, by every possible detail of ornamentation, comfort and color—love, sensual gratification—that man in the main moves, and by that alone. Protean as this impulse may be, and it takes many forms, it stands revealed as the underlying reality of a thousand astounding impulses or disguises—pathetic, lying, simulating, denying, but the same old impulse everywhere and under all circumstances. Refracted as it is by opposition, misunderstanding, failure into a million glistering and lovely or pathetic things, it may seem to be what it is not; but hold fast, trace it back, and there, at bottom, sex appears, a craving for love, and its accompanying sensual gratification, and there is no other.

But the thing which is especially interesting about America is its infantile blindness to all this and the pathetic and at least semi-neurotic condition into which we have fallen in consequence. As one views American life to-day it can be safely asserted that scarcely one of a hundred American men or women view this phase of life intelligibly, although they respond to it normally enough in some of its other phases. Usually before their so-called vision, and between them and their daily deeds, hangs an inane and miasmatic cloud of cant and make-believe. The physiologically and biologically informed know, of course, how ridiculous is the assumption that sex union is the narrowly "moral" function which the religionists would have one believe, although moral it may well be in some larger constructive sense, as is any other life process, if life itself can be termed moral. But that it can involve, without becoming profoundly ridiculous, a narrow or sectarian religious interpretation, is open to question. That it has a sad, tragic, even ruthless aspect (read Maeterlinck's description of the struggles of some flowers to be born and continue the species) is not, scientifically at least, to be combatted. In its biological aspects it has many, many tragic sides, although so dull is the race to all but its most individual ambitions and needs that it cannot be expected to sense this either. Indeed, as expressed by the impulses in man (concocted by what psychic meditation below and on the part of what?), sex is an unregenerate and only partially controlled passion which has more as its aim perhaps than is dreamed of in the philosophies of man. It is a fire, a chemical explosion, really. It concerns not so much the individual as the race, the endless unbroken chain of men and women, however much any individual may think it concerns him alone. Instead of denouncing the individual for his mood in regard to all this, it might be more important to inquire how moral in their import are the elements which compound and bring about the explosion and to treat him as one of their victims.

The truth no doubt is that in this much-maligned impulse which chemical forces beyond and above the willing of men are compounding lies the destiny of man (if he has one), only we are not as yet able to fathom that destiny. Here we come, bottles of fluid dynamite (prepared by what satiric super-soul, and why?), and somewhere in the world is, or may be, another compound which will set us aflame—and we are supposed to connect this with a narrow religious order or theory! I will admit that for the necessities of social arrangement and relationship here, the necessary balances and inter-adjustments that go to make up a workable society of beings, some form of equation between the less and more avid sexually, the too hot and the too cold, must be and is struck, willy-nilly and regardless of individual or man's moral theory. But by what rule and rote? Is there so-called "justice" in it, or "reason," or a fixed social order or method of procedure? We see that in spite of our fixed methods of moral procedure the tragedies continue, the waves and flames of morality and immorality come and go. Our divorce rate! Our sex tragedies and districts! And what guide has the individual? The Golden Rule? A more liberal method of adjustment? In the past, Nature has tolerated polygamy, polyandry and an abbreviated monogamy, and may do so again. The stress and strain which the present social arrangements show are almost premonitory.

But one thing is certain: no hard-and-fast rule governing this impulse has worked with accuracy for any given length of time, anywhere. If there are discovered or discoverable rules for its control and best management in the interest of the race and so in the interest of the Creator they have not yet been announced. We hear of the duty of preserving the sanctity of the home, maintaining a wife and raising a family according to the monogamic theory. Well and good. But, outside of raising endless children to be slain in wars, vegetated in a routine factory life, worn threadbare in a vast and internecine struggle for existence, there is not so much to be said for that, either. Routine home life, even an artistic breeding-pen, can scarcely be the be-all and end-all of human existence, any more than may unrestrained license. And however comfortable or admirable or encouraging the average home may be to given individuals, it is not necessarily so to all. There are those who find it confining, destroying. And, again, religionists and theorists, moral and otherwise, as well as the great greedy syndics and master minds in business or politics, prey upon the fruit of the home and collect "spiritual" and material taxes and establish "spiritual" as well as material autocracies or over-lordships which in no wise make for sex morality any more than for the forces which destroy it. Vice, suborned by the wealthy and powerful, as well as the avid and perverse among the weak, feeds upon the fruit of the so-called moral home. The bull seal still conquers his fifty or a hundred, and the weakling none. In fact, in a so-called Christian realm the mistress abounds, and the high divorce rate attests much private dissatisfaction with the theory. Laws come and laws go; and still we are about where we were before. The gardens of Aphrodite still exist. The hetæra of Greece and Rome are still with us—in our back streets or our high-priced apartment houses. If we no longer have our streets of the so-called "fallen" or "evil" women, who walk in the dark, is it not because caution has become the better part of trade? Are they not to be found behind closed doors in response to special rings, by card of admission, in our best streets? The endless pother! And still sex is as vigorous and dominant as ever it was. The riant scoffers nod and smile and accept the new rules.

Personally, after all this time, my conclusion is: (1), that no individual, however well or ill compounded physically, can make or unmake his moods or add one jot or tittle to his moral desires or perfections, although he and society (or convention) can exercise a certain amount of restraint—a restraint that will almost invariably prove irksome and which he will seek to evade; (2), that however much theorists, hypocrites and sincere religionists, chill-blooded or otherwise, may revile sex or attempt to restrain or destroy it, yet Nature (God or the devil, or the two in one) permits these wild fires to be generated in man, and, in spite of all punishments and hindrances, sees to it that his passions overleap his fears and judgments and cause him to do all the things that may be strictly forbidden him but which may nevertheless be of value to the race itself; (3), that man is not temperamentally or chemically a monogamous animal, however much the social conditions and necessities by which he finds himself surrounded in certain lands and times tend to make him believe so or fear, and that a rough balance or equation is all that is ever struck between his outward public deeds and his inner chemic condition; (4), that, to this hour, there is no city without its percentage of prostitution or hetæra of one grade or another; (5), that there is no city or town where some women or girls do not walk, secretly or openly, to accomplish prostitution and where men do not, secretly or openly, encourage and pursue them, the chemic necessities of their being as much as poverty impelling them to do it; (6), that there is no city or town or countryside, anywhere, where adultery or fornication is not indulged in outside wedlock for love or pleasure; (7), that a high percentage of men in all walks, including priests and clergymen, look after some one type at least of woman and lust after her; (8), that a moderate percentage of women, in marriage and out, seek the affection of a given type of man temperamentally or chemically agreeable or appealing to them, and offer their bodies as a bid for or sacrifice to that affection; (9), that women crave monogamy where their affections or the interests of their children are involved; (10), that love of one woman or one man, or their several or joint love of children, is likely to overlay and put at rest, for the time being, the usual roving desires of sex; (11), that law in all special instances is absolutely helpless before passion, powerless either to interpret its psychology or fix a just measure of praise or blame; (12), that convention has not made, and cannot make, any headway against a chemical scheme of life which puts sex desires first and all else as secondary or socially contributory.

Do I seem illogical or inclined to exaggerate? Think well over the things I have said. The world has a partially traceable history covering more than ten thousand years; in that time nations have risen and fallen, law codes have come and gone, religions have dominated and been swept away. In no law code and in no religion of any nation has the sex question, the need of moderation, duty to family and the like, been ignored. But in all that time the social expression of sex has never been so much as modified, let alone done away with. The Mosaic law is all of three thousand years old, yet what has it availed? Are our women all pure, our men all moral? Yet, in the face of history and present-day occurrences, the facts of divorce courts, night courts, streets crowded with prostitution and kept women, men seeking constantly to lure women, and vice versa, all the million and one evidences in books, plays, newspapers and social life generally that sex is the keynote of existence, there are those who would bar all mention of it, harry the prostitute, unduly punish the fornicator, ostracise the woman who strays from the path of virtue or seeks in divorce a way out of a troubled marital state.

What to make of the brain of man under such circumstances? What to say of the thing that causes him to fight the passion of which he is a victim? Necessity for equation and balance in all things, a very rough balance which cares no more for the individual "good" or "bad" than we care for flies or gnats? Inherent love of moderation in some? Love of peace in some? Love of the reverse in others? The tendency of all things to become static, even passionate temperaments? Surely that, and nothing more. Yet, aside from that, there is something which does not care for the equation-seeking mood of either individuals or society, which is busy manufacturing and pouring into the world new individuals with all their new dreams, passions, lacks of equation, lack of a sense of self-restraint, and sweeping away the old, the conservative, the religious, sanctimonious.

One of the sanifying recourses in life is, of course, to fix one's eye on youth and note what it desires. Plainly, it is a fair expression of the thing that creates it, the chemic mood of the biologic force, for plainly it is closer to that which creates it. As the human or physical machine ages and wears out it is prepared, and then only, to accept the restraints and the equation which society, in order to maintain itself, requires; but not before. In the main, youth blazes with non-equational fires and it best represents that which makes it, the concocting chemic impulses below or behind life. Is youth wrong? Then so is the life impulse, for it builds youth freshly to its needs yearly, daily. The physical laws which seem to govern the biologic impulse after it expresses itself in the shape of youth, or man, and compels it for purposes of social expression to submit to restraints and equation, is another matter, inherent, perhaps, in the constitution of the universe itself and not to be avoided by the biologic impulse or its creatures. But this, as I have said before, does not provide us with *exact* rules for conducting ourselves here or how best to subdue or balance with other things the enormous fires with which we sometimes find ourselves lit. Better admit at once that hard-and-fast and cock-sure rules or laws are of no avail, and trust to the crude accidents of life to caution youth. A happy balance between the fires of youth and the fears and chills of age may be desirable, but, freely admitting that, can it be fixed by exact rule? We are inherent in some greater thing than man—Nature Herself. Only She knows.

One thing is sure: we are not done with the conflict and amazing super-impulses of sex, and are not likely to be soon. And if we were, would life be the varied, fascinating, humorous, poetic, tragic thing we see it to be? Suppose the moralists ruled, with their stiff and narrow balance, and man accepted their quiescent dictates—then what? Contrast it with some of the freer, more distinguished periods—Greece, Rome, Italy during the Renaissance, France under the Louis, England under Elizabeth and Charles II. Consider. I for one see no immediate solution, and firmly believe there is none which does not end in complete mental quiescence—balance or its equivalent, intellectual and emotional or temperamental nothingness, decay and dissolution, with something not so balanced and therefore alive, to supersede, if we are to have any form of life at all.

SECRECY—ITS VALUE

IN the face of a rampant and inane morality which is constantly seeking to befog or misinterpret a world which needs to be seen quite clearly if man is even partially to understand himself or the conditions by which he is confronted, it is well to remember that life is secret, nearly entirely so, in all its phases. Nature reveals Her secrets to no man, save grudgingly and peradventure. By dint of slow searching and because of his own necessities and sufferings he has discovered a few things—how few, as contrasted with the vast sea of the all but undiscoverable, not even the wisest can guess. And, even só, it is all a process of inclusion, and hence exclusion. How little included? And how much excluded? And Her secrecy is by no means moral or ethical or generous in any way. Yet, confronted by all the iron and pagan mysteries of a catch-as-catch-can world, and seeing daily and hourly that only the strong or shrewd or gifted, or those befriended by them, survive, and the weak and untalented are left to fester in want, and that only a rather loose and not very protective or comforting balance or equation is struck between extremes of any kind (even between his so-called God and devil), man still persists in interpreting his needs or hopes or dreams as the result of a super-tender administration of some kind, and sniffs rather disconsolately, if not quite unbelievingly, at the hard facts by which he is confronted. He is so anxious to think Nature kind, generous, non-secret. Indeed, any well-reared-and-ordered moralist or religionist would be inclined to contend, I am sure, that the world is not in the main secret, or at least not maliciously so, and that, even if it is, it should not be—innate desire for balance and equation between so-called evil and good always urging him to this conclusion.

But, Nature is secret, quite maliciously so at times, and Her secrecy is not to be escaped, even by those most anxious to condemn that phase of Her character. All of us, as a part of Her, reflect this chiefest characteristic as well as the most powerful instinct implanted in us by Her—namely, the desire to preserve ourselves and propagate our kind as against the lives and interests of all others. And, being confronted also by one of Her sternest regulations, that only the shrewd, the cunning, the appropriate or desired or presently essential or fit shall survive when assailed by millions of other creatures not so fortunately equipped, we are compelled to admit that we are at least a part of a more or less internecine struggle and so do our best, willy-nilly, as time and occasion may warrant or suggest to escape via secrecy, intrigue, cunning and the like. In other words, we are compelled to conceal that which is important to us and possibly inimical to others, showing, in times of stress, only that which will help us; hence, we, along with everything else, are compelled to be secret whether we wish to or not.

It may be mentioned here that there is a certain fish whose scientific name is Mycteroperca Bonaci and whose common name is Black Grouper, which is of considerable value in this connection. It is a healthy creature, growing to a weight of two hundred and fifty pounds and living a comfortable existence because of its very remarkable ability to adapt itself to conditions. Now while that very subtle thing which we call the creative power and which we endow with the spirit of the Beatitudes is supposed to build this mortal life in such fashion that only honesty and virtue shall prevail, still it builds this fish. Moving in its dark world of green waters, Mycteroperca has the very essence of secrecy, the power of almost instantaneous change into something quite different in so far as appearances are concerned. Its great superiority over other fishes lies in an almost unbelievable power of simulation, which relates solely to the pigmentation of its skin. In electrical mechanics we pride ourselves on our ability to make over one brilliant scene into another in the twinkling of an eye and flash picture after picture before the onlooker. The directive control of Mycteroperca over its appearance is so wonderful that you cannot look at it long without feeling that you are witnessing something spectral and unnatural, so brilliant is its power to deceive. Lying at the bottom of a bay, it can simulate the mud by which it is surrounded. Hidden in the folds of glorious leaves, it is of the same markings. Lurking in a flaw of light, it is like the light itself shining dimly in water. Its power to elude or strike unseen is of the greatest. One might go far afield and gather less forceful indictments—the horrific spider spinning his trap for the unthinking fly; the lovely Drosera (Sundew) using its crimson calyx for a smothering-pit in which to seal and devour the victim of its beauty; the rainbow-colored jellyfish that spreads its prismed tentacles like streamers of great beauty, only to sting and torture all that falls within their radiant folds. Man himself is busy digging the pit and fashioning the snare, but he will not believe it. His feet are in the trap of circumstances; his eyes are on an illusion.

But what would you say was the intention of the overruling intelligent, constructive force which gives to Mycteroperca this ability? To fit it to be truthful? Or would you say that subtlety, chicanery, trickery were here at work? An implement of illusion one might readily suspect it to be, a living lie, a creature whose business it is to appear what it is not, to simulate that with which it has nothing in common, the power of its enemies to forfend against which is little. The indictment is fair.

Yet is it not ridiculous that where all Nature is working in shadow, each thing hiding from the other its processes or thoughts of power and its intentions, that we ask of poor, spindling, cowardly, scurrying man, dodging perpetually here and there between the giant legs of chance and, in so far as he is concerned, all but malign forces, that he stand up and speak *the truth* in all things (would that he could discover it!) or that he say boldly and on all occasions what is in his heart, what are his intentions? Of old we know that men do not, anywhere, save in consonance with their interests, and yet the silly, self-interested request persists; a demonstration of how thought or observation and deduction and principally self-interest lag behind fact. The only thing which opposes secrecy and brings it to light is the skill for secrecy in others; another illustration of the law of balance or equation in Nature, the necessity of give and take in life, the desire of the other person to be protected from too much secrecy on the part of others. But the folly of the appeal in its ideal form, the charm that would disappear with the arrival of absolute frankness, the mystery that would go!

Ninety-nine and ninety-nine one-hundredths of all the interest or charm of all the creatures of the earth and of the circumstances and spaces and conditions in which they find themselves, is the secrecy—or, what is the same, the mystery or subtlety—which attaches to them. We do not know them; we do not understand them; we wonder at their states, their thoughts, their moods, what they will do, which way turn, when attacked, whom attack, whom deceive, whom praise, whom reward. Secrecy—secrecy—mystery. If it were gone the illusion of life itself, which is all that it is, would be gone also. And we are cautioned to love truth and to say truly and to our own hurt if necessary! And some advocate this so earnestly as part of the service due the other person, or of life to us. Yet, in the main, it comes to this: every other is to speak the truth to *us*, to conceal no important fact that might be helpful to us from *us,* to do justice to *us,* to think kindly of *us.*

A fine program, and absolutely consonant with our desire to live, prosper, succeed, regardless of the well-being of every other.

But let us reverse the program and advocate to ourselves, even in jest, that we do strict justice (if we could discover what that might be) to every other or tell him the exact truth about ourselves (heaven forbid!), our adventures, dreams, schemes; to think kindly (yes, even to think kindly in the face of the little that we know) of him. The Catholic hierarchy—which, by the way, has little to do with Messianic Christianity and its fine-spun ideals—so thoroughly understood human nature of the middle centuries as well as to-day that it introduced as an intermediary between man and his own conscience, his private shames, regrets, fears: the confessional (secrecy) in order that the average individual might free his soul of crimes without exposing himself to the fierce light of criticism which a public confession or truth-telling would entail. And the hesitation and even shame, for all its cloak of secrecy, with which the confessional is approached! The Church knew that man was not equal to the task of confronting his own accusing conscience in the open or before others but must confess in secret, if at all. Hence the drawn curtain and the reward of absolution for confession!

War, in the main the result of economic pressure, is an illustration of the necessity for secrecy, or rather the methods by which war is made—strategy, no less. Mere brute numbers clouting each other to obtain a numerical supremacy is nothing. A soldier worthy the rank of corporal would smile at such a program. Secrecy is the thing, the devising of traps and lures whereby the enemy may be betrayed and to his undoing. The spider weaving his net, the trapper devising his traps, the snake moving in grasses the color of itself, is no different to the general who by strategy (and what general without strategy is worthy the name?) seeks to encompass the enemy. Shakespeare in Macbeth, by means of the witches, suggests so archly the value of secrecy to the so-called good or just (in that instance MacDuff) in fighting evil (Macbeth) by having the soldiery of MacDuff simulate Birnam Wood by cutting off and carrying the branches of its trees towards his castle, thus lyingly fulfilling the prophecy of the witches to Macbeth that he should not be injured until Birnam Wood should rise and come against him, and so destroying his self-confidence. And, indeed, is not stark, threatening secrecy, non-moral force that it is, the thing which gives color if not joy to life and which lends surprise, uncertainty, fear and hence freedom from ennui to life, and, by contrast, hope and calculation, the greatest and most charming of all our gifts? For what game or sport, implying, as they do, friendly contest, would be worthy the name if it did not involve the element of chance or uncertainty, or, in other words, secrecy, to the extent that one cannot beforehand determine the outcome?

Again, are not all of our ambitions, if not as to their purport at least as to their outcome, secret? Nature provides secrecy, or uncertainty, which is the same thing, or darkness as a condition for the development of quite everything, from seeds to human plans, and builds and builds with us in countless ways and to astonishing results, and yet we are not permitted to share Her secret. Our petty brains and bodies are but mere implements of sorts in Her hands whereby She is constructing something, the significance or purpose of which we cannot even guess and which She is at no pains to reveal. She builds us to contain, or rather to comprehend, but a modicum, a minute fragment, of the enormous information or secret which is Hers. Secrecy on Her part, you see.

If one turns to the pages of science, what a masterly array of natural diplomacy and artifice is there displayed! The fishes of the sea imitating the coloring of the grasses or shadows of the deep in which they hide and by means of which they escape their enemies (protective coloring is the scientific name); insects the same, in so far as foliage and grasses are concerned; birds the same; reptiles the same; man, for all his noble theories and dreams of a generous and unselfish mode of conduct, the same; as artificial and secretive as any, he. The stripling lawyer imitates the look and manner of his intellectual superior—words, phrases, carriage, side-whiskers even—in order to seem his equal, or in other words to conceal (secrecy, you see) the fact that he is not his equal, from some trusting and unsophisticated client. Protective coloring, as it were.

Take again the instance of a man beginning to rise financially and wishing to appear the equivalent of men far richer than himself. His office is in their vicinity, his residence in their neighborhood. He is in their club if possible, their church, their directories. He is not as rich as they are, but wishes to conceal the fact. It is not good for the world to know that he is not what he is not. His few public deeds would not be as acceptable or he would be compelled to doff the uniform he so much desires to wear, the manners, along possibly with the emoluments thereof, or the hope of them. Secrecy—secrecy—secrecy. A seeming only, where reality would leave life bare and hard.

And is it not the same with doctors, merchants, professionals of all kinds? To this day is not medicine, like most other professions, fond of mystery and secrecy. . . . Latin for instance, in preparing its prescriptions, thereby giving them an air of superiority which is not necessarily there at all, or to prevent the patient from knowing what is being put into his stomach, or to make the cure seem more formidable by being mysterious or secret. And to this hour, lawyers delighting in magnificently darksome briefs, which in simple language would be understandable to all and far less fearsome. Again, religion, the Catholic and many other versions, rejoicing in a ritual which, if presented or sung in English, would be just as impressive to the really intelligent if it possessed any genuine merit or appeal. But to the ignorant laity, according to the thoughts of the churchman, it might not be; hence the Latin. And perhaps it is as it should be, for do not the ignorant and the savage invariably crave that which they cannot understand? It may be that they desire something more symbolic of all they feel but cannot express, a quantity and quality of mysterious inner moods and emotions which no human spoken words, especially those of their own tongue, would even suggest.

Hence the priest and preacher, Shi'ite or Sunnite, Dervish, Buddhist, or Brahman formalist, one and all, although ordinary human beings like ourselves, are trained, and most carefully, in the protective coloring of their profession. For essentially they are no different, or, with very rare exception, no more spiritual, no more self-sacrificial—in other words, no more unnatural—than any of their fellows. But, in due process of time, the manners, customs, rules even of those who by chance or peradventure (the accident of disposition or revulsion from too much of something else) have been tender, self-sacrificial, humanitarian, have given these latter their cue. They now know, let us say, what "good" or self-restraining or humanity-loving men and women in times past have, at one time and another, been like, how they walked in humility, denied themselves the pleasures, even the necessities of life, divided a cloak with a beggar or gave it whole, went with an importunate enemy two miles instead of one, turned the other cheek to one who had smitten them on one, gave the last of money or food to one who was hungered, shelter to the shelterless, warmth to the cold, ignored frivolity or laughter because of so much existing misery. And so those who, without performing similar discomforting services, would like to appear thus, now know what to do, how such an one, assuming that he minister to the weak, the erring, the deficient, should conduct himself, his most appropriate airs, manners, moods. Hence—but does one need to call attention to the vast system of protective coloring which now produces saviors, samaritans, ministers by the hundreds of thousands throughout the world, all presumably embracing the qualities which make the self-sacrificial character important, if it is important, yet who perform few if any of those deeds which the coloring implies: the "cloth," the hats, the reversed collars, the severe *black,* sign of abstemiousness, self-sacrifice, putting aside of the vanities, shows and pleasures of this world.

Of course there is always the rare individual born so strong, so wise, so courageous, that he needs few if any disguises in order to make life palatable to him, or his way in it. But he is rare, and, even when present, may not always proceed with ease or fearlessly but must disguise the courage and intelligence which he possesses (secrecy). Even he, when dealing with weaker, as well as stronger, individuals and groups, dare not show forth his true strength, save in their behalf, unless he would evoke their destroying anger. For masses, lacking power as to their individual units, are infuriated by one who is not so constituted, who offends by his strength their own futility. All lesser strengths, whether represented by individuals or masses, are envious and jealous of power. And the strong hate the strong quite as much as they do the weak when the latter are opposed to them. And, vice versa, the weak look upon the strong as driving masters, but the strong look upon the strong as rivals seeking power equal to their own, or equal to the task of displacing them. Hence their bitter and destructive rage; the hate of tiger for tiger, for instance, bull for bull. Secrecy, secrecy, here as elsewhere apparently the best policy Nature has been able to devise the only or the essential one, the one most employed. Truly the wise, however powerful, disguise their power and wisdom. They go softly, speak kindly, advocate justice or equation in all things, as well they may, seeing that they themselves may stand in need of it at any turn; and, if they work their will, work it in the dark and alone as much as possible.

What, then, shall we say of life when confronted by truths such as these—that it is offensive, unbearable, a thing to be wept over, shunned, departed from as quickly as possible? I think not. Nature has always been so, and men for millions of years have undertaken life with all its difficulties and subtleties and have done well enough. Indeed, they have thrived, like all those who sharpen their souls against difficulty. It is Nature's way. With steel She cuts steel, with subtlety subtlety, and the whole process appears to be one in which a more capable device for enduring the inherent restlessness and changefulness of Nature Herself is steadily prepared. It is one of dull wit upon whom, like barnacles, illusions fasten. And he is in error who assumes that the processes of Nature are different from those of man. We are like life, like the chemicals and forces of which we are composed, and have always been so. Only theory and dogma, growing upon and obscuring sluggish minds, have permitted the rise of a contra-conception. We should brush the cobwebs from our eyes and do away with illusion. In so far as possible, and as did the gladiators of old, we should face life with such weapons as we may, some with raw strength and short sword and shield, others with net and trident; one relying on brute strength if need must, the other on the skill and craft with which he may enmesh and slay. There is no other way. Life is so, and only the cowardly or the dull or the weak will either fail to see or endeavor to evade so solemn and even terrible a truth.

IDEALS, MORALS, AND THE DAILY NEWSPAPER

FOR two centuries now if not longer the newspapers, rather than the preachers and reformers generally who preceded and still parallel them, have been elevating themselves to the rôles of soothsayer, prophet, and guardians of all phases of virtue, honesty and the like, to say nothing of those shibboleths of the would-be intellectually dominant, "justice" and "truth." And the particular views of these papers have come to have an undue weight with those so moderately equipped intellectually as to look upon them as moral leaders. Experiments in government and phases of moral self-control, public and private, are there constantly advocated for the good of the other man, yet nearly always in accordance with the current bias or the direction of the interests of the paper. Yet back of these papers, and in spite of a public following which is supposed to regulate or control or suggest their policy and viewpoint, is always, or nearly so, an individual or group of individuals, possibly a self-interested organization (commercial, religious or otherwise) with perhaps no more intellectual grip on the social and spiritual complexities of the world than any other individual of average capacity and judgment, possibly not so much. Yet with the tremendous leverage of circulation, plus a serviceable and profitable and aggressive counting-room to help out, their moral and social pronunciamentos ridiculously enough become all but sacrosanct, irrefutable, colossal! Yet after all is said and done, here is nothing more than an individual, all too human perhaps, or if not that, a group represented by one individual possibly, seeking via this same lever (circulation) the special, particular things which he or it or they crave. And as a rule he or his group is truckling and hand-rubbing to that which he or it or they imagine the time requires, but seeking always circulation first, as though that were the be-all and end-all of all value, wisdom and duty.

And yet, in America at least, where will you find a citizen who does not to a marked extent reverence the opinions of his paper? The slavish manner in which in certain regions to this day the voters follow a paper and the manner in which the American press has successfully clouded issue after issue since America began—the currency issue for one, the slavery issue for another, the tariff issue for a third, the trust issue for a fourth, the profiteering and European war issues at the present moment. And where will you find a newspaper not advertising passing panaceas that it knows cannot heal (I am not talking about patent medicines), or admitting that a satisfactory social solution for the woes of the millions cannot be found, or admitting frankly that human law is the widespread net that it is, through which great and small alike skip briskly, chance and accident restraining some and releasing others? Only when the big skip through the lesion is greater. Or where will you find a newspaper that will freely admit that the Ten Commandments are not after all God-given law (do not think for a moment that they privately believe they are), or that they constitute anything more than a form of social agreement based for their validity on the will of the majority and not holding where men do not believe them to be true and not followed by any spiritually destructive consequences where men do not accept them to be spiritually true? Life pours through the reportorial, editorial and counting-rooms of the average newspaper pell-mell quite as it does elsewhere, only a little more so. Those at the head note well the secrecy, the self-interest, the "policy" running through all things, the struggles of all individuals and organizations to grow, usually at the expense of everything else; yet editorially, and at the very best, a balance or dependent equation between rival clashing interests—rival, hungry, self-seeking hordes—is all that is ever struck here, although this is all but invariably announced as the Sinaitic command of an all-wise, omnipotent, omnipresent intelligence, the newspaper editor or owner posing as its especial mouthpiece and forwarder! Is it not too ridiculous that so human and fallible or greedy and venal a thing as the average newspaper should set itself up to be a moral and at times even a religious arbiter of a community?

Yet where would be the circulation of the average paper if it did not so do? And where would it be if it attempted to practice what it preached, literally and for itself, as it so freely advises others to do? As all those well know who have anything to do with the organization or control of anything in life, newspapers included, the Beatitudes, as Christ laid them down in the Sermon on the Mount, are not workable and never have been practically. Yet where will you find a newspaper honestly so stating, or even whispering a serious doubt? On the contrary, is it not the absolute workability of these that has, hitherto at least, been most violently insisted upon, and by organizations which well know the pagan complexities of life and are in no way representative of even the faintest approach toward a beatific conception of anything? "Do not as I do but as I say." That only quiescence and decay could follow the enforcement of any such program as the Beatitudes or the fixed rules of justice, truth, etc., advocated by the average daily paper or any one else, is not only scientifically demonstrable by chemistry and physics but is a truism to the average, and even less than average, constructive and even newspaper mind. Nearly every one with any claim to intelligence or experience understands this, yet where will you find a newspaper or any other public medium of expression venturing on this simple truth? The average man is still in leading strings to various silly theories, religious or otherwise, fostered by self-interested groups, or to his hope of temporary human prosperity, and these are the things which still keep him in the wake of various sophisticated journals which cunningly play upon his illusions. Indeed he flees exact fact as though it were the plague. Blessed words or the sweet milk of romance and prevarication are the things which entertain and soothe him most. In other words—think of this ridiculous and paradoxical fact!—a creature invents a bugaboo and then kneels down and worships it. It forges chains for its so-called intellect, and then groans or rests content under their binding weight.

But (to continue this slight diatribe) imagine the staff of any newspaper even attempting to follow any rules save those which govern the survival of the fit, or failing to cast the Beatitudes out of doors when it comes to their special interests or the prosperity of the several functions which they perform! Editorially the Beatitudes prove profitable as texts for moral preachment and mass consumption, but in the counting-office or the gathering of news how different! And as for going two miles with a traveler when he had compelled you to go one, or turning the other cheek when the first had been smitten! These things do not fall within the realm of the practical and are therefore not in the purview of any newspaper organization except in the editorial or pulpiteering department, and that intended to catch the pennies of the religionists.

So daily we have the spectacle of pages that in one column misrepresent the motives of the social or political enemies of this or that particular newspaper organization, or that play up to the subtleties of vice or crime for their news or dramatic values, or that display to the eyes of the young and old alike all the misadventures and incalculable subterfuges of a treacherous universe, while in another column, constantly reiterated, appear the words right, justice, mercy, truth, tenderness, duty, etc., as representing a definite program for conduct for the other person always, easily followed and easily achieved—by him. Yes, for the other person, outside of any given newspaper office, there are always God-given and immutable rules which spell peace and happiness for him, that are invariably to be practiced, if you will believe these same papers, by the majority, especially of their readers. And indeed these rules are by them persistently represented as the will and thought of a definite, definable God—He who spoke from Sinai, or who walked to Calvary (quite different Gods, by the way!)—to fly in the face of whom or which leads only to destruction. Yet all that is needed, as they well know, in so far as a reasonable guide to conduct is concerned (and all that we ever get, whether via the law or the average motivating impulses of man) is the perception and the fact of the necessity for a certain equation or balance in all things, i. e., the Golden Rule, mystic heavens or hells and the clerical representatives of the same with their collections and false notions to the contrary notwithstanding. Yet where will you find a newspaper with sufficient courage to say so? Where? Is it not here that one should pause and inquire whether the newspapers, aside from their purely reportorial functions (which latter might well be viséd under stricter libel, perjury and false witness laws than those prevailing at present), should receive so much as even a moment's serious consideration?

EQUATION INEVITABLE
A VARIANT IN PHILOSOPHIC VIEWPOINT

IN society, where man is constantly scheming out methods of procedure and how his ideas and feelings and appetites can be brought to a harmonious workable state, a certain reciprocating smoothness of exchange and balance must be, and apparently has been, achieved. It is like those constructive adjustments which make any machine possible, and has apparently given rise to such conceptions of the necessary conditions for exchange as are indicated by the words "harmony," "justice," "truth," possibly even "tenderness" and "mercy," all of which mean but one thing, if they mean anything at all: the need of striking a balance or achieving an equilibrium between plainly restless and conflicting elements. (Why restless? Who knows? Why conflicting? Who knows?) However, it is this same equation or balance which conditions so large a thing as a universe, whose prime impulse apparently is to achieve endless variety in homogeneity, and vice versa.

But these have been assumed, in an absolute and not a relative sense, to be attributes of a Supreme Being who is all-just, all-truthful, all-merciful, all-tender, rather than as mechanic or, if one accepts the created theory of life, as an intelligently and yet not moralistically worked-out system of minor arrangements, reciprocations and minute equations, which have little to do with the aspects and movements of much larger forces of which as yet we know nothing and which at first glance hinder rather than aid the intellect in perceiving the ultimate possibilities of the governing force in any direction. Indeed the rough balance or equation everywhere seen and struck between element and element, impulse and impulse, need and need, while they might seem to lend color to the existence of absolute right, justice, truth, honor, etc., really indicates nothing more than this rough approximation to equation in everything—force with matter, element with element—as an offset to incomprehensible and, to mortal mind, even horrible and ghastly extremes and disorder; nothing more. For in the face of all the schemes and contrivances whereby man may live in harmony with his neighbor there is the contrary fact that all these schemes are constantly being interfered with by contrary forces, decays, mistaken notions, dreams which produce inharmony. This can mean nothing if not an inherent impulse in Nature that makes for change and so rearrangement, regardless of any existing harmonies or balances, plus the curious impulse in man and Nature (inertia?) which seems to wish to avoid change.

In spite of all man's laws, taboos, social understandings, agreements and beliefs, there are certain things done under the sun which do not make for perpetual peace, harmony, order, exact justice and so the welfare of the race *as he conceives it;* nor do they argue for the domination of a harmonious, all-powerful God *as man conceives Him.* Shocking as it may seem, certain individuals and groups contrive to live and thrive under conditions which, according to other masses and individuals who live and contemplate them, are apparently inimical to the so-called best interests of the race and the plans of its Creator. Indeed the latter is constantly, according to man or his theorists, trying to overcome them and so save Himself.

Who and what are these inimical forces which are supposed to defy God Himself? Criminals, liars, lechers, murderers, self-aggrandizing intellects of all types and sizes, plus accident, disease, cataclysm. At the same time and as if working in harmony with them, and to the dismay of the religionist at least, there are vast legions of inimical non-moral and seemingly socially non-helpful or even destructive microbes and animals which seize on man, the image of God, whose welfare God seeks, and which live and thrive without sign of consciousness of God, equation, or anything else. I am thinking of the germs of cholera, smallpox, yellow fever, as well as plagues of locusts, worms, wood-lice or scales, rats and the like, which while destroying vegetation and wealth most necessary to man at one point at the same time may and do nourish birds inimical or helpful to him and cause all things to develop methods of defending themselves and so aid their growth. The chemic or mechanistic interpreter of life discovers equation here well enough, and even a kind of rough harmony, although the religionist does not, and so while it is entirely possible for a monistic or evolutionary mystic to believe in a series of individually severe but racially helpful checks and balances which in some of their aspects are non-moral but are still driving man on to something, good or ill, it is not possible for the religionist or the moralist, taking him at his own dogmatic valuation, so to do. God must be good, exactly just, always merciful, as man understands those things in the realm in which he moves. Though a world of scientific data may now be brought forward to demonstrate that God is not a personality with a given moral direction or bias, as we understand morals, or with a here decipherable purpose, yet he must deny that. The nature of God, if not revealed by a voice of thunder from a mountain top, is, according to him, seen in the works of Nature; and the works of Nature are good.

But if God, or Good, is imminent, working for some far-off, Divine event, why the intermediate pother? I wonder at times why those who ponder these things with a view of "saving" the race and so eventually establishing truth, justice, mercy here on earth, are not permanently confused or hushed into silence by the overwhelming evidence that no one thing, however put together by the human brain to endure, succeeds ultimately in maintaining itself or that which it dreams it will maintain. Religions come and go. Laws are written and fade away. Moral laws change with groups and climates. There remains only this necessity for equation, some form of adjustment, reciprocity, balance between the integral factors of each group, good, bad or indifferent, which no one thinks of translating as the *only omnipresent evidence of so-called Divine Will.* Indeed, since it is not necessarily directly connected with the welfare of the individual but is something to which, willy-nilly, he must at least roughly adjust himself, however successfully he may temporarily evade it, if he wishes to live, it has come to be looked upon by him as the machinations of a devil who opposes his God. In other words, dogmatic morals, as we understand these, have been introduced, although these same, or our interpretation of what is essential to the welfare of life, may not agree with the larger chemic urge and the import of this compulsion of balance as Nature views or uses the same.

It follows, then, that many things which we now consider essential to our racial or spiritual development, especially those which are intended to fit us for a purely mythical heaven, may not be essential at all. Especially may this be true of the many taboos and so-called moral social arrangements which we have established here to make comfortable our little passing state and which, by a process of egoism and self-interest, we ascribe to the will of God. Asceticism in morals, as well as self-imposed deprivations of any kind intended to bring us into conformity with the exact righteousness of Nature or God, may have nothing to do with any Divine mandate or impulse whatsoever. The investigations of the mechanists and the monists throw a very disturbing light on Nature (Loeb; Crile; Snyder). Excess, we know—or its equivalent, strain—is destructive to any organism, and the dogmatic moralist may well caution against it. Yet does a Creator who creates by billions and allows whole races, such as the American Indians, for example, to disappear almost in a generation, care particularly whether this, that or the other organism is broken down by this, that or the other strain or excess? It may be that excess is entirely gratifying to Him or It—like a shell maker pleased with the explosive power of his shells. What is one man, one organism, one race of organisms, to a thing that produces them by quintillions, age in and age out? So a conditioning law of equation or balance which compels a rough reciprocity between parts, all parts, may not remove the effects of or the necessity for strain or excess in the relationship of some men or some races, or all men and all races. War certainly indicates as much, and all the plottings and struggles and injustices and deaths which are concomitants if not essentials of all forms of progress. Again, what *we* might consider necessary in the way of equation or balance, and what *Nature* would, are two very different things. Our very finite minds can see but finitely. So our seemingly necessary limitations on individuals may be accidental and trivial and so detrimental to the larger purposes of Nature, which must betimes sweep them away with huge murderous wars or movements and so restore the changeful balance which she must keep in ways different from the minor arrangements which spring up here.

Even now Nature may be constructing individuals and forces which will completely undo, or at least enlarge, our theories of individual limitations and powers. We do not as yet know what Nature is seeking through man, if anything—certainly not his immortality; there is no evidence as to that—nor can we guess how she is seeking it. One thing we do know: our impulses do not always accord with moral or religious law, the so-called will of the Creator here on earth, and yet our impulses are assuredly provided us by a Creator, if no more than the mechanistic one of the chemists and physicists. We do not compound ourselves. We cannot always by any means control the impulses of our compounds. Only the warring, frustrating impulses of other compounds (or individuals or forces, social opinion being a phase of them) do that for us; hence we are not privileged to say that God, or the Creator, wishes us to do thus and so. We can only say that changing conditions compel us to or prevent us from doing thus and so. Nature may wish us to be forceful in many strange ways in order that we may contest, bicker with other things equally forceful in other ways (all created by Her) so that out of the contest such as we see may come something which we can never see. Who knows?

In other words, all we can say is that Nature has supplied us with certain forces or chemic tendencies and responses, and has also provided (rather roughly in certain instances) the checks and balances which govern the same. Our puny strengths will permit us to do only so much; no more. That these strengths are being enlarged from time to time is rather obvious (consider a man like John D. Rockefeller, or Napoleon, and an ape). At the same time the limitations essential to balance, reciprocity, part with part and force with force, are apparently never set aside entirely. Both Rockefeller and Napoleon find themselves decidedly limited in their powers, compelled to compromise with many things in moving to attain their dreams. And their wishes in the main have far transcended the dictates of ethics, as these have hitherto been conceived. For the most part they ignored reported or written ethics, sticking by seemingly unethical forces, subtlety, craft, the power to do all that their strength or their instincts permitted them to do. And Nature appears to have no objection to them or their results, has furthered them indeed, nor has She apparently to millions of creatures like them in spirit, or worse, as we see *worse* here, for She permits their appearance and uses the result.

Let me vary the argument slightly.

The shelves of our law libraries are packed to suffocation and moldering to decay with laws ethically intended to govern things which man has never yet been able to govern entirely and probably never will be, although the instinct so to legislate probably conforms to the mechanistic instinct for balance and proportion in all things. In England they hung men for sheep-stealing a few hundred years ago, and yet sheep were and still are stolen in England. It is death to kill your neighbor, and yet when did man ever cease killing his neighbor? Is it not as often and as indifferently done to-day as ever? It means from one to twenty years in the penitentiary in America to steal, and yet men steal. It is written that one should never covet his neighbor's wife and that adultery is a crime, yet when has the ultimate conception of these things been more than a dream? Man, or at least a part of him, a fragment of the chemical whole of which he is a part or an expression, wishes and writes laws to confirm these, but in spite of all so-called spiritual instruction, an ordered scheme of spiritual rewards and punishments, he is still not chemically able to accommodate himself to these things—not all of him, at least. Nature, his sheer, rank human nature, which sinks deep below into mechanistic, chemical and physical laws and substances, will not let him. Instead he resorts to subtlety, craft—a very unspiritual but plainly natural or chemical thing. The fact is that the power of certain individuals to do is only limited by the power of certain other individuals to resist, and their natures and tendencies are by no means the same. Yet this squares with the first or pyknotic law of energy, as laid down by Vogt.* The self-integrating force of one individual is limited by the self-integrating force of all other individuals; which is, if it is anything, Newton's law working out in human affairs. There is a rough law of balance indicated by this opposition and strain, but nothing more.

I once talked with a discouraged, or let us say pessimistic, humanitarian, the twenty best years of whose life had been devoted to corrective and ameliorative work among dependents and defectives, young and old, criminals, the physically undermined and the insane. This man had worked to have various

* J. C. Vogt: "The Nature of Electricity and Magnetism on the Basis of a Simplified Conception of Substance."

laws passed in various States which would tend to lessen the brutality of their treatment and also to bring about some method whereby their self-reproduction would be painlessly stopped. His idea, after twenty years of experimenting, was that the processes by which the criminal and defectives generally were being gathered and governed and improved, however laudable in theory, was destined to eventually prove economically impossible and so shirked. The tares were too many, too elusive, too expensive to gather and govern. "The thing can't be done," I remember his saying. "As society is at present governed or constituted something which is by no means humanitarian or ideal prevails, and in spite of the best intentions of idealists or philanthropists you have the enormous toll of inefficiency and nepotism to contend with. Always the old Adam breaks loose somewhere, and by the time you have investigated and reinvestigated and built institutions and passed laws and elected officials the thing becomes a social and financial burden beyond reckoning—lost," he added, "in abstrusities and bad management. Politicians juggle with it, and newer reformers or reactionaries undo what you have done. Besides," he concluded, "normal, healthy men and women do not appear to be able to concern themselves with the day-to-day variations and aberrations of dependent defectives and criminal types. You have the spectacle then of official and even medical neglect, brutality, rotten meat being served to criminals or those detained or cared for—in short, all the horrors that spring from some curious opposition in Nature to anything which is not able to take care of itself. Her plan apparently is to let them die. I tell you that the law of the survival of the strongest cannot be set aside. Any attempt to do so merely begets a vast tangle of effort and expense which results in the final operation of that law anyhow."

My own observations of the working of various plans and theories calculated to improve or "save" mankind coincide with this and suggest to me the conclusion that there is, on the one hand, inherent in the chemic impulses and appetites of life (which man does not create), an instinct toward individuality which may be for good or for ill, plus, on the other hand, this law of balance or equation but over which neither the humanitarian nor the idealist, any more than the criminal or indifferent or self-seeking realist, has any control whatever. If this were not true there would be no explaining such strange social developments as the lusts of certain individuals, the vast animal hungers and abnormalities which seem to contradict any possibility of an exact social equation. While the ascetic passions and self-sacrifice of such men as St. Francis, Jesus, Buddha and the like may belie an entirely material or animal interpretation of this very material scene, the more material one of an Alexander VI., a Medici, a Morgan and a Gould do suggest that an equation or balance between the types is holding in Nature. Men do fight and die for idealistic or moral beliefs just as plainly as they do for material ends. This would indicate, as I said before, a desire for rough balance or equilibrium in Nature between the starkest extremes of its creative impulses—equation, equation. Nothing more nor less.

But a God directing and calling?

Oh, no; not that necessarily, but a condition in Nature itself perhaps which will not permit it to move save by a process of checks and balances—variety in unity, and vice versa.

If one takes no more varied types than Christ and Nero, or Alexander VI. and St. Francis, one sees how plain this is, in so far as our earthly state is concerned. God, or Nature, or Life, permits both, creates both. In these examples one sees how the impulses of the flesh always vary and how difficult it is, where millions outrival these in secret tendencies and impulses, to suggest a working harmony; and yet there is a harmony and they do harmonize; or, by triturating the one the other maintain a working balance, the tendencies of the one being offset by those of the other, and vice versa.

No less latitude, perhaps, could or would serve in a world

or a universe which breeds individuals by quadrillions, momentarily perhaps, and which conceals or contains forces of whose impulses, emotions, necessities we know nothing, and so equation is and can be the only answer. What can we know, for instance, of the impulses or morals of the Sun, whose heat apparently breeds all forms of life we know here, horrific and otherwise? And yet we also know that heat is balanced by cold in the universe; light by no light; matter by force; tenderness by savagery; lust by asceticism; love by hate; and so on *ad infinitum.* No thing is fixed. All tendencies are permitted apparently. Only a balance is maintained.

The thing which the evolutionist has discovered and put forward with considerable enthusiasm is this: that life in every form has tended to evolve from the simple to the complex, and only through a vast complexity or organization has it managed to attain this spectacle of things which we call life or beauty—division of itself, as it were. The complexity of the individual thing which we call a tree or a flower or an animal, or, if you please, a social state (and indeed those more or less abstruse things which we know as arts and sciences), are but a further evolution of the complexity of the world machine, and life has brought them about and apparently saved them to the world, possibly for the purpose of partial self-expression. At the same time there has always been involved in this process the law of the survival of the strongest or temporarily and accidentally most favored, a process which the humanitarians are never prone to accept because it belies the theory of saving anything except by a compensative condition of slaughter and neglect of other things less strong—or, as the phrase has it, unfit things. In the theory of the religionist and the moralist the horrific processes that work in the sea and the jungle, and other unsocialized and enigmatic phases of imminent life, are entirely outside the scheme of a just and merciful God or Creator, not countenanced by Him! When His will is known and His suggestions are obeyed, these will be overcome and disappear! Well, this may be true, only it does not appear from any material or mental examination of the scene.

Even now, as we talk of sweeter and less avid processes which might be brought into play by a superior power, life is maintaining its ancient balance of evil and good, or extremities of one kind balanced against extremities of another. Even now, under the very noses of the religionists and the moralists, these processes are at work and show no sign of being abated. For every neighborhood of taste and comfort, witness the vast areas of poverty, poor taste, neglect, dull thought, inefficiency. For every comfortable man a lean one, or many. For every mind of the first order a million of a weaker, fumbling character. For every tender, Christ-like soul how many of another kind—avid, selfish, cruel, hideous almost! Are the poor governed by the rich—and well? Do the shrewd rule the ignorant, and to their advantage? Do the strong control the weak, and to their advantage? Are the inefficient well or badly housed, well or badly nourished, neglected, left to stew in their own juice of misery and live and die as best they can, or are they looked after, as the religionist and moralist suggest and hope for? Only the dull or dishonest among the moralists and religionists can, it seems to me, fail to perceive or dare deny what even the dull or the ignorant now being trampled upon do already vaguely perceive and understand.

And yet behold! the song of ultimate perfection continues yearly, from century to century, to be sung. The Divine, far-off event (which, if anything, is Nirvana) is surely coming. A sweeter and less avid process will be brought into play. Man is to be saved from hunger, cold, thirst, lust, undue material ambition, by telling him how horrible they are and asking him to be kind. Well, he may make a comfortable social organization for himself here on earth, but that will by no means prove that the universe or God is moral. For, behold—man himself is superimposed upon other forms of life, a ruthless Lord or devil to them, and thrives only by their destruction. Do you suppose the ox, the hog, the horse, the fish, or any of the multitude of creatures man slays or enslaves in order that he may be comfortable and spiritually at rest, could be made to look upon him as tender, merciful, a creature necessarily to be saved to a higher spiritual state—representing, for instance, an all-kind God? I doubt it. What about the God who allows their organization and so-called right to life to be disrupted in our favor? Where the universal harmony, justice, mercy there? We are to develop a social organization in which gentleness, mercy and harmony will prevail among us, but we do not hesitate to curb the efforts or aspirations of lesser creatures, even rival nations—the Indians, say—in the same direction. In the great days to come no man will contest with his neighbor, but only with the universe—which of course raises the question of why fight the universe. And where do the rights of the universe come in, which we are hoping to rob to our own advantage and its enslavement?

Aside from the confusion involved as to the character of man and the governing forces of life, there is no quarrel with a portion of this theory. To a certain extent harmony, or a "dependent equation," as Spencer was pleased to term it, will always be attained between individuals assembled in vast numbers on earth or in the sea perforce, because it may not be escaped. If one reads chemistry and physics correctly it is a condition which underlies everything. An equation between matter and force and the elements to which apparently they give rise, must be struck, a balance attained, if life as we see it is to appear or go on. The slightest disturbance of the existing equations which produce life as we see it, as Loeb and Crile and others have shown, ends in monstrosities or confusion, and life as we know it ceases. In our own social life, if equation did not hold, internecine contest would soon decimate and gradually eliminate the vast majority of us. The late great war indicated as much. Indeed there is scarcely any doubt that social life as we know it will yet need to be organized upon an even more closely balanced scale than at present, since the elements and powers which make for contest and self-defense are becoming more numerous. Hunger, cold, thirst and many other ills to which the flesh is heir may yet be eliminated among men, or the individuals of one dominant state. It is now, by certain orders of men and insects; the bee-hive and the ant-colony offer suggestions. But it does not follow that the basic elements of Nature or God, or man, would thereby be changed. Is it not more likely that here and now, in a small way and for the time being, only their disruptive as opposed to their constructive characteristics are restrained? Such stabilized centers of motion do occur in Nature from time to time in small ways and places. All human and animal bodies, machines and forms of government even, are illustrations in point. But does that prove or augur that the changeful elemental conditions everywhere prevailing outside these delicate arrangements in Nature may not eventually sweep in and make over that which has been established here into such a condition as we find in the sea, for instance, where life insistently and apparently mechanistically preys on life? Why not? The glory of pagan life and art—were they saved? Or was their knell sounded by the advent of Christianity?

Many, observing only the satisfactory results of harmony or equation or balance, and entirely failing to note the essential disharmonies out of which alone harmonies may take their rise, have assumed the existence of an emasculate God whose virtues are all negative, ignoring the positive horrors by which we live and progress. For them the cataclysms of physics, the fumbling failures of biology, are meaningless, if they exist at all. Yet plainly the creative force is neither as generous nor as amiable as they think. Rather, brilliant as is all this evolutionary process, and it reveals startling harmonies, beauties and seeming intelligence, it still only argues some such fumbling hit-or-miss mechanistic scheme as the chemists and physicists are beginning to outline and which allows for far more latitude in morals and conduct, as well as invention and discovery even, than the religionist has hitherto been willing to grant. The only one who appears to sense the true process or processes of Nature is the mechanistic chemist or physicist, who does not deny the possibility of extremes and horrors existing in the Divine mind or will of the creative impulse. "Murder," say these scientific seekers after truth, or at least their facts point to this, "is a disturbing and disrupting process. It destroys the equation best expressed in 'Live and let live.' It affects individual peace. If you do so unto others they will do the same unto you. Chemically and physically, according to the law of reaction or equation, they cannot very well avoid it. Therefore do not murder." Yet where is there any Divine command in that? Is it not rather a simple and easily understandable interpretation of a very obvious and inescapable law of equation, under which nevertheless, so roughly is this law adjusted and so casually does it work, murder and many other forms of non-equation may and do take their rise and do persist? If that is God or Good, then God permits murder, repays with murder, or asks you to be the judge as to whether you will tolerate murder in your State. Rather, to the physicist and chemist, it appears to be not so much a Divine command as an accidental and inescapable condition of equation.

We are told, by way of dogmatic moral comfort, that man has achieved somewhat that the animals have not, and that therefore he is superior. But also, as is now becoming perfectly plain, he has been able to discover and perpetuate for his own satisfaction crimes and iniquities for which no animal apparently within its small range of instinct or mechanistic control has the skill. Nature makes both, yet she does not, or cannot, or at least has not, made the animals as delicately and resourcefully evil in some things as is man. That is why he is able to dominate them. In one way, then, man is worse than the animals, and in another better—a balance presumably in the favor of man, though not necessarily so. The truth is that most of the ways wherein man has been differentiated from the animals by forces over which he has no control concern not ethics, as we understand and act upon them, but mechanical articulations and utilitarian comforts, the construction and normal use of which lie entirely apart from the realm of ethics. There is nothing either moral or immoral in the development and use or non-use of steam, electricity, plumbing, the tractor engine, automobiles and so on. They are mechanistic and non-moral. Thus we have developed architecture, machinery and the arts. It is true that in so far as man himself is concerned these are helpful to him in his mass phase and provide a larger freedom, which has resulted in a large experience, hence intelligence or comprehension in every direction. Yet have they improved his morals? Or lowered them? Who would say so? Yet perceiving this development or change, and, more faintly, the need of balance and equation which runs through all and underlies all, man has set about the task of writing about it, framing the inescapable equational laws which all changes suggest and compel into definite unbreakable commands from a definite God, singing songs about Him, painting pictures of Him, and directing attention to what man has ignorantly assumed to be a universal source of supply which will or should permit the greatest possible number to live under some such scheme of equation as is here suggested. Unfortunately this has not been proved as yet, and at any rate it is not the same as the presumably provable scheme of moral order which has been foisted upon man by the dull, designing or poetically enthusiastic of all ages, and which involves the laying aside of nearly every forceful, vigorous, natural, or human or pagan, attribute. Quite the contrary.

In this connection I should like to reiterate that to the Christian and other metaphysical idealists neither dishonesty nor vice nor any crime is contemplated by God, and therefore should not exist, any more than any other variation from that perfect state, best indicated perhaps by what the Ten Commandments forbid and the Beatitudes imply. God does not will them. He personally resents and will punish their appearance. The first part of this (i. e., that He does not will them) might be accepted as true if the fact that he permits them, or at least that they *are,* in spite of Him, not denied. But of course religion, as all those who philosophically struggle with life now know or should, is an abstraction, an ideal, whose dogmas can only in part be approximated in life. For life, as we nearly all know by now or should, is a shifty and evasive mechanism, chemic in part at least, and material and inscrutable, with which the abstractions of the religionist have little if anything in common. The best that religion and ethics have so far done is to take credit for the inherent and necessary tendency to compromise which has previously been indicated and which is manifested by all phases of natural energy, as much by that shown in our body politic as anywhere else. Indeed, the very best that religion can show is no better than that which life, or Nature Herself, could and did long before any religion appeared, namely, a rough equation, a balance struck; so that if a man had done a consciously wrong thing in one place he was chemically or emotionally moved to do a right thing in another, and if his actions were bad in one way it might be that he was compelled by forces outside his control to counterbalance them by good ones in another. All animal forms above those merely mechanistic or tropic (those governed by tropisms of various kinds) appear to display most of the virtues exercised by humans—the care of their young, for instance, distress at their loss, loyalty, ability to organize and so observe group laws; characteristics celebrated by man, where exercised by him, as virtues, beatitudes and what not else. Yet these lower forms cannot possibly know of religious or moral precepts in any revealed or instructed sense, via a Messiah or Redeemer. Instincts or tropisms as developed and verified by oppositions or aids (accidental or otherwise)—once more the law of balance or equation—appear to have been their sole guides. Hence to the religionist and moralist, thus far at least, they have been beyond the pale of ethical consideration, things almost beyond the willing, and so beyond the care, of the Creator Himself. An especial opponent of God or Good had to be devised in order to take care of them. And yet are they not an excellent illustration of this same creative and governing force in Nature which, while apparently seeking variety in unity, is itself subject to a law of balance or harmony as well as one of disharmony or change, and this without any evidence self-conscious on its part? At least the investigations of the chemists and the physicists thus far appear to indicate as much. "Vengeance is mine" declared the old Hebraic Jahveh, and by that very assertion he admitted that he did not expect to establish the abstractions of right, truth, justice and mercy on earth but rather, since he could not, he would at least attempt to strike a balance and would exact, in the form of pain or disaster, repayment for things done in opposition to his code.

Well, that requires no Sinaitic command or religious law to make it true. It is not a matter for great churches and confessionals and pence and genuflections—or is it? It is true, whether God or Moses or any one else ever said so or not. It is a material and an economic fact as well as a chemic or psychic law. If you wish to glorify God or Nature for that, well and good. Your mood may be admirable or interesting, if not exactly necessary. But certainly, whether one admits the existence of a self-willing Creator or not, it is too much to say that man obtains exact justice or that an exact return is made anywhere for energies expended, ideals struggled for, efforts, good, bad or indifferent, made. We know that is not true. Nor is it true that there is not a counter impulse to withhold it. There is. And men, fellow-units in the great self-balancing cosmos, all too frequently reflect that impulse. Man is no more essentially just than he is unjust. He is an impulse, a will to live, a sharply reflected chemical and physical impulse in Nature, which acts or reacts as the nature of other chemical and physical stimuli in immediate contact with him suggests or compels, and which same may be by no means as moral as we think. Man, as a representation of chemical and physical impulses coming from somewhere, has an innate desire for power for extreme movement for himself; but so have all other mechanical or physical representations of that impulse. And it is but the balancing pressure of his fellows which keeps him in position at or near a median line. If you examine him carefully you will find that in the main he desires so-called "justice" for himself only, a fair balance for himself, liberty for himself, or that which is related to him via pleasure or profit, and so on *ad infinitum.* At the same time he is a slave, a tool, a medium for something, an intruded if not self-intruding, self-seeking insect, but without power to control or fend against major impulses and powers. Still, between man and man, tribe and tribe, nation and nation, there are these necessary equations or balances plus their internal hopes or chemic tendencies, each one for himself, to change and achieve; yet the same being but roughly worked out; on the one hand to balance or equation in favor of all the others, on the other hand to supremacy or extreme liberty of movement for each. Where only failure is achieved there is either a lull, temporary only, or a storm soon or late (revolution), or periods of horror in which chaos rules, or peace in which nothing is achieved. The world is sad over its inability to obtain freedom, great scope of emotion, for itself, or gleeful because of its triumph in this direction. But all the time it is struggling and maintaining but a rough and in the main brief balance, part with part or unit with unit.

One might go on indefinitely contemplating other phases of this same equational law, its relation to love of parents, love of country, love of home, love of one's neighbor, love of this, love of that. Are not all of these held up as duties, virtues, perfections even Sinaitic commands, as in "Honor thy father and thy mother," when as a matter of fact and inwardly we know that this is a matter of equation or balance and cannot absolutely as a commandment from on high exist where no reasonable return in kind is predicated. What, love a shameless, brutal, unparental or non-filial father or mother, son or daughter, in whom, let us say, exists not one redeeming trait or quality of all that we consider essential to or characteristic of those states? It is not chemically therefore not humanly possible. What is meant is that it is not only possible but natural to make a reasonable return where affection, kindness or care has been extended. Now while it is entirely conceivable that one might love one who was cruel to oneself and generous to others, or generous to oneself and cruel to others, who in some way or some one direction fulfilled some phases of balance or equation, in however weak or impossible a way, still one could not possibly love one who was in no wise kind or generous to any one, a thing without reciprocal or balancing relations in some direction. The law of balance or equation which governs in all processes, even thought, will not permit it. There must be something given in some way, directly or indirectly, before anything can be returned or evolved, even in thought. And if one reverses the picture and attempts to conceive of hating some one or thing equationally just, fair or balanced, not attempting to take from any one or thing too much and not withholding from any one or thing that which is equationally his, it is quite as psychically impossible. One cannot cerebrate inimically toward that person or thing as being evil, reprehensible or what not. It cannot be done. Sometimes, where by reason of plenty or inherent weakness of mind or force, or carelessness of thought or interest, an individual is in any way indifferent to a "reasonable" or balanced return to himself for effort made, labor given, thought expended and what not, and where this results in no injury to himself or others, it is entirely possible to look upon him with indifference or as a fool, or as one who is weak-minded or not capable of balancing himself against the shrewd and self-interested minds of others. But such indifference or lack of self-interest would not indicate that one looked upon him as being evil, scarcely even a discreditable force, save possibly where his operations, or lack of them, affected the interests or rights or privileges of another or others.

Not love of God, then, it would seem, nor fear of God, although these abstractions have come to be real enough to some minds, prevents one individual from overriding the dreams and hopes of his neighbor, but fear of retaliation which his selfishness might produce. "Thou shalt not" springs plainly from "Thou hadst best not, it is dangerous," to which might be added the strangest quality of all, the tendency in large or small bodies or masses to quiescence, the love of peace, or inertia. Our evoluted mechanistic chemism has become so diffused or varied that we may even now speak of such intangible and yet vital forces as love of the fixed scene, which appears to be little more than a reflected form of helio, or ego, or some-other form of tropism, the inherent power in everything to attract something to itself and so maintain itself, for the time being anyhow. That things are inclined to a static or inert state or to congeal and so stratify and endure in that form (Nirvana?) is as true as that they must change; and, under certain conditions, Nature seems to abhor too much speed, as too little.

Is there anywhere in this to be found that universal right, truth, justice, mercy, as we have hitherto deemed it or them to be or exist? Perhaps not, but it is all of so-called right, truth, mercy or justice, universal or otherwise, that we will ever know, all of it that is involved with life. Does this, by any chance, contain truth? Yes, indeed, it is truth, for it is a fact. Is it right? Well, for life as we find it conditioned it is apparently the only way. Who can suggest a better? Should the fact that we find ourselves thus conditioned, confronted by Nature in all Her complexity and with only this necessity for equation to fall back on, disconcert or dishearten us? Need it or must it take the savor out of life? No; not, at least, in my judgment. Life in its most terrible as well as its most halcyon aspects is at once an enticing and a fit game. It seems well enough suited to our capacities, and we to it, since essentially we are of it—it, in fact. At least it leaves or provides us much to strive for, and strife is the only key to knowledge or sensation and life that we have. Abstractions and theories are good as games at which the human mind may play if it chooses, and whenever life becomes too severe for any group or part of it it is easy enough to invent a theory or abstraction which will then make it seem different. And this is almost invariably done, as witness all the impossible religions and theories that at one time and another have filled the world. Like chess or checkers, they furnish a diversion or relief to life-weary minds. If you have nothing better to do even a religion may be worth while. At worst it can only narrow your vision, and if that is a comfort—well, it is a comfort, but you do not thus escape the essential facts of life. You merely invent a shield against their too-sharp blows. Regardless of whatever dogmatic moralities may have been dreamed, or yet may be, or attempted, life is still avid, treacherous, astounding. Our little safety, if we have any, lies not in the desires or intentions of our fellow-mortals, good, bad or indifferent, or in their churches or creeds, or ours really, but in their limitations. *They dare not do unto us for fear of what we will do to them,* or *of what the machinery of equation which life has set up or is conditioned by and now operates, will do to them.* All else is a poet's dream.

What, then, shall man do? Weep for that? Shall he despair and call life a failure and a torment? Shall he say that it is limited, that there is no opportunity for progress, or that the sweetness of those things defined as love, charity, mercy, neighborliness and race sociability are by such a governing condition destroyed? Not at all. Wherein is the temperament of Nature Herself, Her sweetness, if such there be; Her romance, if such there be; Her beauty, if such there be, altered by this? Life is as it is—active, dancing, changeful, beautiful, at once brutal and tender—regardless of how our theories would seek to make it seem, and though it does as it chooses at times, or appears to, and invents or assumes various guises of perfection, it is as it has always been, both good and bad, yet held in a kind of equational vise or harmony—neither too good nor too bad—or we would not now be here at all, any of us, to tell the tale. As it is, and well within its equational swing or law, there is room for the will to superiority in the super-man as well as the trembling fears of the least of created creatures. Nor is it impossible for man, with his puny strength or with such force as he may gather, to attempt to upset this very equation and so rule all; or, on the contrary, choose to live in sweetest peace with his neighbor, if he can. He may, and great will be the wonder and charm of his existence if he no more than try. But that he should succeed in permanently so doing is not within his scope unless he should grow to be the universe itself. On the other hand, under this same controlling equation, a man may be a Colossus and bestride the world without upsetting the equation ultimately. Like Alexander, he may sigh for more worlds to conquer; or, like Hannibal, take refuge in despair and death. Or, better yet, like some forceful and yet humble laborer at some small task, he may seek to hide himself away in some simple peaceful realm, free of the storms which rock these greater worlds, and still be secure in one of those minor equilibriums which in the shadow of some of the greater ones are always holding somewhere in part. For, roughly, equation is always holding in one or many forms--dependent equations, which consist of many, many equations or balances, joined in some still greater one or synthesis—and apparently always will. Who shall say? To our present senses the ultimate facts of life are not altering; although that is not for petty man to know.

On the other hand, I should say that the condition of equation which is everywhere evident does not deny or belie any elements of softness, color, beauty or art which now sweeten, or seem, to, a picture which must seem to many inherently grim. God, Good, Nature, Force, is not now, and never has been apparently, without some of these aspects in part, nor bare of the easing limitations indicated by the Ten Commandments, the Golden Rule and the Beatitudes. For before these were *it* was, and if they are or ever were true they still are so, for they took their rise out of it and so must be and remain in it, forever and ever, emanations or adjustments (equation, no doubt) suggested by the desire for expression on the part of the cosmos as a whole. Yet the knowledge that they are the result of a condition or equation which the universe, the life force itself, cannot escape, is or should be most encouraging. Nature must let many things live in reasonable equation or peace, for it is in them and they in it. "I am in the Father; the Father is in me."

If, then, man is savage he is also tender, inherently so apparently, for by what measure would he measure savageness if not by its contrary? And if he is avid, centripetal, individual, is he not somewhat of their contrary also? In truth, somewhere in the scheme of things is implanted a love of beauty and order as well as their contraries, which can only find expression via equation, and this it is, chemical, inherent awareness of it no doubt, which eases the ache of existence for us all (God, man, devil). For if life loves change, movement, difference, contest, it also plainly loves their contraries, for these exist, and we could not know the one without the other. Order exists as a half of its opposite, disorder, and the one could not well be without the other, and peace exists, if at all, as the complement or antithesis of what is not peaceful. Yet through all and all, and in all and all, are the sting and gayety of change and the consciousness of it, and these remain, possibly forever and ever, outside Nirvana, which Nature may never wish to see or know. It may be impossible for Her to die or be still.

Equation, then, is that which is involved in the lust of the lover for his sweetheart, and her acceptance; the husband for his wife, and her faith; the mother for her child, and its love; the citizen for his neighbor; the individual for his friend. Art, the love of life for itself, is nothing more than a synthesis of many equations whereby many lovely harmonies and their opposites are expressed or implied. Hunger, balanced against satiation, creates more beauty. Life builds and wills far beyond the ken of man or his companion animals, and all that he can know is the chemic thrill of life, its joys, the necessity of equation and so-called fair play, or rhythm and balance. For, behold, life is ever dancing and does not will to be still. Not to want too much, because one cannot get too much; not to seek to devour the whole world, because one cannot; not to threaten, because of vanity and self-appreciation, all else with extermination, because one cannot possibly exterminate all else without disturbing the general balance and so bring the weight, the conditioning and crushing force of equation itself upon oneself, is to say what may offend the individual life-lover but which nevertheless produces the only condition in which the general totality in all its glittering variety, which it appears to crave, can best express itself outside Nirvana. And this it is which should drive the fog of religious theory out of our minds.

For why pray in beggarly fashion for that which will be, whether we pray or not—which, as the mechanists believe and show cannot escape its own destiny? Rather sing and be joyful, I should say, for one's unescapable share in so great a spectacle. The game is open, free, a thrashing, glorious scene. Our God, if we have one, is not a namby-pamby, milk-and-water solution, suitable for the stomachs and optics of still more namby-pamby men, but a vast somewhat which offers a splendid universe-eating career to the giant, if he wills, an opportunity to thrive and grow to even the most spindling of beginners. Our God, if we have one, is a vast somewhat too great for the perception or understanding or destruction or solution of any minor portion of Him, such as we are. He is a creator of spectacles, a slinger of thunder-bolts, a breather of fire, a master of cataclysm. His, or Its, least breath is storm. Its sigh is earthquake or orbital derangement. No attributes such as man can conceive can apply—neither good nor evil, virtue or its opposite—for these apply only as mild suggestions at moments of equation in one minor part of the great whole or another. Our God is tragedy and comedy, terror and delight. He is limitless opportunity and endless opposition and destruction, for His way is extremes in equation, and nothing more and nothing less.

What then? Despair over that? Is there not, in all conscience, under a loose equation (loose and operative only in extremes) room for all the lusts, the terrors, the wonders, the simplicities of the greatest as well as the least? Alexander may yet be again, or the devil himself in all his power and lurid glory, before he is crushed and set aside, for the time being, by his inherent antithesis, the thing which is not devil.

And as for the religionist, may not Jesus, St. Francis, St. Simon Stylites come again? Let man fight for their return if he will. Who is to gainsay him?—not God, Force, the Universal Substance. Obviously it does not care how it expresses itself, so long as it achieves avid, forceful, artistic expression.

PHANTASMAGORIA.

CHARACTERS:

THE LORD OF THE UNIVERSE
BEAUTY
AMBITION
PITY
LOVE
HATE
DESPAIR
REASON
HOPE
FEAR
GREED

FIRST SECOND THIRD FOURTH FIFTH SIXTH	} POWERS OF DARKNESS

SERAPHIM
CHERUBIM

Clouds upon clouds of birds, snakes, fish, animals, men, flowers, trees, planets, suns.

SCENE I—*The House of Birth*
SCENE II—*The House of Life*
SCENE III—*The House of Death.*

SCENE I. THE HOUSE OF BIRTH

SCENE: *Darkness and illimitable space. Æons of time, as measured by the illusion of time, elapse.* THE LORD OF THE UNIVERSE, *as force, inert, yet all-in-all, rests quiescent. A faint pulsing begins. Without thought or reason, restless, chaotic, the idea of separateness and individuality generates—an insane dream. The cloudy length of a giant outlines itself, reclining in endless space. It appears and disappears, now a thigh, now an arm, only to fade again. The vague outlines of a brow and cheek appear, only to fade again. Æons of time elapse. The illusion reasserts itself. Cloudy fire-mists pour from his nostrils. Poles of light erect themselves from materialized temples. Blazing suns and meteors burst forth and swirl about his head. Strange and multitudinous forms manifest themselves—animals, birds, fishes, horned and winged things. They appear and disappear, as thoughts form and fade. He is blind, aged, insane. He erects imaginary titanic arms and rubs his changing, stupendous face with his changing hands.*

THE LORD OF THE UNIVERSE

Oh, ho, ho, ho! Oh, ho, ho, ho! *(He sinks back wearily, all but the outlines of his head disappearing.)*

BEAUTY (*a thought*)

(Leaping, pink-limbed and perfect, from his brain, a figure of delight.) Lord, thou hast created me! I am thy perfect thought, thy happiest illusion! I will be worshiped! I will be worshiped! (*She springs sinuously among the spinning, changing spheres, a radiant smile upon her face, her arms tossed upward in delight.)*

THE LORD OF THE UNIVERSE

(Materializing himself fully, a paretic smile upon his lips. He rubs his face and imagines eyes, giving himself sight, and surveys her broodingly.) Have I created thee? Oh, ho, ho, ho!

(He rubs his flaming hair.) I must not forget thee! I must not forget thee! Oh, ho, ho! Thou art Beauty! *(His expression changes; an unimaginable weariness settles upon his face, aged, æonic. He frowns and leers and partly fades, re-establishing himself after a time. As he does so,* AMBITION, *a sinister thought, club in hand and darkling and scowling, a figure of terror, leaps from his eyes.)*

AMBITION

(Brandishing his club.) I will be obeyed! I will be obeyed! Out of thy terror, Lord, thou hast created me! War and strife will I have! War! War! *(He struts and stares.)*

THE LORD OF THE UNIVERSE

(The darkling mood passing, a light of momentary peace settling on his face. He gazes at the figure tolerantly.) Have I created thee? Weary! Weary! I am weary! *(He stretches his arms.)* But stay! I am lonely. Be thou what thou art. *(He draws himself to a sitting position, all the height and depth of space.)*

BEAUTY

(Threading a necklace of suns.) I will be worshiped! I will be worshiped! *(She croons joyously.)*

THE LORD OF THE UNIVERSE

(His mood changing, a giant despair creeping into his eyes.) Forever and ever! Oh, ho, ho, ho! Forever and ever! It is a dream! *(He staggers to his feet, the great shadowy arms flailing wildly. As he does so he imagines Space and Time, and begins to wander down their lengths, staggering as he goes. From his brow leap* HATE, DESPAIR, PITY, HOPE, FEAR, *thoughts all, the last two with great round eyes and open mouths. At the same time clouds upon clouds of unimaginable forms and characters, previously non-existent, come into being, the product of his fancy. Suns, worlds, fire-mists, swarms of birds, snakes, fishes, animals and men are born, strange wraiths that float in wreaths about him and traverse all immensity. They circle, murmur, mutter, cry. The avatars of men come*

forth, huge forms of gas. They are preceded and followed by vast clouds of thoughts of their own—ravening, embodied fancies that bicker and contest. These immense companies and semblances appear and disappear, as the primary figure thinks or loses memory of what he has thought. He alternately laughs and groans, maundering.)

BEAUTY

(Dancing on before.) I will be worshiped! I will be worshiped!

AMBITION

(Gathering at his back vast clouds of restless, threatening figures like himself.) I am his thought of strength! I am his thought of power. I am his thought of rage! I am his thought of contest! Oh, ho, ho, ho! Follow me! Follow me! See, we will sow destruction! We will spread despair! We will slay! We will burn! Oh, ho, ho, ho!

THE LORD OF THE UNIVERSE

(Wildly, his fancy flaming furiously.) Oh, ho, ho, ho! I am God! I am that I am—all in all! I am my dream of myself! I will dream me dreams, visions. These are my creations, all! *(He turns and surveys his endless fancies of horror and delight.)* Oh, ho, ho, ho! Come, Art! Come, Love! Come, Hope! Come, Death! Dream as I dream! Create destiny, suffer! I am God! I cannot die! Insane! Insane! Insane! Oh, ho, ho, ho! *(He shouts in agony, then joy, then sobs, staggering as he does so, ending in a gale of lunatic laughter.)*

PITY

(To LOVE, *hovering near.)* We are his children; and we can do nothing?

LOVE

Nothing, save he think on us.

PITY

(To HOPE.*)* Canst thou do nothing?

HOPE

Nothing, save he think on me and thee.

HATE

(Clasping the hand of DESPAIR.*)* Come aside. Are not we his thought also? What have we in common with them?

DESPAIR

(Darkly.) Nothing! Nothing! Yet are we his thought also, but not of them! No, no, no! He should sleep again! He should sleep!

THE LORD OF THE UNIVERSE

(Staggering and writhing.) Oh, ho, ho, ho! Oh, ho, ho, ho! I am God! I dream me dreams! I build me endless wonders, endless pleasures, endless horrors! Oh, ho, ho, ho! *(He staggers madly on.)*

BEAUTY

Build thou me temples of beauty, Lord! I will be worshiped! I will be worshiped!

AMBITION

Make thou me worlds and legions! Worlds! Worlds! And legions! I would rule! I would slay! I would burn!

LOVE

Oh, but wilt thou make flowers and vast realms of quiet places, Lord? Or but little valleys, if thou wilt? Make streams and pretty shelters! Give not all to Ambition, Lord! Give not all to war!

HATE

(Springing before his face.) Make thou me implements of terror! Create thou me forms of horror, of evil! Spin thou me dark chains and darker places! Make thou tortures of failure and regret, Lord—tortures! Tortures! *(He glowers about him.)*

PITY

Nay, Lord, let not all be of horror and hate! Think thou on me, Lord, of sweet pity and tender things! Or, if thou canst not, think thou but of ways that I may heal what Hate will destroy, what Ambition would crush. Think thou thus, Lord! I am a thought of thine also!

THE LORD OF THE UNIVERSE

(Wearily.) Oh, ho, ho, ho! *(He staggers on.)*

FEAR

Lord, do thou protect me! Do thou conceal me! Forget me not, Lord! Forget me not! I fear! I fear!

DESPAIR

Why dost thou not sleep, Lord? Of what avail are we, thy fancies? Oh, why dost thou not sleep? Sleep! Sleep! Sleep!

THE LORD OF THE UNIVERSE

(Staggering on.) Oh, ho, ho, ho! Oh, ho, ho, ho! Space—Time—I have made me these! Suns—Planets—I have made me these! Love—Hate—I have made me these! Hope—Fear—I have made me these! Beauty—I have made me this! Oh, ho, ho, ho! Oh, ho, ho, ho! *(He staggers on, gesticulating and laughing stupendously.)*

BEAUTY

(Wildly.) I will be worshiped! I will be worshiped!

SCENE II: THE HOUSE OF LIFE.

SCENE: *The cloudy realms of space. At a point, halls of illimitable and indescribable splendor, the colorings of the dawn. Beyond, a swirling belt of suns and satellites glittering thinly against the dark. Beyond this, in measureless nothingness, the suggestion of other clouds of suns and planets, spinning. At the center, the Presence, couched upon gold and porphyry, high-piled, cloud on cloud. Poles of outpouring thought, great flames, radiate from his brows; about him a nimbus of fire. He is now fully self-materialized and concentrated, but sits quiescent, weary, lonely, a compendium of vagrom, changeful, insane emotions and ideas. Immediately before him,* BEAUTY, LOVE, PITY, HOPE, REASON—*colorful shadows all—as well as beasts, birds, fishes, reptiles, flowers, trees; men and women in cloudy, wraith-like masses. Above him, immense legions of* CHERUBIM *and* SERAPHIM, *figures of translucent light, radiant, choral. In the background,* AMBITION; *about him swirl, darkling,* HATE, FEAR, GREED, DESPAIR, *and behind them, cloud upon cloud, sinister figures, emissaries, dreams, the darker products of the Lord's fancy.*

SERAPHIM AND CHERUBIM

(Fanning with glittering wings.) Hail, our Creator! Hail, Lord! Do thou remain forever in thought our Creator, our Thinker! Blessed be thy reality! Hail! Hail!

BEAUTY

(Surveying from a glistering footstool, nearest of all the swarming universe.) Am I not beautiful, Lord? Am I not thy thought of Beauty? Art thou not content to think on me, thy first thought? And shall I not be thy last? Thou hast but commanded, and they worship me! Thou but thinkest, and I am supernal in beauty! *(She smiles.)* They worship me! They worship me!

THE LORD OF THE UNIVERSE

(Broodingly.) Sweet thought—my dearest thought!

AMBITION

(Clanking ponderous armor, a cloudy giant in moody meditation.) We wait! We wait! He thinks not on us! He thinks not on us. Now are his thoughts of drooling pleasure—of Beauty, of Hope, Peace—pale nothings all—Seraphim and Cherubim, mere fluttering figures of light! Beauty reigns! Hope and Reason and Pity are at her feet! See how the universe peoples itself with these, his fancies! He dreams but fair dreams!

THE LORD OF THE UNIVERSE

(To BEAUTY, *turning slowly and viewing complacently the immensity and beauty of his fancy.)* Art thou pleased, then, with what I have made for thee? See, see—dreams, dreams, sweet dreams all—mad fancies all—mad! Mad! That which I make is madness all—disordered dreams! I am mad, mad!

BEAUTY

Wondrous, Lord, of whom I am the first! Great Creator! Thou art wonder and beauty all. Sweet are thy dreams! Sweet thy madness! Sweet am I! But sleep no more, Lord! Dream on. It is sweet to be worshiped so! I would be worshiped! I would be worshiped!

THE LORD OF THE UNIVERSE

Sayest thou so, perfect thought? It is sweet madness? Oh, ho, ho, ho! A thing of now, and then no longer! Thou art a fair dream, a dear one, but nothing—nothing! Is not that transcendant sorrow—madness?

BEAUTY

(Caressingly.) Oh, think not so, Lord! Think not so! A dear dream! A wondrous dream!

THE LORD OF THE UNIVERSE

(Darkly and broodingly.) What am I? What art thou? What are these? *(He waves a vast hand.)* What it all is I

cannot think—or why—or whence—or where. I dream and sleep—I sleep and dream! Oh, ho, ho, ho! Oh, ho, ho, ho! A dream! A dream! Sayest thou a sweet dream? A sweet dream! Oh, ho, ho, ho! I have lost the key! I have lost the key! *(He laughs loudly, sadly.)*

AMBITION

(In the background, rumbling.) He has lost the key! He has lost the key!

BEAUTY

A sweet dream, Lord! A sweet dream! Sleep no more, Lord! Sleep no more! It is all too sweet! Sleep no more! *(She smiles.)*

AMBITION

(Restlessly.) He dreams but useless things! We grow to thin nothings! *(He clanks his armor weakly.)*

PITY

Think kindly, Lord! Kind and tender thoughts! It is best ever!

THE POWERS OF DARKNESS

(Rumbling.) Hail! Let Hope be forgotten! And Love! And Pity! Hail!

BEAUTY

(Rising and laying a hand upon his brow.) Lord, I am thy first-born. After me came these. *(She motions to* HOPE, PITY, REASON.) I am thy first thought, thy thought of Beauty! Say it! Remember me! Forget me not! All else avails so little! And think thou not on Ambition or Hate. They would destroy—even me! Even me! *(She smiles.)*

THE POWERS OF DARKNESS

(Thundering:) Yea, even Beauty, Lord! What is Beauty to thee?

THE LORD OF THE UNIVERSE

(Gazing dully.) Beauty! Beauty! Can I remember thee always, even though I would? Thine eyes! What is it I

meant by thine eyes? *(He gazes into them.)* Mad! Mad! Mad!

AMBITION

(Angrily, clanking his armor.) He drools and dreams! Me, his best thought—his greatest—he forgets! I am his horror, his strength, his despair, his power—yet he thinks not on me! Beauty! Beauty! And I wait in shadow! I, his rage—yet he sleeps in vagrom thoughts of beauty! Awake, Lord! Forget these pale shadows! Are not thy darker thoughts better? Think thou on me! On Power! Come, Hate! Come, Anger! Come, Despair Come, Fear! Sit ye all with me!

FEAR

Only let me return unto thee, Lord! I fear! I fear!

BEAUTY

(To AMBITION, *angrily.)* And if he thought on thee, what then? Storms, horrors, all blackness and rage! Thou art such! Is not Beauty better?—this light?—this song?—these Cherubim and Seraphim? Wilt thou have naught but shadow? Avaunt! To think on thee is death, destruction, the end of all! Oh, no, Lord! Oh, no, no, no! Put them all hence! Think thou on me! Are not all thy fair dreams, in which suns cluster and lovely forms bud forth, more to thee than these, thy darker? *(She smiles winningly.)*

THE LORD OF THE UNIVERSE

(Heavily) I am that I am!

AMBITION

(Fiercely glowering and sulking.) Yea; Terror, Might, Strength, Death thou art! Think thou on me!

BEAUTY

Nay—Love, Beauty, All Perfectness, Light, Joy, Song—so art thou, and so only! Think thou on me, Lord! Think thou on me! *(She smooths his hands.)*

HATE, FEAR, GREED, DESPAIR

(In chorus.) Think thou on us! Are not we of thee?

LOVE, PITY, HOPE, REASON

(In chorus.) Think thou on us! Are not we of thee?

CHERUBIM AND SERAPHIM

Thou everlasting glory—Hail! Hail!

AMBITION

(Angrily.) Vanish, vain things! Dream, Lord, no more! *(He glowers and sulks.)*

THE LORD OF THE UNIVERSE

(To BEAUTY *sadly.)* I know not whether thou art best or worst. But stay, stay! Stay thou with me but yet a while! Let me not forget this thing that thou art—wonder, light, a glorious dream! *(He sighs.)* Oh, ho, ho, ho! Let me think no more of horrors! Of that I am aweary! Mad! Mad! Mad! Yet now I have thee—thou art a pleasant thought, thou joyous dream of fair things! Beauty! Beauty! Oh, Beauty! *(He smooths her cheek.)*

A CLOUD OF SERAPHIM

(Fluttering nigh.) He dreams of Beauty! We will not die! Hail! Hail!

A CLOUD OF CHERUBIM

He smiles on Beauty! We will not die! Hail! Hail

AMBITION

(A hovering, terrible figure in the gloom.) He rests and drools! All is light and song! He thinks not on death!

(The shadows recede into the darkness, to all but nothingness; the endless legions of suns twinkle; the clouds of CHERUBIM *and* SERAPHIM *swirl and turn.)*

SCENE III: THE HOUSE OF DEATH

SCENE: *A chamber of unimaginable horrors, vast, murky, involute, in which serpents twist and writhe; tortured figures crawl and groan; beasts of many heads and paws prowl to and fro, and all slimy odorous forms interlace in welters and sloughs and draperies and festoons. At the center, the Throne of the Lord, a mound of unclean beasts and serpents, hung over by clouds of evil spirits; his present embodied thoughts. At his side, huddled in despair, faint, pale shadows of their former selves, the thinnest of dreams*—BEAUTY, REASON, PITY, HOPE, LOVE. *Before him in glowering fullness, grown to vast proportions,* AMBITION, *and behind him the legions of his fancy, black and fulgurous, drawn close about. Insane, fevered, maundering, the LORD OF THE UNIVERSE bellows of destruction.*

THE LORD OF THE UNIVERSE

Oh, ho, ho, ho! Oh, ho, ho, ho! Death! Death! Death! Thou dearest death! Bring thou me heaps of dead—the endless slain! Breed winged and forked things, horrors all! Bring thou me shames, despairs, disasters, with which to torture and slay! Go forth! Go forth! Sweep thou with Hate, with Rage, with Despair, with Fear! Breed me vast powers of evil, and still vaster! Rank thou me them rank on rank—file by file! *(He thinks on tortured forms.)* Make me armies of horrors, of woes, of immedicable griefs! *(As he thinks, from his brain leap forth, many-headed, forked, winged, the first six Powers of Darkness, and after them, clawed and winged forces of ravening aspect and disaster.)*

BEAUTY

(Sadly, in a thin voice.) Lord, am I forgotten? *(He makes no answer.)*

LOVE

(In a thin voice.) Lord, canst thou no longer think on me? *(He makes no answer.)*

HOPE

(Weakly.) Lord, am I no more to thee? *(No answer.)*

PITY

Canst thou not remember me, Lord? *(No answer.)*

REASON

Lord, am I as nothing to thee now? *(No answer.)*

AMBITION

(To the clouds of darkness behind him as the first of the six great Powers leap forth.) Join them thou! Forth!

FIRST POWER OF DARKNESS

(Hundred-headed, winged and fanged, leaping from the brain of the Creator at illimitable speed). Hail! I go to harry! To slay!

SECOND POWER OF DARKNESS

(Hundred-headed, winged and fanged, rushing forth at illimitable speed.) Hail! I go to rack, to torture!

THIRD POWER OF DARKNESS

(Hundred-headed, winged and fanged, rushing forth at illimitable speed.) Hail! I go to ravage! To gall! To flay!

FOURTH POWER OF DARKNESS

(Hundred-headed, winged and fanged, rushing forth at illimitable speed.) Hail! Where Sorrow is not, I carry it!

FIFTH POWER OF DARKNESS

(Hundred-headed, winged and fanged, rushing forth at illimitable speed.) Hail! Where Happiness is, I destroy it!

SIXTH POWER OF DARKNESS

(Hundred-headed, seven-horned, winged and fanged, rushing forth at illimitable speed.) Hail! Hail! Where Peace is, and Love, I make them as not! *(They speed to his right hand and to his left, above and beneath him, before and behind him.)*

THE LORD OF THE UNIVERSE

Forth! Forth! Fury upon fury! Bring me masses of destruction! Undo! Undo! Undo! I would have change! Death! Woe! Tears—bring me tears, tears, tears! Wipe out all dreams! Make ashes of fancies! Destroy! Destroy! Destroy! Let all be of horror, of death, of sorrow, of pain! Make of life an ending in misery! Mad! Mad! I am mad! Oh, ho, ho, ho! *(He bellows in insane rage.)*

AMBITION

(Raveningly, to the clouds of Darkness behind.) Join thou these! Forth! Forth! Out upon his glistering thoughts! Undo! Undo! He is sick of pity, of peace! Harry thou with these! Destroy! Make dust of suns! Breed distempers in all flesh! Reduce, level, macerate, decay! Make of everything nothing! Forth! Forth!

THE LEGIONS OF DARKNESS

(Rumbling in anticipation.) Hail! *(They speed outward.)*

THE LORD OF THE UNIVERSE

(Rocking to and fro in insane pain.) To my right hand and to my left! Above me, and beneath! Before me, and behind! Out—on! Harry! Destroy! Cease, Time! Be nothing, Space! Oh, ho, ho, ho! Oh, ho, ho, ho! End thou me the weariness of this! *(He weeps in frenetic misery.)*

A CLOUD OF SERAPHIM

(Faded to but pale rays.) Oh, Measureless Wonder of all Wonders! Oh, Creator of all Things! Canst thou not think on us? We die! We die! *(They begin to fade.)*

A CLOUD OF CHERUBIM

(Shrunken to a thin line.) Nor on us—on us? We die! We die! *(They slowly fade also.)*

BEAUTY

(Rising and viewing all with weary eyes.) He dreams on me no more—on Beauty no more! Oh, mad, mad, Lord! Oh, fevered, useless dreams! Gone all the sweet Seraphim and Cherubim—the halls of light and wonder—his suns and jewel-

stars! His dreams have changed. These his horrors are now his mood. And death—and nothingness—for all of us, his mood! *(To* DESPAIR) Hail! Hail! thou unutterable one. *(To* AMBITION, *glowering near.)* And thou, great evil one, his torturous swelling thought! Now is thy dark hour! But sleep and nothingness is the end of this for thee and all! Thou wouldst destroy even me, oh evil thing! Yet if he but thought on me, how different! His singing world again! But wait, wait! If he think on thee for long comes death and the end of all this—of thee, as of me! By death, sleep! And by sleep, if he sleep—where then is his thought of thee or me? Pray that he change!

AMBITION

(Arrogantly.) Avaunt, thin thing! Now is my Lord awake—he thinks on me, not thee! To harry, burn, slay! To his right hand and to his left! Above him, and beneath! Before him, and behind! He is for strife, strength, conflict! To harry, slay, lay waste! It is as it is! He knows thee not! *(The destroying legions rumble.)*

PITY

(Drawing near to BEAUTY.) He thinks not on me again! I am grown so thin! Is there no change? Is peace worth nothing—the tender heart—the end of agonies and storms?

AMBITION

Avaunt! He knows thee not! (PITY *shrinks exceeding small.)*

LOVE

(Drawing near, a pale shadow.) Or all the lovely thoughts that fluttered into happiness—are they worth nothing?

AMBITION

Avaunt! He knows thee not, thin wraith! *(She fades to a point.)*

REASON

Nor me? Not even order?

AMBITION

Hence! (REASON *steps aside.)*

HOPE

Nor yet the thought he had in me? Can he not remember me?

AMBITION

Vanish! Thy Lord is for destruction! He thinks not on thee—but on me! Hence! (HOPE *pales to a thin flame.)*

BEAUTY

(Proudly.) Yet am I Beauty, his first thought! Rage on, thou evil one! Of what avail, since thou wilt end also? Destroy as thou wilt, he will not forget me! I am that which he is—Beauty! His first thought! Think madly as he may, yet will his last thought, as his first, be of me. I am in him, and he in me. From him, when he wake, if ever, will I come! I will be worshiped! I will be worshiped!

THE LORD OF THE UNIVERSE

(Writhing in a last insane agony.) Oh, ho, ho, ho! Oh, ho, ho, ho! Let me have done with Life! Let me have done with Thought—Pain—with Order, Beauty, Hope! Let me have done with all things! Oh, ho, ho, ho! Sick—sick! Death! Death! Burn! Harry! Slay! Oh, ho, ho, ho! I will have done with all! *(He tears at his snaky locks.)*

REASON

(Sadly.) Great Master of us all, so this then is the end? I, who was thy thought of order, am disordered! I, who was thy strength, am thy weakness! So sink I back to nothingness! *(He re-enters the brow of the Lord.)*

LOVE

And I, who was his thought of happiness! So come I to nothingness again! *(She re-enters the forehead of the Lord.)*

PITY

And I, who was his thought of tenderness! *(She fades into his brain.)*

HOPE

And I, who was his thought of love and peace! *(She disappears also.)*

BEAUTY

(Paling.) Yet is he not done with me! Mad though he be, even though he sleep, now I feel his thought! He is in me, as I in him! I will be worshiped! I will be worshiped! *(She re-enters his brow undiminished.)*

FIRST POWER OF DARKNESS

(Returning and entering in.) All that was to thy left hand is not!

THE LORD

'Tis well!

SECOND POWER OF DARKNESS

(Returning and entering in.) All that was to thy right hand is not.

THE LORD

'Tis well!

THIRD POWER OF DARKNESS

(Returning and entering in.) All that was before thee is not!

THE LORD

'Tis well!

FOURTH POWER OF DARKNESS

(Returning and entering in.) All that was behind thee is not!

THE LORD

'Tis well!

FIFTH POWER OF DARKNESS

(Returning and entering.) All that was above thee is not!

THE LORD

'Tis well!

SIXTH POWER OF DARKNESS

(Returning and entering.) All that was beneath thee is not!

THE LORD

'Tis well!

AMBITION

'Tis well! Hail, Lord! As thou wouldst, I have ended thy dreams! Canst thou not rest?

THE LORD OF THE UNIVERSE

(*Writhing.*) Oh, ho, ho, ho! Oh, ho, ho, ho! I dream! I dream! It is too much! Destroy! Destroy! I will have peace! I will have peace! *(He turns and writhes, sinking in weariness as he does so, and partially disappearing. Æons elapse.)*

FIRST POWER OF DARKNESS

(Beginning to fade in the brain of the Lord.) It is of me that he ceases to think! I fail! *(He disappears.)*

AMBITION

(Sadly.) It is the end!

SECOND POWER OF DARKNESS

(Beginning to fade in the brain of the Lord.) It is of me he ceases to think. Oh, ho, ho, ho! I fail! *(He disappears.)*

AMBITION

(Sadly.) It is the end!

THIRD POWER OF DARKNESS

(Writhing and fading in the brain of the Lord.) It is of me he ceases to think! I fail! Oh, ho, ho, ho! *(He disappears.)*

AMBITION

It is the end!

FOURTH POWER OF DARKNESS

(Fading into the brain of the Lord.) It is of me he ceases to think! I fail! *(He groans and disappears.)*

AMBITION

It is the end!

FIFTH POWER OF DARKNESS

It is of me he ceases to think! I fail! *(He disappears.)*

AMBITION

It is the end!

SIXTH POWER OF DARKNESS

It is of me he ceases to think! I fail! *(He disappears.)*

AMBITION

It is the end!

THE LORD OF THE UNIVERSE

(Stretching prone in space and all but vanishing. Only faint outlines are visible here and there, the brow and face intact.) Peace! Peace! It is enough! It is enough! I have done! Let it be as it ever was from everlasting to everlasting —a dream—a dream! Oh, ho, ho, ho! *(He sighs heavily. The last writhing beasts thin and are gone.* AMBITION, *paling and thinning, stands wide-eyed, agape, before the fading brow of the Lord.)*

AMBITION

At last! And I—it is of me he ceases to think—even me! I have done! I have done! *(He vanishes.)*

BEAUTY

(A thin star in the brow of the Lord, glistering and yet paling.) It is even of me he ceases to think! Lord, hast thou forgotten thy first-born?

THE LORD OF THE UNIVERSE

Peace! Peace! Enter thou into me! *(He sighs and begins to vanish completely.)*

BEAUTY

(Fading into his sleep.) I will be worshiped! I will be worshiped! *(She smiles.)*

The illusion of reality ceases. Suns and planets are gone. Time and Space are not. That which was is as that which was not.

ASHTORETH

WHAT has impressed me most about life, always, is the freshness and newness of everything, the perennial up-welling of life in every form; the manner in which, as age steals on for some, youth, new, innocent, inexperienced, believing, takes charge, its eyes alight with aspiration, its body ablaze with desire. We know that the world is old, old, and societies also in every form, while the average span of life for the individual is little more than forty years—yet step into the streets and witness the immemorable clangor and newness, the present visible portion of the unbroken thread or pattern that reaches back into eternity. And for all that life is so old, old, and atoms of the life pattern or chain are feeble, is life old? Does the bit of thread or pattern that we see here now show the least evidence of wear or tear? Is not the race as new, as fresh as ever? We rise betimes and the ancient sunlight streams fresh and strong and *new* into our passing window—this window which, in a few years, will be as forgotten and as non-recoverable as we ourselves shall be.

And the ways without—are they crowded with the aged, the worn, the soul-weary? Here and there, perhaps, a halting, bent or time-worn specimen that attracts attention for its *age!* In the main, at every turn, youth is in charge, laughing, singing, whistling, the newest modes of the *Zeitgeist* adorning it, the latest coats, the latest hats, the latest shoes heightening the charm of bodies utterly evanescent. The percentage of the really aged abroad is as one to one hundred—one thousand. Viewing the swift tides of life as they burble in the great thoroughfares they are utterly negligible. And it is always so. A large crowd of the old and the weak and the defective would be an astounding sight anywhere in life that is so old.

Yes, life is careful to do away with all evidences of age in the public places where it runs so gaily. The sick—are they here or in hospitals or darkened bedrooms? The maimed, the blind, the defective in any way—are they here, or hidden away in institutions where the young and the hopeful may not see? Life apparently resents them. It will not have its ways bestrewn by its discarded implements and shells. Out, out, since it is done with them. Away! There is much talk of charity and the beatitudes, but let one lose an arm, a leg, an eye, a hand. Practically the entire world shudders and withdraws. Better, indeed, a criminal, whole and exhibiting that self-sufficiency which the life impulse demands, than to have been injured in any worthy or even glorious contest. Rarely if ever, and never willingly, does Life obtrude upon our unwilling gaze a suggestion of the brevity of our own strength or charm, or present to the eye even a faint suggestion of the inscrutable and astounding and even wholesale cruelty of itself. Indeed, where Nature with her illusions has her way, pain, weariness and death are never to be accepted as the huge controlling facts that they are.

What—Nature cruel? Look at the freshness of Her face, the joy of Her perpetual youth, the glory of Her springs, the richness and variety of Her facets and changes! Quite so. She is the subtlest of all our enemies, the wisest of all our craftsmen and managers. Her instinct and therefore Her business is to keep the eternal freshness and durability and zest of life uppermost, and this She does with unbelievable skill. For although we are here, young and new, believing vigorously in our destiny, the grand sum of our future and its durability, still only forty or fifty years ago there were all of a billion people here who were as fresh and as vigorous and as youthful as we are now. They believed in their grand destinies as we believe in ours, and where are they? Gone. No trace—no memory even—no care. Only we are what is left of what was them, their descendants.

And the astonishing tragedies, the painful diseases, the most grinding and wearing of denied hopes, by reason of which they are no longer here and we are—how adroitly even the memory of these have been removed! The wonder! Yet *life* is as fresh now as it was then. *It* has not aged. *It* has not gone. The endless chain is as bright and strong as ever—stronger, maybe. To-morrow when we are where they are it will be as taut and shining and swift-moving and as new as ever.

But these young bustling souls swinging their canes, lighting their cigarettes, whistling and dreaming of a perfect to-morrow—do they know aught of this? Not a word. And will they? Not, in the main, until it is too late to affect their lives. And, better yet, and what is really more important, they do not care. Life has one admirable trait: it limits the sensibility of many. "Never mind, dearie," it seems to say, "do not worry about me, or older days. The old was nothing, the new is all. Eat, drink, be merry and forget. It is best." Thus life, and it is her intention that they shall. Each sorrow or deprivation or disaster as it befalls them is painted in their consciousness as special to them. Never before was there one such to equal this. No, no. Life would not be so cruel. She would not intentionally do this to any one. "What!" she whispers artfully and convincingly, "life induce such bitter tears? Life ruthlessly and cruelly deprive any one of a hand? an eye? of life itself? Never. To be injured thus indifferently, when so many are not, was never intended by her for you, as you can see. If that is not so, why is it so many are well, hale, happy?" So she lies, for well she knows that each can know but a very little, has no time to learn more. And she sees that he has not.

But in the dark places, the back rooms, the upper floors or cellars of tenements or great houses, the hospitals, the asylums, the jails, the farms and homes for the aged—and the enormous graveyards! Look and see. Here are those who but a little while since were a part of this pell-mell vigorous scene. They were her tools, as you are now, her victims. She fashioned them as one might a small machine, used them for a while for something and then threw them aside. Like a knife or any tool, they grew a little dull, and it is so much easier to fashion a new one. We are intended to last only a little while. While your strength is budding that of others is failing. While your cheeks are reddening theirs are paling. While your eyes are sharpening in shrewdness theirs are weakening to a dim myopia, and you may soon out-see them and push them aside. Yet the bodies of the old that so offend you now were as lithe as your own, and they in their hour were grumbling at the ineffectiveness of age.

But the darkest part of it is that aside from the small modicum of service which you may render at top speed and with the utmost enthusiasm, Nature has not the slightest care for you or yours. With the same cavalier air with which She provides a hundred drones for the single love-flight of the queen bee, all the failures to die, so She provides a thousand, or ten thousand, or a hundred thousand, that one—and only one—may think the necessary thought, invent the necessary machine, build the necessary bridge or lead the necessary army. The rest may die as they will. They are chaff. Lay them out in hundreds—in millions—to be blown whithersoever the wind listeth, to poverty, to death, perchance even to fortune, a brief hour. Who cares? Not She. Only the ways of life must be kept fresh and new, the illusion of newness and vigor maintained. Only through new bright instruments will She work, and none other. A tasteful maid. In the blood-stream of your body are quadrillions of little entities—so many millions to the single blood drop—whose total destiny, apparently, is to your life about as yours is to the race—and no more. They hurry that you may live. They toil that you may smile, seek, yearn, blaze with ecstasy. A fraction of a minute each, and their little cycles have been run. So yours here. But do they know? Or care? Or do you? There is that much wisdom or tenderness or practicality in Nature, that for the majority She inhibits the power of memory or perspective or too great sensitiveness to joy or pain. Else what a cursing, else what a wailing, else what a ceasing—even in the face of Her imperial will.

THE REFORMER

AMONG the interesting phenomena of life is the periodic appearance in every walk of life of the reformer, the individual who, according to some theory based on clear perception or some delusion that has developed in his brain, seeks to readjust conditions as he finds them to something more in accord with what is agreeable to him, and who accordingly, by a process of transference akin to that which has been so adequately set forth in psychoanalysis, seeks to represent himself to himself as a world need. Always it is life, not himself, that is in need of this new condition, and so him. And what is it that as a rule he offers or seeks? Without exception, if you trouble to examine the great instances—Buddha, Christ, Confucius, St. Francis, Luther, Mohammed—it is a revision of a current, and in itself passing, condition which has become irritating to his sense of balance or proportion or equation in things mundane, his personal and physical reaction to or sensory repulsion from conditions which have become chemically (socially, spiritually, anything you will) too far removed from a norm or mean or equation which appeals to him, his eternal and special view of harmony. But this after all is chemic and natural, and when he is successful he merely represents an inevitable tendency in nature to maintain a balance or equation between one type of mood and another, only one of which can be dominant for a time and of which he becomes the passing representative.

It is the only way apparently in which the moving spirit which creates us can express—or, better yet, change—itself. Our self-propulsive emotions, moods or appetites have somehow a tendency, if uninterrupted, to lead us too far in some one direction—to the place, for instance, where a chemical or physical non-balance is threatened to that dependent equation of rival forces in which we all find ourselves immersed or held. Then, apparently, by an inhering law which compels balance or equation in all things, a counter-tendency which is most likely to first present itself in the shape of a reformer, or instructor, or warner, always chemical in his significance, appears (Buddha, Christ, Mohammed, Luther), and you have a readjustment toward a happy medium again, as it were. One phase of life, let us say, grows and presses too dominantly on another. Forthwith a spokesman or mouthpiece of some kind arises, the antithesis of the dominant thing, by no means remote or divine but plainly human and simple and easily understandable, if he is to prove of any value. That is why it is always esoterically safe in gross material days to look forward to the coming of a Christ or Messiah, or reformer, or changer, of one type or another. He is in reality a chemic and psychic sign. He cannot help coming. He is merely an individual expression of the general tendency toward balance or equation. And he will surely come when things swing too far in any given direction. Any one can be a mouthpiece for an extreme lack of balance in human affairs, any one. The accident of circumstances usually distinguishes that one.

But by that we are not told that extremes, either of the gross or material, or on the other hand of the spiritual or ascetic, are to be permanently done away with or "reformed," or that either, when dominant, is essentially evil or good, or that the replacing thing is essentially better and so should remain forever. Rather, what is new and ameliorative—be it religious, ethic or economic—is merely one or the other half or portion or face of that which was before it came, a change from, or the obverse of, the other. Indeed the essential character of God, or the biologic force, or the Universe, is not made much clearer unless we see in this tendency to change or equation in all things that it or he is both good and evil. Since chemically or spiritually we are compelled always to seek a level or balance and maintain it, roughly enough it is true; since to live is to swing to and fro, past a mean and between extremes, may we not deduce from that that equation, balance, is an attribute of God or the life force, a conditioning attribute, and one under which it *must* express itself?

For in life, as we may always note, and at the very moment the greatest reformers are operating, there are also working —and quite as vigorously, else the reformer would have little to do—anti-reformers, or anti-Christs, or reactionaries, if you will, creatures who represent the obverse of what is sought by the reformer or changer, and who will by no means be permanently disposed of by him. Life apparently goes on two legs, or opposites, always—heat: cold; high: low; external: internal; strength: weakness; little: much; excluded: included. Side by side with millions or billions who wish one type of thing are always millions or billions who wish another, whose impulses, desires and necessities are the very antithesis of those advocated by the reformers, saviors, adjustors then operating. Thus as Christ walked the earth there were Herod, and the whole brood of Roman, Greek and Egyptian philosophers—pagans all—scouting his beliefs and dreams, and their descendants are with us yet. About St. Francis were the millions of gourmandizers and lechers of France, Italy and the European world generally (to say nothing of the skeptical Innocent III.), too gross to perceive the significance of that which the saint represented. Yet St. Francis was little more than a chemical reaction against a too-heavy materialism that enveloped Europe—nothing more, truly. He was, as it were, poetry as opposed to the grossest and most sodden type of materialistic thought. This is equally true of Luther and so many others. Christ the same; Mohammed the same. Yet plainly the creative force which we worship as God, the underlying chemistry with its cell mechanism, was as much the maker of the fat sensualists who surrounded and enraged Luther as it was of Luther. It was and is in both, and both in it. Else how explain their joint presence and conflict, their psychic as well as chemic necessity to each other, the one useless without the other—no devil no saint, and vice versa? I for one am convinced that the Universe, or God, or Good, is no more concerned with our saints than with our sinners. Both may be essential, no doubt are. Certainly both are in it, from it, necessary to it, expressive of different moods of it, and as such necessary to each other, in order that it or life shall exist, express itself, at all. From this I see no escape by any path.

The great aim of all reformers—that of permanently reforming man in his social as well as his religious ways or intentions, in his lusts after sensuality and the like, from a (in their estimation) condition of too great license to one of none at all—is of course ridiculous. Although always "Justice," "Right," "Truth," "Eternal law" are supposed to be involved in their commandments or demands, and presumed to represent a permanent and unchanging state of perfection of some kind—the all-good in some direction, and as such to be the direct commandments of God Himself—what is really, often unintelligently, sought is an easement of a too-great social swing in any one direction. Not perfection, but a better balance, is all that is really sought or ever attained. Yet so errant and nonsensical is life, its social or chemic drift—mere idle rocking of force in one direction or another at times—that man, for a time at least at one period or another, may be made to believe in or at least conform to, even coincide with, some current conception of the ideal which may or may not be in line with his greatest need, equation, in his affairs here or elsewhere at the time—which, indeed, may be absolutely inimical to his mental progress, as in the case of Mohammedanism, Shintoism, Christianity and the like. In other words, the necessity for obtaining a better equation in one place may very well upset a very excellent equation elsewhere. Thus, while it might be of passing advantage in one country—Arabia, say—that a readjustment via the thoughts of a Mohammed would be in order, it does not follow that his local "Rights," "Truths" and homilies would elsewhere be essential. Yet essential or no, an impetus flowing from such a center may well disturb a better equation elsewhere. This was illustrated when Mohammedanism assailed Christianity in Europe.

The truth is that what the reformers are always seeking, ignorantly or otherwise, is a better balance in things social or mental or moral, less accentuated tendencies of any kind—usually away from the too-gross, although at times away from the too-ascetic also, toward which extremes life appears to swing at times. And what they do is to identify their meager, if equational, perceptions of life with eternal thought or order, and to insist that the half of the balance which they represent is the whole of it. As a rule they are quite unfitted by ignorance as well as by the time mood of which they are the expression to see that without that against which they war neither they nor their divine creator would have the least excuse for existing.

To me, not violent extremes of any kind, although these are productive of great suffering at times, but the suave inanity which imagines it wants only unchanging good or, on the other hand, unchanging evil, is the thing to be feared. Fortunately or unfortunately, as one may view this thing, a strictly median condition, while excellent as a haven of refuge from extremes, is nevertheless never wholly or easily attained in life, and never, apparently, seriously desired by it, as an end in itself, and never quite satisfactory. Indeed it is the equivalent of nothingness and would produce just that if the world sought to persist in it. Yet wise Nature is our rescuer in this as in many another plight in which betimes She places us for ends of Her own, for Nature seeks, if She seeks anything, motion, although apparently in no straight line. Her mood, if anything, is synchronic, rhythmic, pendulumic. She wishes, if one may interpret Her wishes from what may be seen here, to swing in a semi-balanced way between extremes of so-called good and evil—never all good and never all evil, but a little of both, or plenty, in order that there may be contention, strife, something to live *about* and for. These violent extremes of any kind—ascetic, religious, barbaric, or repulsive—which affect life and irritate our souls, or the souls of some of us, are not at all offensive to Nature in Her entirety apparently. She appears to like extremes as well as a median line, the latter as a fence or break between them, and will have nothing of perpetual anything in any one direction. And life, it seems to me, would be more understandable, less disturbing to most of us, if in hours of stress of any kind we were able to realize this—that Nature adores extremes, with always a happy medium as the guiding and dividing line to which She can return and on which She can fix, as the mariner on the North Star. And if some such more liberal conception of God, or force, or life, or the creative impulse, could be introduced, it would be better. What we really need is a better stomach for life as it is, and Nature, in the course of time, may possibly build us such.

MARRIAGE AND DIVORCE

"Whom does not love rule? And where is he not Lord?"
Epiphanes Soter.

"There is no advisable love unless it is as reverent as it is romantic, as permanent as it is passionate."
George M. Gould.

"Faithful monogamy must ever be woman's standard in love, because only in its still certainty can she fitly prepare and keep the place for her child."
Beatrice Forbes-Robertson Hale.

"Too many have forgotten that love is as much a subject of the law of evolution or progressive development as any other biologic thing."
Haeckel.

N. B. The attached six questions, to which I have appended answers, were once submitted to me by an American publication for comment or solution! At the time I was unable to make an intelligible reply, but having since given the matter thought I have answered them, largely for my own satisfaction. They are submitted with no faith in any possible fixed solution but merely as meat for passing discussion.

I

Why is it, when there are so many evidences in favor of marriage as we practice it, that so many marriages fall short of just the purpose they seem meant to serve?

In the first place, are there so many evidences in favor of marriage as we practice it? In part the question contains its own answer when it states that so many marriages fall short of just the purpose they seem meant to serve. Statistics for marriage and divorce show that one out of every seven marriages ends in the divorce court. For every one thus openly disrupted, how many others are restrained or concealed for reasons of religion, morality, children, society and business policy or permitted license? Many a couple agree to go their ways separately, doing as they please and shielding each other in their privileges. Others drift into a quarrelsome or unhappy state from sheer inertia or lack of means or charm or courage to establish or create a new condition. Millions sink in the slough of despond because they have not strength of any kind. Age, poverty, thickness of wit does for them completely.

Now there is no need, and should be no desire, to evade the biologic necessity implied by marriage. Children must be brought into the world and reared if life is to go on. All the why-fors of this are given in a thousand biologic and anthropologic volumes, and so no need to discuss them here. But this much may be said, that among animals the limits of the control of the maternal feeling or instinct are rigidly confined to simple necessity. Love seems to disappear as soon as the young can possibly walk or fly and get their food—proof of its mechanistic or chemic quality and origin and its lack of any sacrosanct and "for eternity" spiritual character. Indeed, under most phases of animal life the father is absolutely indifferent to the fate of his offspring. In many, perhaps most, animals he seems to care no more for his children than if they were moving bushes. Certainly he cares no more for his own than for those of another, and the idea of any love toward grandchildren is absurd. Not even the mother shows this.

But it is of the greatest interest to note that with the appearance of humanity and its ideas of home and property (both products of maternal instinct or the chemic necessity in her for the care of her young) there has arisen a natural extension of the scope and control of the family instinct, so that the interest of the parents continues into or through adult life. Support and protection of the mother continues beyond the child-bearing period, grandchildren are beloved, more distant relatives are held within the family affection, and the patriarchal type of society is established. Since the higher ideals of society and civilization have been permitted to arise the ægis of love has extended over the nation, and patriotism, with its great influence in war and history, has appeared. Finally that highest development of humanity, ethics or love of humanity, has arisen (still an actual outgrowth and extension of maternal instinct or love apparently), as well as the theory of the existence of a Divine Father-Mother of humanity and of all life.

Yes, since the period of the law and the influence of Rome and the idea of love, the practice of it by enduring families has become rapidly more complex. To the force of sex compulsion and instinct, never omitted, have been added permanency, monogamy, home-keeping virtues, pedagogy, public health, civic and political honor, democracy and a thousand such compounds. Has it stood up well under them? Is the load too great? Our riotous divorce practices and statistics, as well as the so-called sex or prostitution problem, raises a sharp question. Does the average strong successful man confine himself to one woman? Has he ever? Does the exceptionally beautiful and dynamic woman confine herself to one man? Has she ever? Has not fear frightened the weak into a kind of rat-like dodging or a sniveling, quarreling, complaining compliance? It may be and no doubt is true that the so-called "building of the future," contemplated by the mechanistic or biologic impulse, if by anything, cannot be based on sensuality entirely; but the retort may be that Nature never seems to desire or achieve a wholesale debauchery any more than she desires a cold and narrow monogamy—the religionists and ethic-mongers to the contrary notwithstanding. At best she strikes a balance, wishes apparently virtue opposed to debauchery, *and vice versa,* for ends of her own.

But to return. However mechanically and instinctively it may have started, Life has since developed the more or less gorgeous chemistry of love with which now, if never in the past, it is invested. Human beings are apparently capable of higher and more enduring synthetic and chemic affinities, and this to many has seemed to warrant the second thought wherewith this interview is prefaced. Yet, for all this higher development, the strain of practical life appears to be too much for it. Besides the compulsion imposed by the biologic process which draws two people together there is a process of self-evolution and variation which seems to conflict with the marriage tie. How subtle is that problem which is to keep two people, subject to internal and external chemical and physical changes, harmonious for the eternity for which they are supposed to be linked? Nothing short of this is the theory which the religionist propounds. The moralist, not bound by religious dogma, will make the bond for life only. The philosopher or chemist transmutes the bond into a problem and speculates on how many weeks, or months, or years, the unstable equation may endure.

In considering the validity of our ideas in regard to marriage we either accept the current religionistic or moralistic theory, or we do not. For those who do there is no problem: they must accept their chains and slavery, if so they find marriage to be, and make a virtue of their sufferings. For those who do not there is the agonizing problem of the need of an equation in the matter of change. Somewhere they must draw the line, or necessity, increasing age, the difficulty of living in a moving-van, will fix the line for them. Again, there is a limit to any individual's capacity for change, however kaleidoscopic that may be. After all, any individual, male or female, however attractive, is but single in quantity, and the choice offered to either of a suitable helpmate or companion is not so very large. One may be forever lowering a hook into the water, but not all the fishes in the sea may take it even if they would. Solomon may have had three hundred wives and seven hundred concubines, but it can scarcely be said that he needed them or that they got much out of it; and while it is conceivable that a man or woman in swift kaleidoscopic search, and devoting him or herself strictly to the task in hand, might enjoy as many as a thousand or so of the opposite sex in the course of a lifetime, it can scarcely be considered valuable from the point of view of public policy and little less than difficult and, as it would seem to one at least, profitless from the point of view of the individual himself.

On the other hand there enters into the matter the very serious problem suggested by question IV, which I will include and touch on here for a moment only: "Are the children of any union better served by successive marriages than by a home where parents are held together, even though not by love but rather by a sense of duty to their children?" Obviously, Nature intended marriage for the reproduction and care of children, but I beg to call attention to the fact that Nature, or God, or the biologic process, or what you will, is no better planner or executor of any given theory or scheme it may have in mind than man himself. If this were not true there would be no physically imperfect men or women. The student of the pathology of sex, as well as of the sources of life itself, is confronted by a thousand variations from that happy norm on which the moralistic marriage must be based. Nature has not provided all its creatures with the capacity for a happy marriage. Plainly, it has cursed or endowed many of them with strange and horrible vices, with vast and self-torturing passions, with immeasurable longings and desires, which unfit them for the proper fulfillment of the monogamic conception of the perfect marriage, hence of the care of the ensuing children. What then is to be done? Who is to blame—Nature or man? And if Nature is to blame, or God, cannot we charge the presumed misery of the children up to Him also?

Personally, I am not prepared to admit that children are made miserable or destroyed by divorce and change. But granting that, certainly man is not to blame, for from the very beginning he has been crucified upon a rood which is not of his devising. He did not institute marriage; it was instituted for him, the biologic process having devised it long before he appeared apparently. I would gladly have all living creatures endowed with every capacity which would fit them for a peaceful and contented enjoyment of a moralistic life, if that were intended or important, but since in the vast and secret laboratory of Nature alone can man be properly outfitted for the adventure, and since, obviously, in many cases he is not, I submit that the matter of matrimony and the welfare of the ensuing children cannot be solved by talk and that Nature and its concomitants, change and divorce, must be permitted to take their free and unlimited way as they will. The great tides and forces of life which burst upon men and animals and change them do not always give notice that they are about to rise and change things. They rise in their great strength, and man, to his bewilderment, finds himself changing and changed. Hence I would say that the trouble with marriage is that in its extreme interpretation it conflicts with the law of change, or balance and equation, and hence suffers a severe and seemingly destructive defeat.

II

What would be the result were we generally to adopt Ellen Key's conception of marriage: "Marriage is only moral when it grows from an inner necessity, and not from outward pressure?"

Very pleasant, I should say, if logic and ideal syllogism ruled in life. The trouble with this world is that no ideal, however eagerly pursued, is guaranteed a happy fruition. You may lay down your formula for happiness and say : "Thus and so being done all will be well," but can you make human nature do anything according to any one finite individual theory? Man does not make or regulate Nature: Nature makes and regulates man, and She makes him any way She pleases—vile, lovely, strong, weak, simple, complex, and so on. There is no one theory that fits all climates or types of people. Life would be very dull if this were true.

But I presume by "inner necessity" Ellen Key means intense desire plus a marked affinity of two people for each other, and if the union is for only so long as this endures I should see no drawback to it whatever. I should say that humanity would be much better able to endure the stresses and difficulties of the world if they were all so happily mated, and indeed there might not be so many stresses and difficulties to endure. No doubt we all wish that this would come true, but not all people are motivated by either love or passion. They would not marry for love if they could but rather for social precedence, material luxuries and the like. They accept children as a somewhat unfortunate concomitant, and so you have the curious problem of whether this state and its results are good, bad or indifferent in so far as society is concerned. For my part I would paraphrase Christ's idea and say: "Render unto Materiality the things that are Material, and to Love the things that are Love's." Then the world would remain just about as it is now.

III

Would a succession of unions, expressing different phases of true love, be of higher value to the individual soul and to the life of the race than one unbroken although loveless marriage?

My answer to this question, based on my own individual temperament, would be Yes, but I cannot help speculating as to the opinions of those whose temperaments are so cool or so unemotional that they can put social precedence, material comfort, or the general welfare of the state, as they see it, above affection or passion. Thousands of people are by temperament sacrificial, one might almost say masochistic. They never put themselves first, and that for the very simple reason that their emotions or desires do not compel them so to do. The religionist, the moralist and the fanatic, for reasons of order or material development, as he sees them, would and does look upon love and passion as a disturbing, unsatisfactory and almost unnecessary element in life. Passion is sin or weakness to him, and the individual who requires more than one union to express his emotional necessities is either a lunatic or a criminal. His first impulse is to drive him out of society, to lock him up and reform him by some iron system of training; failing this he will shun him and form little communities of his own into which the victims of emotion and passion must never venture save as thieves steal into a house at night. This last is well and as it should be no doubt in his special case, but on the other hand he is the type of man who is determined that there shall be no divorce for others very unlike himself, who would make wife-desertion a criminal offense of the first order and who would almost punish adultery with death if he could. He is a puritan soul. He does not see Nature in all Her subtle ramifications and climatic and chemic variations, and he helps to make that endless war between the so-called light and darkness of life—between sin and virtue—and these special phases of asceticism or temperamental coolness are the foundation of all religions apparently.

Such individuals would argue, for instance, that the child of a loveless marriage is as well off as a child of a marriage of any other kind, provided he is clothed and fed, washed and schooled and thoroughly inculcated with the belief that sex is a crime. The less love enters into the child's life at any time the better, say they. Children will do better, make better men and women, and make more money, if they do not love too much. Thus stands the world, divided between the hot and the cold, the stern and the tender, the fools of passion and the fools of material order and well-being. Is the one better or wiser than the other? I do not know. You may pay your money and take your choice, for you cannot well serve passion and materiality at the same time. Personally I stand with the fools of love, because I think for all their follies and errors and Lear-like ends they are happier.

IV

If the answer is Yes, are the children better served by successive marriages than by a home where parents are held together if not by love by a sense of duty to their children?

I would not say that children are, in the main, better served by successive marriages due to changes of temperament, because I do not know, but I can truly say that I am fairly well satisfied, from my personal observation, that they are no worse served. In the first place the fate of the modern child is not nearly so much in the hands of individual parents as it is in those of the state, the public schools and their teachers, the newspapers and their editors, the judges of courts and public and private citizens generally; for the modern child can almost say to-day that the state is both my father and my mother and it will take care of me. When it can really say this we will be much better off, for we are all going to be happier. The extremes of misery in childhood are going to be done away with.

In the next place it is a part of my personal observation that children of warring or troubled homes, where they are made to endure them, are worse off than are those who have escaped through fracture and been thrown on their own resources or are assisted by the charity of the state. or relatives, or the citizens of the country generally, to say nothing of the love or obligation of one or both of the separated parents. There is a deal too much sentiment attaching to the home as such to-day, sentiment not justified by facts. All homes are not ideal rearing-places for children, by any means. Consider the vast factory communities everywhere, too easily forgotten by the comfortable intellectual classes, and again the slums. The homes in these are, if one were to pay strict attention to the moralist, as ideal rearing-places for children as any other; yet we know that life offers pits of horror as well as abodes of sweetness and light in the guise of the modern so-called home. Again, it should be remembered that the home was made for man, not man for the home, and when the home fails as a vehicle of comfort and aid it should be done away with. It is, after all, only wood or stone or plaster, an economic convenience at best. And, anyhow, where the heart is is home, though it be a bed under the open sky or in a new lodging-house every hour. And this generalization is not intended to exclude children either. The children of troubled warring homes live in a kind of hell of temperament from which they are glad enough to escape as they grow older, and from which they evolve the dream of building something better for themselves, for they realize the horror of the thing they have endured.

The basic reason for destroying many a home is that the children may not be injured. All life administers its sternest reprimands to those who abuse children. Life loves children. It really prefers them to their elders—the biologic process so does. There is a public obligation to them which we all acknowledge. But this is not to say that all parents should therefore be compelled to rear their children. It may well be that they are not fitted economically or mentally or otherwise so to do. Their whole duty is, or might well be, done when they support them properly. The state should do the rest, for, as I have just suggested, most people are not fit to rear their children; and I say this with the greatest respect for the human and very charming impulse which causes them to wish to. The intellectual standards of the average individual are not much; those of the state are in the main better and should and may be trusted to do better by the children than any of millions of parents.

V

Under what circumstance is divorce justifiable?

When there is inharmony, schism, and in consequence bitter contention. I recommend this question, first, to the religious dogmatists of all creeds; second, to the anarchists, socialists and economic thinkers generally. They represent purely individual, and to them justifiable, points of view. Hence the world's collection of dogmatic and radical literature.

VI

What is the key to making marriage do its work in the world?

? ? ? ? Unchanging love possibly, or an ingrowing and harmonious sense of duty. Without Napoleonic skill or tact, however, I fear me much even then, and so would end with——

? ? ? ? ? ? ?

P. S. To sum it all up I should like to advance another theory of mine in regard to the duality of sex. It is quite probable that in the beginning (biologically speaking) the sexual progenitor of the human race or of evoluted species contained in itself the full chemical content of what has since been evoluted into the so-called male and female. Such being the case its chemical responsiveness to the movements of the universe, chemical, physical, spiritual, or let us say emotional, and to its immediate surroundings, was complete in itself. It was not divided into two sexes and therefore not dependent on any alienated portion of itself for its chemical, spiritual, emotional or physical satiation. What happened to it individually and momentarily was all that could happen to it. It needed no complementary organism, no other half, to make its understanding of, its reaction to, life complete. That is not true to-day. Man (male or female) appears to be individual and complete, but it is an illusion. He is complete and separate as an organism in everything save his chemical responsiveness to the universe which requires his union, not merely physically but spiritually, with his sexual companion to be complete. Their union sexually, temperamentally, emotionally, intellectually and so on is required before a full measure of chemical responsiveness to life can be attained in either. It may seem otherwise in individual cases, but it is not so. Such being the case (and a world of biological data might be here introduced), you have the amazing spectacle of love which confounds all theories of life, which laughs at death, and, in its fullest expression, defies all human theory and understanding, acting as a *new* non-understandable thing, and letting in dreams, emotions, conditions from a deeper world than any we know and whereby this shadow called existence is resolved, modified, made over into something else so that it bears no resemblance to its former state. It becomes apparently what it well may be: a dream and an illusion of beauty or pain or delight, or all. Evolutionary progress seems to be based on this non-understandable, mysterious, idealistic reaction and contact which baffles the most searching suggestions and intuitions of the imagination and leaves us awed and dumb before the great classics of desire and passion.

But the great fact, not to be lost sight of, is that love, complete chemical responsiveness to the universe, is only attained in the reunion of the separated chemical constituents of the original asexual individual, and without love or this union there is no full chemical-spiritual responsiveness to the universe. Man does not soar emotionally into the empyrean except in love, and by "in love" I mean when stirred by the sex impulse which makes for mate-seeking and union. It does not follow that there need ever be physical satiation to complete this union. Spiritual pollination can spring from the merest accidental contact for a moment with a mate. But the fact remains that the greatest, most complete spiritual and physical responsiveness to the universe (which after all is a mere matter of chemical reaction) springs from this responsiveness, which springs from love, and as such our so-called love (desire, passionate chemical response, physical and spiritual) becomes the most significant fact in the universe as we now understand it. For what is the universe without intellectual perception on our part, the beholding of it with the eye, the perception of it with the senses, the responsiveness to it through the emotions?

MORE DEMOCRACY OR LESS? AN INQUIRY

IN my youth no country was so significant to me as the United States, of course, so wonderful, so fully representative of the natural spirit of aspiration in man, his dreams, hopes, superior and constructive possibilities. All that America did, could do, had done, was in line with the noblest and best principles in Nature, as I then understood Nature. And I still believe that this nation might be one of tremendous significance in connection with intellectual development, but some marked changes will need to come about.

Plainly, in a material and (socially speaking) internal organic way, it has accomplished much, even if thus far its intellectual stature has not proved so tremendous. We are, as I see it now, a deeply-illusioned people, concerned solely with material things when they are really no longer very important —certainly not as much so as when the land was new and without material means—and yet we remain almost entirely interested in such things when our minds should be beginning to grasp the wider possibilities of life—still fighting over beef and coal trusts and railroads and cables, the mere money return involved—who is to have the control of them—when we ought to be intensely concerned with the mysteries of chemistry and physics and a more pliable form of government.

Though my personal feeling once was that America was destined to take high rank, if not complete leadership, in the intellectual world, I am now not so sure. At this writing it looks as though it might retrograde, and that speedily, and give place to newer lands—newer in spirit, I mean. It may not, but the signs are somewhat against it. Our literature has plainly developed to the level of the best seller and then stopped. Our art is sporadic, and with a few exceptions lymphatic and strongly suggestive of older forms. The futuristic dream did not originate here. Our science—well, who are our American scientists anyhow? Loeb? Carel? Tesla? Bell? All foreigners.

In architecture, markedly allied, I must say, to mechanics, in which we flourish, we have done better—yes, and in anything and everything which relates, or has, to mechanics, trade, commercial organization. In those things, indeed, we have appeared to do most astoundingly, although I am firmly convinced that the boundless and virgin resources of the land have had as much—more, in fact—to do with this than anything else. We have not had so much to create as to develop, and other countries and other financiers—their trade geniuses—have done quite as well if not better in some instances than have we. I refer to such concerns and individuals as the English East India Company, the Royal Dutch Shell, the Allgemeine Elektrische Gesellschaft, the Cunard, Allen and other such organizations, to say nothing of such individuals as Lord Strathcona, Baron Shibusawa, Cecil Rhodes, Lord Cowdray, Alfred Harmsworth, Sir Thomas Lipton, etc.

Indeed the one thing I would like to point out most definitely in passing is this: that the by now ingrown idea in every average American's mind that all of the most significant inventions and discoveries, mental as well as mechanical, of the last hundred years or more are entirely of American origin is not true by any means. Far from it. Those great prime movers—for instance, the steam engine, the electric motor, and the gas engine (as well as its natural child, the automobile)—came to us from abroad. So did the telegraph, the railroad, radium, X-ray photography and—what is most remarkable, considering that the ironclad came from here—every step in steel manufacture. The telephone was invented by a Scot who was twenty-five years old when he became an emigrant to our country.

Other countries, so I was condescendingly taught—Egypt,

Greece, Rome, France, England, Spain (for a little while) and Holland—in times past and even approximating our own day, had been blessed with some opportunities and had done considerable toward fulfilling what I was taught was not so much the material as the spiritual and moral well-being of man—his intellectual and therefore his mental and social happiness. But nevertheless and never before, however (or since), had any country had, or could have, the natural, noble and spiritual impulse, to say nothing of the amazing opportunities, which America, the United States, was enjoying—a vast and fertile soil, an equable climate, engrossing varieties of scenery, a people given over entirely to industry, frugality and proper social and spiritual ideals. In other words America, according to my teachers, was destined to lead the world in thought, truth, beauty, liberty, justice, industry, and what not achievement, among other things.

Well, consider Greece in its day, faced by or placed in a virgin and undiscovered world. To the south and east Egypt and Phœnicia, to the north and west darkness, mystery, an unexplored world. No ships but oared boats—not even the trireme at first—no compass, no machinery, no implements of agriculture, and consider that to-day we quote Galen, Hippocrates and Æsculapius, its doctors; Euripides, Sophocles, Æschylus and Aristophanes, its playwrights; Herodotus and Xenophon, its historians; Demosthenes, its orator; Homer, Anacreon, Pindar and Sappho, its poets; Æsop and Helodorus, its writers; Pythagoras, Socrates, Plato, Aristotle and twenty others, its philosophers—the greatest in all the world—Solon, Alcibiades, Pericles, Aristides, and ten others, its statesmen. Also we marvel at Praxiteles, Phidias and Skopas, its sculptors; Alexander, Miltiades and Themistocles, its generals; and Archimedes, its mathematician. Nations, like individuals, are apparently born with genius, or they are not. They think, or they do not; they are dull merchants and tricksters like the Carthaginians and Phœnicians, or they are not.

America at the present moment, these United States, suggests nothing so much as the trading Carthaginians and Phœnicians. We have, apparently, no soul for really great things intellectually, and yet we have done a few things, too—fought wars for our own integrity, invented a number of very useful machines—the cotton gin, sewing-machine, flying-machine and U-boat—grown rich and great in size, freed the slaves (which England did in her realm without a war), liberated Cuba (no exploitation since?), struggled with the Philippine problem, the Mexican problem, and some others, but to no definite end as yet, however. And yet our deeds are plainly so incommensurate to our power. For we still have with us the Negroes, the clash and plotting of various rival sectarians, easily allayed by a truly educated race, the growth and almost complete independence of various private interests and individuals—puritanism run all but mad and to the death of genuine intellectuality, artistic or otherwise, etc. And yet to the average American it remains a belief or fact that within our borders, safe under the control and guidance of a human and helpful Constitution or form of government, are all the social, commercial and mental opportunities to which an ambitious citizen of the world may logically aspire—freedom to think, to grow mentally and in every other way, to acquire tremendous wealth and be a person in whom the inventive and constructive processes of Nature can take the liveliest interest. Indeed, whatever may have befallen him socially or economically in recent years, he is still convinced that he is absolutely free—freer than the constituent individuals of any other nation, that he is a great thinker and leader in things intellectual and that America is the best and most carefully administered country in the world, administered entirely, or nearly so, on his behalf.

Well, I have no very great quarrel with that as a theory, a method of expressing one's private vital force, but is it true? In my personal judgment, America as yet certainly is neither a social nor a democratic success. Its original democratic theory does not work, or has not, and a trust- and a law-frightened people, to say nothing of a cowardly or suborned and in any case helpless press, prove it. Where in any country not dominated by an autocracy has ever a people more pathetically and ridiculously slipped about afraid to voice its views on war, on freedom of speech, freedom of the press, the trusts, religion —indeed any honest private conviction that it has? In what country even less free can a man be more thoroughly browbeaten, arrested without trial, denied the privilege of a hearing and held against the written words of the nation's own Constitution guaranteeing its citizens freedom of speech, of public gathering, of writing and publishing what they honestly feel? In what other lands less free are whole elements held in a caste condition—the Negro, the foreign-born, the Indian?

When one considers the history of American commercial development, the growth of private wealth, of its private leaders—the Rockefellers, Morgans, Vanderbilts, Goulds, Ryans, et al., indeed all the railroad, street-car, land and other lords—a, until the war, practically stationary wage-rate, an ever-increasing rising cost of living, cold legislative conniving and robbery before which the people are absolutely helpless, Tammany Hall, the New York Street Car Monopoly, seven hundred and fifty-three different kinds of trusts that tax people as efficiently and ardently as ever any monarchy or tyranny dreamed of doing—I should really like to know on what authority we base our plea for the transcendent merits of democracy, and I am as good a democrat as most Americans, if not more so.

Government everywhere, in monarchies and republics, as well as tyrannies and despotisms, has, other things being equal, always kept step with the natural development of the intelligence of the mass, a thing which has been as much developed by the goads of tyrannies as by the petting of republics. But could you ever convince a full-fledged American, raised on

Fourth of July orations and the wonders and generosities of the American Constitution, of this? For him, of course, liberty began in 1776 at Bunker Hill or somewhere near it. Before that was no light anywhere. Since then we have gone on—doing better and better, making all men richer happier, kinder, wiser.

But have we? Is our land and its progress so absolutely flawless? Aside from love of country and individual vanity which might make us want to think so, have we not developed as many flaws, anachronisms, social and governmental irritations and oppressions as any other country? I call attention to the deliberation and ease with which the trusts organize our legislatures, dictate to the jurists of the land, deny even the permanence or sacredness of contract when it concerns them; rob, pillage and tax to their hearts' content while a pitiful mass at the bottom march to and fro wondering where or to whom to turn for relief. And, on the other hand, life here, as much as elsewhere—the struggling mass—is as savagely pushed by necessity as any mass anywhere. Our labor unrest is as great, our poverty as keen; five per cent, or so it is alleged, of the population controlling ninety-five per cent of the wealth; thirteen per cent of the population illiterate; at the top gorgons of financiers as fat and comfortable and dictatorial as any the world has ever seen and as unpatriotic and un-American, in so far as its original theory goes, as may be. Worse yet, it is absolutely true that ours is, or was, materially at least, a rich land, boundless in its opportunities at first, which latter fact has contributed greatly to our optimism but not to our comfort. More rapidly here than anywhere in the world the rich have divided themselves from the poor, and now here as elsewhere necessity and pain are and will remain no doubt the goads to comparative ease. Yet the tramping American when he utters the marvelous word democracy believes that he has it, and when he is not complaining and the newspapers tell him so, believes that he is perfectly happy.

At the same time, considering our aggressive and progressive financial leaders—and heaven forbid (on humanitarian grounds, at least) that I should defend them, for a more selfish, cruel and undemocratic pack never lived (consider the packers, the street-car corporations, the railroads alone, not to mention a thousand others)—there is this to be said, that although nearly every crime in the decalogue may be charged to them, bribery, perjury, murder, even a total indifference to individual welfare (twelve and a half cents an hour, for instance, up to six years ago for hard, grinding day labor on a railroad or in a canning factory), as well as greed, love of power, and lust after it—still much if not all of America's boasted financial supremacy is due to them and to none other. We jeer at John D. Rockefeller at home perhaps, or Morgan, but when abroad among envious strangers who is first to thrust out his chest and boast of what America has done—its financial leaders, no less? Who? The average American? You know so. Such being the case one often wonders what is to be done with a country or a people that can so readily blow hot and cold out of the same mouth. Can it be made to follow an austere democratic program—the sharp, taut socialization of everything—or will it succumb to autocratic or to financial domination, and if so, which? At the present moment the air hums with the rival theories. To me the chief problem in connection with America, if it has one, and as I see it, is that of finding itself mentally as well as finding a formula that will allow and encourage leadership without submitting to the abuses which in the past and even the present the latter tends to give rise. For here as much as anywhere else the average small American is as much a petty tyrant as may be found. Consider only the food profiteer, the small dealers, jobbers and wholesalers. And here, as elsewhere, are all the petty tyrannies of small and large enterprises in regard to wage-earners, the scorns, the brutalities, the exactions. Can these be outrivaled if readily duplicated in any autocracy or democracy ruled by a dictator anywhere? At the same time, is it not true that, if the country is to succeed or at least progress materially, a place must be made for the selfish, self-aggrandizing individual either as leader politically or as creator? Will life go forward without some such process or opportunities for immense rewards or honors to the individual—the right to satisfy his feverish if ridiculous ambition for supremacy? Will patriotism, love of country, alone do it? Can it be discovered?

What made Rome great? *Senatus populusque Romanus.* The Senate supplied the leadership, the people the impulse and force, which spread the dominion of the shepherds of the Seven Hills until it ruled the world from Scotland to the Nubian Desert and the confines of India. What is the secret of the Roman church's preëminence? Leadership? Autocracy? In the early Christian church these were lacking. Think or say what you will of its results, but consider it. In so far as the early Christians were concerned they were all "brethren," like the Russians of to-day and the citizens of the French Revolution. Each early Christian community elected its deacons; the deacons elected the priests; the priests elected the bishops; the bishops elected the cardinals; and the cardinals the pope. Before the Catholic church began to attain to its strength, however, the process was reversed: the pope appointed the cardinal, he the bishop, the bishop the priest. Then the deacons were selected by the priest, in certain cases some deacons were elective, but then the priest and deacon, appointed by the bishop, constituted the majority of the board. It was then, and then only, that the Roman church began to flourish truly. The ambition of man had full scope, his vanity. Apparently the world hitherto has not been able to do or live without it. On the authorization basis of leadership the Roman church, the most impressive organization in human history, has stood for seventeen centuries.

But take our own Standard Oil Company. Who built it? Who used to caution all his lieutenants never to talk, to keep everything a secret, particularly its prosperity? And has not the blessing of cheap oil been extended to all the world? Who selected strong, ambitious men and set them to planning the monopoly of oil for their personal and private benefit, dickered with the railroads and cut the throats of his rivals via the rebate? Does his name have to be written here? Call him a scoundrel, scoff at autocracy and high and mighty plutocrats. After all, can a man or a woman become a safe or dictatorial plutocrat without having something to offer which makes his plutocracy and his dictatorship bearable? Have mere dull tyrants anywhere ever lasted long? Have they ever had brains enough? Most of Rome's worst emperors were slain in anywhere from three to five years. The tyrants of Asia and Africa last, if they do, because the people are as dull as themselves, or their rule is agreeable to them.

Every great business corporation, as we know, is built about the personality, the leadership, the autocracy, of one man. We hear of love of country, of putting the needs of the mass, one's country—all countries—above that of one's personal or private needs. There are noble examples no doubt (off-hand few occur to me) of unselfish public sacrifice of many, many private lives, but are they the rule or the exception? Does not the average individual now as heretofore consult his own interest, his advantage, his purse, his survival, his fame? Once one is large and secure, easy in the possession of fame, money, love even, it is possible, of course—and even with a grandiose air—to do generously, to give freely, to seek the advantage of the mass. Scarcely any other avenue of personal satisfaction remains open. I am not sneering; I am contemplating a possibly chemic, physic or psychic law. Who knows?

Taking the average individual, with life (necessity, hunger, drouths of one kind and another) pressing upon him as fiercely as it does, and contemplating America as it is and the world as it is, is it not fair to ask whether it is possible to make over man—his ambitions, his soul, into the likeness of what is suggested by the average modern democratic or republican or socialistic program? Can he be adjusted to it? Haven't we just had two thousand years of an attempt in one form? Possibly he can, but is it wise that he should? Are not striking, centralizing figures more important and, save during extremely patriotic moments, when some danger, say, threatens the national organism as a whole, is it not extremely difficult to cause the average individual to enthuse over a crowd or the needs of a crowd? And on the contrary, is it not most pathetically easy to cause him to enthuse over a man or a woman—to cause any of us so to do? It would almost look as though it were Nature's way, would it not—the love of the mass for leaders, for grandiose, grandiloquent figures? Is not life, in the main, personal, individual? Think how we insist on identifying God as an individual. Will not such leadership as was offered by Alexander, Hannibal, Mohammed, Napoleon, Washington, Lincoln, always be popular? The leadership of lesser or more self-aggrandizing individuals—such as, for instance, that of the late James J. Hill, of the Great Northern Railway; E. H. Harriman, of the Union Pacific; Cornelius Vanderbilt, of the New York Central; Jay Gould, of the Missouri Pacific; Jay Cooke, of Civil War Finance; Armour, Field, Leiter, Morgan, or, to come down to the present moment, John H. Patterson, of the National Cash Register; Henry Ford, of the jitney; F. W. Woolworth, of the five-and-ten-cent store—if never popular, still does it not remain necessary? Must not some one lead even in the home and all forms of private commercial adventure? It may not be an absolutely invariable rule, but is it not near enough to make it seem so? I am not quarreling with the possibilities of love, generosity, self-sacrifice, public and private. We all hope for them, do we not? In various minor ways at least, and even in some public and large ways, they exist. But how about self-interest, cold, savage and yet constructive if feverish self-interest? Has that been abrogated?

Indeed, ought not we Americans, of all people, learn, and

learn quickly, that autocracy in whatever form you find it—absolute or otherwise—is never real autocracy, not absolute, and that on the other hand so-called democracy is never real democracy but always something tempered by private autocracy in a thousand—nay, in a million—forms? For after all, who tells such people as Rockefeller and Woolworth, to say nothing of kings and emperors—fallible and seeking souls, all—how, what, why, they must do?—how far they may go? What to interest themselves in? Consider the fall of the French kings, Charles I., the late Czar. They deal with the mass, and therefore to a certain extent they must respect it. They cannot escape it. It is their fate. At the same time, in attempting so to do, to whom do they not listen really for sound advice?—often to the least of their subjects or hirelings. The stockholders in any modern corporation—are they any more as to voice and weight in that which their money makes possible than the people out in the street of a republic or a kingdom with their ultimate veto power? They elect a board of directors as we elect a senate, or a monarchy, a legislature. And this leadership perpetuates itself, or at any rate holds things together, as does officialdom at Washington, until a leader appears. A weak king or emperor is run by strong men, a weak President is dictated to by a strong Senate or House. When the Roman Senate was strong the dictators were weak, and vice versa. In calm, peaceful days leadership is not necessary. It is or may be a disturbing factor. But when changes are coming, when Nature is brewing a storm—then. So life, with its endless brewing of storms and leaders, ought to give a hint to republics or democracies or corporate organizations.

And, having said so much, is it not plain that room must be made always for the leader, the passing autocrat, if you will? Must he not be given—if he have brains—the right of initiative and power, for after all is he not also a slave to life, chance, labor, the time-spirit? It is to be assumed, of course, that men shall demand first that he command their admiration and loyalty, as he certainly will if he is a real leader. Rome admired her Cæsar, France her Napoleon; Germany evidently liked her Kaiser, France her Clemenceau, England her Lloyd George. They thought them, apparently, necessary and great leaders. In our contest with Germany we perhaps, for one nation, were fighting to make her dislike something which she craved and needed, could not probably very well do without.

The trouble, as I see it, is that too often, in spite of all the current palaver and enthusiasm of some for special individuals, we have too little real or popular leadership. Middleweight idealists and theorists are too often at the steering-gear here as well as elsewhere. In this country we have the crowd, the extraordinarily well-educated (or we think so) and disciplined crowd, willing and eager for leadership. But what leadership? As it stands, all democracies are organized with elaborate systems of checks—legislative, executive—which are intended to and do tie the hands of all possible leaders, until a very, very great emergency arises. In the ordinary run of days and events only the ordinary politician or parlor-diplomat need apply. But when an extreme necessity calls, these minors must give way, but does the true leader always appear in time? Will he? Did the Allies have a truly able anti-Teutonic leader in the recent great struggle? Joffre? Asquith? Lloyd George? Kerensky? Wilson? Nicholas Romanoff?

Our Federal Constitution, theoretically at least, gives us a crowd government; only, owing to the wholly undemocratic character of the American people, this has long since been replaced by money or trust government, the rule of the wealthy by right of subornation. And our state and municipal governments, modeled on that of the nation, have gone the same way. Even such little individuality and leadership for the mass as might possibly exist under these conditions is lost or discarded nearly every two or four years in the regular and money-controlled changes of administration. The old and experienced are replaced with the new and untried. Perhaps under conditions as they are this is best. I am not sure. But for efficiency, after the manner of the great successful private corporations, is it? Personally, I think not—not yet, at any rate. As yet democracy does not take sufficient interest in itself, is too indifferent to its real interests and needs. It is too easy-going, not sufficiently self compelling. Every one wants to be his own boss and to be a great, undemocratic, individual success, hence there is very little true effective organization outside private institutions and what they compel in a public way. We make no provision for the continuation of leadership even under emergency.

Personally, I think the defect cannot forever go on unremedied. Democracy must do at least as well as autocracy, or it ought to shut up shop. And if it cannot obtain the efficiency exemplified by the private corporataion it will, and it will deserve to. Perhaps our recent sad experiences in meeting the expanded demands on governmental efficiency should show us how to lay a new basis for that efficiency in modifications of our governmental structure. But will they? What I think is that more autocracy, behind which should be a livelier sense of power and control on the part of the people, should come into our democracy, or our democracy will really cease to be. The present drift toward money control cannot go unchecked. Our leaders will either become much more forceful, and the mass more watchful and jealous, as it should be, or we will have no democracy of any kind. There is scarcely any now. Congress should be used more against the President and the Supreme Court, and the latter against both, only the judges should be plainly responsible to the people, closely and fearsomely beholden to them—as much so, at any rate, as they now are to the corporations and wealth. Both the leaders and their weapons—the laws—should become more vigorous. Democracy will have to step up, and step lively. Then will it be any more of a democracy than some of the older and more historic autocracies and monarchies? Will it?

THE ESSENTIAL TRAGEDY OF LIFE

The Serpent to Eve, Genesis iii, 3:5: *"For God doth know that in the day ye eat thereof"* (the Tree of Knowledge) *"then your eyes shall be opened and ye shall be as gods, knowing good and evil."*

Jehovah to the Serpent, Genesis iii, 14;15: *"Because thou hast done this"* (urged Eve to seek wisdom by eating of the Fruit of the Tree of Knowledge) *"thou art cursed above all cattle, and every beast of the field; upon thy belly shalt thou go, and dust shalt thou eat all the days of thy life; and I will put enmity between thee and the woman, and between thy seed and her seed; it shall bruise thy head and thou shalt bruise his heel."*

Jehovah to Eve, for attempting to obtain wisdom via eating the Fruit of the Tree, Genesis iv, 16: *"I will greatly multiply thy sorrow and thy conception; in sorrow shalt thou bring forth children; and thy desire shall be to thy husband and he shall rule over thee."*

Jehovah to Adam, because of his following the advice of Eve: *"Because thou hast hearkened unto the voice of thy wife and hast eaten of the Tree, cursed is the ground for thy sake; in sorrow shalt thou eat of it all the days of thy life; thorns and thistles shall it bring forth to thee, and thou shalt eat the herb of the field. In the sweat of thy face shalt thou eat bread till thou return unto the ground."*

"Prometheus (forethought), son of the Titan Iapetus and Clymene, and brother of Atlas, Menœtius and Epimetheus (after-thought), is represented as the creator of man, out of earth and water, and his great benefactor, having given him, in spite of Zeus who was apparently opposed to it all, a portion of all the qualities possessed by the other animals. He also stole fire from heaven in a hollow tube, and taught mortals all useful arts. In order to punish Prometheus for this, Zeus gave Pandora to Epimetheus, his brother, in consequence of which diseases and sufferings of every kind befell mortals. He also chained Prometheus to a rock on Mount Caucasus, where during the daytime an eagle consumed his liver, which was restored each succeeding night. Prometheus was thus exposed to perpetual torture; but Hercules (strength) killed the eagle and with the consent of Zeus, who in this way had an opportunity of allowing his son to gain immortal fame, delivered the sufferer."

Smaller Classical Dictionary.

The significance of these several references to and quotations from the supposed creative power of the elder pagan world is, if anything, that man is a waif and an interloper in Nature (or things celestial or intelligent), a machine or toy, created by something which desires to use him or work through him in some way, with no essential power to make his own way and no "right" to seek either knowledge or wisdom, lest, in the words attributed to Jehovah, his Creator, in Genesis, he becomes "as one of us," a minor god, for instance, as the Creator via this phrase writes himself down to be; not the Supreme Ruler of the Universe, by any means. And in this phrase ("one of us") is contained a hint of a possible condition or order in the universe which, since the Christian era, has been put aside as untrue, namely, that the Creator of man, our two billion two-legged citizens stalking this earth, may be but (to use a very crude and yet for that reason understandable description) a "side-line" manufacturer, as it were, or a lower-level competitor for life and pleasure, along with many others of his kind—Creators or "Gods" or avatars of, let us say, mosquitos, flies, bulls, cats, dogs; in other words the specific and singular Creator of some one thing as opposed to other Gods or powers who might well be creators of other things of equal rank. And these "Gods," in turn, should one choose to follow the thought, might well be the special product of some greater "God" or manufacturer or Creator who is finding a rather peculiar expression through them and their creations in turn; also the various rivalries which exist between man and the lower animals for the possession of the earth might thereby be explained or have something to do with that.

The thought is not new. Alfred Russel Wallace, co-discoverer with Darwin, Lamarck and Spencer of the theory of evolution, has pointed out that "the organizing mind which actually carries out the development of the life world need not be infinite, need not be what is usually meant by the term God or Deity. The main cause of the antagonism between religion and science seems to me to be the assumption by both that there are no existences capable of taking part in the work of creation other than blind forces on the one hand and the infinite, eternal, omnipotent God on the other. The apparently gratuitous creation by theologians of a hierarchy of angels and archangels, with no defined duties but those of attendants and messengers of the Deity, perhaps increases this antagonism." He then proceeds to develop a theory of his own in which (I quote) "the vast, the infinite chasm between ourselves and the Deity is to some extent occupied by an almost infinite series of grades of beings, each successive grade having higher and higher powers in regard to the origination, the development and the control of the universe." He goes on to show how this might be done by them—all to the one end: namely, the creation and preparation of man via experiences here, persumably for a higher place in the control of the universe at large, always under the Supreme Ruler of course and his lesser, yet in so far as man is concerned greater, agents. In other words, under these sub-Gods.

The idea is interesting only it does not, although it may be too much to say that it cannot, explain the endless bickering and chaffering in the universe at large, the utter failure of various movements and types here on earth and apparently elsewhere, the astonishing selection of so minute a mote in the material universe as this particular planet for the purpose of working out a higher type of assistant or worshiper of God Himself. It may be true, but the idea is a little fantastic and suggests the labors of an ignorant and yet hopeful being endeavoring to account for himself, his presence, in the best way he can.

To my humble way of thinking, the ancient Greeks and the various theogonies of the ancient pagan world (Egyptian, Chaldean, Hindu) were at least as plausible in their apprehension of a troublesome disorder. The Old Testament and all other forms of ancient pagan literature suggest the general and very natural conception, based on the evidence of life itself, that various gods were or are contending via various forms of life (animal, vegetable and mineral) for some form of expression here on earth, and that the various things which they make (or the one thing which each makes, its image and likeness perhaps) is opposed to all others here. Pagan thought reeked with the feeling of contests between gods or creators or controllers of this, that and the other, and in the Sinaitic interpretation of life just quoted we see something of the same thing; also in what small consideration man was held by his alleged special Creator. Evidently the conclusion reached by the thinking elders of the pagan world was that man, in so far as his own special Creator was concerned, was viewed with sinister opposition by the power which made him. It did not want him to amount to anything. Indeed he was very, very plainly conscious of the inimical attitude of Nature, or rather man's especial God or Creator, toward him. He was not as yet deluded by the Christian phantasm that man is made in the image and likeness of his Creator, who is highly considerate of him, and that the world was made for man, or that because of faith, good deeds, special forms of self-abnegation and self-effacement he is to be reserved to eternal bliss hereafter although there is no especial reward for him here and now. And this is excellent indeed as illustrating a force or forces of a creative turn which might wish to use man as man uses any other minor implement for the accomplishment of any purpose he may have, but not very complimentary to him as an illustration of his own free and creative powers.

And, curiously, modern chemistry with its various tropisms —helio, magnetic, stereo and chemo—together with its legal part, physics, does little better by him. Already they tend to show that he is merely—and, what is worse, accidentally so —an evoluted arrangement of attractions and repulsions, arranged by chemicals and forces which desire or cannot escape whorls or epitomes of complicated motions and emotions or attractions which take the odd forms presented by men and animals.

But aside from this the most effective illustration of the essential nothingness of man is his plain *individual* weakness here and now as contrasted with his mass ideals and the huge vanity or tendency toward romance which causes him to wish to seem to be more than he really is or can ever hope to be. For plainly every life, in the last analysis, however useful to an assumed and carefully directing Creator, or however successful from a momentary analysis it may appear, is a failure. We hear of that curious thing, "a successful life." It is in the main a myth, a self-delusion. How could there possibly be success for a watery, bulbous, highly limited and specially functioned creature, lacking (in the case of man, for instance) many of the superior attributes of other animals—wings, a sense of direction, foreknowledge and the like—and manufactured every forty years by hundreds of millions, century in and century out, made apparently not in the image and likeness of anything superior to himself but in that of an accidentally compelled pattern, due to an accidental arrangement of chemicals, his every move and aspiration anticipated and accounted for by a formula and an accidentally evolved system long before he arrives, and he himself born puling, compact of vain illusions in regard to himself, his "mission," his dominant relation to the enormous schemes of Nature, and ending, if "life" endures so long, in toothless senility and watery decay, dissolution. And in addition some have scientifically placed the creative as well as the generative period of man between his twentieth and fortieth years—twenty years! Others generously extend it to fifty and even sixty. Few venture to carry it beyond that. At seventy old Nestor drools and repeats his fables of his few years and many troubles. At fifty, even forty-five, most men are busy recounting the deeds, adventures and creations of their earlier years!

To me the most astonishing thing in connection with man is this same vanity or power of romanticising everything relating to himself, so that whereas in reality he is what he is, a structure of brief import and minute social or any other form of energy, left by his loving Creator to contest in the most drastic and often fatal way with thousands, one might almost say millions of inimical powers and only significant really in so far as he or it is interlocked with others in some larger unity, either (for illustration) as a soldier in an army or its delegated commander or as a delegated or acknowledged representative of some moving or mass or race impulse, still he has this astonishing power of viewing himself as a tremendous force in himself, a god, a hero, an enduring and undying figure of glory and beauty—as significant almost as the Creator Himself, in whose image and likeness he is supposed to be made!

The wonder! The beauty even!

Sometimes I think all this is the almost inevitable result of something inherently weak but with one clear power: that of visualizing or perceiving strength in other things and so, by contrast, its own weakness; and, by reflex action merely, attempting to salve itself against its own ineffectiveness by imagining itself to be that which it may never be: a victor, a Colossus bestriding the world, an undying potentate, ruling forever, and so gaining strength to go on. For individuals are never masters in any remarkable way. They merely and at best borrow or direct the energies of many, and in the main to no important result to themselves. A Napoleon slaves and starves to the end that he may die on St. Helena and bring considerable profit to many who never heard of him and care not at all. A Cæsar toils endlessly at organization and the development and preservation of Rome, only to be stabbed to death in his fifty-sixth year, practically unrewarded. A Hannibal slaves for Carthage, enduring endless hardships, only to die by his own hand. The category might be extended indefinitely. And yet the world is full of laudations of the powers of men, their satisfactions, their vast, vast rewards and glories; while so many decayed steles and temple doorways, and data unending, bear testimony to their utter material and subsequent spiritual futility.

And when I say this I wish to make it perfectly clear that I am by no means confusing the race with the individual, or vice versa. What a race may do, and what man may, are two very different things. The race, representing the totality of active creations and pushed on by dynamic forces from below, may be, and in so far as one can guess is, a huge success. The God or force or forces using man in various aspects here and now (two billion men at the present moment) may be and no doubt is finding self-expression through and in him and may well be tremendously satisfied with the result. But in what way does that, or can it, add to the comfort or bliss of the particular individual? Endlessly repeated, an oyster-like copy of every other man that has ever been, a mere minute portion of something the significance or import of which he can not even surmise. And within the race itself one need only think of the various types—preacher, actor, lawyer, doctor, merchant, thief, writer, poetic, artist, prize-fighter, all very much alike and all repeated and repeated ad infinitum—to see how impossible the idea of individuality is. The very idea of extreme individuality, even under the most special and favored circumstances, is seen to be all but an impossibility. We are at best, even in our arts and highest forms of special adaptations, copies of things which are and have been as common as pig-tracks—generals, philosophers, statesmen, society grande dames and the like not excepted. Over and over and over we appear, one and all, even our exact gestures, smiles, glances. Who has not seen it in so short a space as three generations? And we speak of individuality, of special destinies!

Herein lies the pathos, and this is the outstanding fact, that man is essentially a creation or mechanism, accidental or not as you wish, of a force or forces which in so far as any one can determine is or are, far more than he in his wildest flights of fancy suspects, the thing which he most craves to be, individual, enduring, but of which he is only a part and of which he is constantly seeking more—*life*. The thing which makes and repeats over and over ad infinitum and *is* two billions of men, or anything else into which it chooses to form itself, may be thought of as having life, personality, success and the like, but as for individual man or any of its minute atoms! Indeed man might as well think of the minute atoms of his internal mechanism as having success, fame, a great life or future, as himself. His day, like theirs, is measured by a minute fraction of time and labor and energy, and so is nothing. Quite obviously there is something which is to man what man in his entirety as an individual is to the least ion or molecule of his inner cosmos: a thing of so vast a magnitude comparatively as to be as far outside his reckoning as must he be to the ion of his inner body. And as for size or force and import, that which creates him is as far above him as he is above the ion. Indeed, although man, in his capacity or proportion as an individual and as contrasted with the least of the electrons of his being, is beyond computation for size, yet viewed again in contrast with his external world he sinks into a mere fumbling, briefly-ended mote and tool. Like the ion of his inner cosmos, in this vast etheric or ionic something which is outside of him and which we see blazing as worlds or suns or existing as immeasurable space, he is too minute and too brief to be discussed. Even the great earth which he treads with so much pride is to this external thing quite as minute as man's electron is to him; and yet his relationship even to this is almost as nothing. For on this so minute thing which, sidereally speaking, is as nothing, he appears nevertheless, insectwise, by the billion every forty (or whatever the average life of man may be) years, to say nothing of innumerable other forms which have the ion or the molecule as the base of their material presence or structure. Still he permits himself to believe that he is something, and in facing all has the stupendous or fortunate ignorance to write himself down as Lord, Master, Great Guider of Things Terrestrial!

One of the things which might modify this supreme romantic estimate of himself, if such a thing were either desirable or possible, would be an even slightly technical examination of the process by which he arrives, as well as the extreme simplicity of the mechanical and chemical formula by which, throughout endless ages, he and all his fellows have been created. There is no longer any vast mystery about it; we are even getting relatively close to the secret, or could if we were permitted to go on undisturbed for a period by wars, let us say, or religious and educational illusions and furies (put forward by what? How brought about?), a persistent inherent mass opposition to thought and change in man himself. What subtle force ever invented that as a race quieter?

As biologists and anthropologists present man and his allied species, the original type structure on which all are more or less modeled is not so wonderful: two eyes, two ears, two nostrils, two feet and two hands or four feet, two of them antecedents of the present hands; or two feet and two wings, the latter successors of former feet; a lung or air-breathing system, not unlike that of any tree or plant; a root or arterial system, modified to meet various conditions and situations as in birds, fishes, moles; a nervous or sensory system of an allied character—no marked diversity in anything indeed, and all brought about by the inescapable chemical and physical reactions and compulsions of seemingly blind forces, as Crile and Loeb have shown. Even now chemists and physicists are at work upon the balances and equations involved in the mechanical and chemical construction of man, the leverage by which he moves, the combinations which control his form or aspect, as well as the chemical combinations which can induce motion or self-propulsion. Even as to his so-called thought how close are the Behaviorists to the material mechanics which produce it? His thoughts also are apparently little more than compelled reactions of one chemical upon another which he can no more escape than can he his form or motions. The one unsolved mystery apparently is why a machine so easily made and controlled should be able to speculate as to the reason for his being or to worry over it.

And yet just here another interesting fact stands out, and that is that whether or not he is a machine, Nature, or his Creator, appears to be quite definitely opposed to his finding out about himself or even to his delving into the matter, and throughout recorded science there is no evidence of the least willingness on the part of Nature or the life constructing forces to yield a single fact of any kind without a struggle. Man has fumbled and stumbled, dying by billions in one erroneous way, or another, until at last, by mere chance apparently, he has stumbled upon one helpful fact or another. It is as if the fable of Prometheus or that other of Adam and Eve were true. The seekers after knowledge of any kind have almost invariably been fought or their work brought to nothing, and even where man has apparently proven victorious or where he has seemingly been aided only that has been yielded which has tended to further him as an ignorant and yet useful machine, never as a thinker. No one who has tended to throw a clear light on the internecine struggles of Nature Herself, Her cruelties and brutalities, has prospered. If one doubts this he has only to consider the fumbling, haphazard progress of man, his warring notions as to his source and import, his strange aberrant evolution and the persistent and discouraging hindrances cast in the way of his intellectual evolution; i. e., the rise of impossible and even ridiculous leaders and religious theories—Christianity, Shintoism, Mohammedism—and the arrival of such dark figures as Attila (self-styled "the scourge of God"), Alaric, and Mohammed with his houris' dream, upon the scene of fairly acceptable intellectual conditions. The deaths of endless prying inventors, their pursuit by the religionists in darker ages, the periodic rise of -isms and world-sweeping folderol, political and other notions, all seem to point to but one thing: Nature's indifference if not opposition to man's tendency to develop intelligence and desire to know—if such a thing can be assumed, for it cannot be proved. For since when has the dulness of the mass, or man, his ignorance or indifference, apparently calculated and conditional, not stood their ground against the overtures of intelligence, science, the arts, philosophy? Nothing flourishes on earth so well as vain theory. Energetic thought is all but taboo. False dreams and false hopes are invariably encouraged by apparently some chemical or mechanical condition in the so-called brain of man himself. It is scarcely so much that he dare not as that he cannot.

And if he should but stop to consider this cloak-and-suit-model repetition of himself previously suggested, this system or pattern after which he and all the endless decillions which have preceded and will follow him are made, do you suppose he could exact anything which suggested individuality or personal persistence as a spirit or thought—self-generated thought—out of it? Is one button wiser or much more important than any other, or at all more likely to outlast another spiritually? Is it in any way essential that it should? The original model for the button might be important, but as for the endless copies! Indeed in the whole program of repetition, in so far as man or any of the animals or insects or of matter itself is concerned, there is but one ray of light or hope, and that is that the ion or electron of which all and everything appears to be composed may after all be the only true base or unit of expression of the so-called controlling spirit or force or forces of life, not the various contesting combinations of them, and that this ionic sea or mass, while controlled by the necessity of division and recombination, if it wishes to express itself at all ("The Kinetic Theory," J. C. Vogt), is still so large and so involute in its creative processes as to be necessarily more or less indifferent to any form of ionic self-expression or combination that might occur under or with it. So that the mere fact that groups or volumes of itself (ions) should combine for any purpose or generate themselves into any special forms of life (via combination, of course)—suns, planets, animals, races, nations, and their special developments again—might be to it a matter of absolutely no consequence. What matter if the electrons of some minute part of itself should organize and set up some special sun or planet or race of individuals, so long as they did not prove troublesome to the rest of the ionic sea? Supposing there are vast galaxies of self-generated suns in space—endless space, composed of but a part of the total ionic mass—so long as they are a mere negligible nothing to the totality of enduring force; what of it? If such were the case it is entirely conceivable that anything might arise for a time, any system of suns or race-life on suns or planets, and also the domination of one organized group of ions over another, but all subject nevertheless in the course of time and according to some equational and inescapable law to the totality of primary ionic or universal force.

In that case such a statement as occurs in Genesis iii. 5, would be plain enough. Some self-generated combination of ions looking upon itself as a creator in its own right (for a period anyhow), and having sub-invented man for some purpose of its own, self-expression or comfort, or the use of other enslaved ions to do its bidding, might say just that ("For God doth know," etc.); and it would be true.

On the other hand man, via the force of the numbers of the ions collected within himself, his race, and by degrees so gaining in numbers, and so power or intelligence equal to that of the ions which had originally enslaved him, might rise and question of this other elemental ionic combination its right to lordship over him. And again, by reason of *laissez faire* conditions which apparently hold throughout all Nature and force, he would then be able to overthrow this higher ionic combination and so set up a lordship of his own—as in some ways even now he appears to be doing. For one need only observe his growing command of machinery and the apparently indifferent streams of ionic energy everywhere moving, upon the backs of which or to the streams of which he attaches his wires and dynamos and engines and permits them to do a part of his work for him, in order to see how this might be. For if we are not an illustration of one ionic combination using another, what are we? And if that which is above us is not a combination of ions using us, what is it? Science has no other answer. At the same time, of course, man would be fought, as apparently he is being fought now, attacked and delayed by the powers which hitherto have made and are still using him. In that case the remarks of Jehovah in Genesis would be explicable enough.

And I here venture this prediction, based on this idea, that in case man is ever capable of awaking from his dream of spiritual enslavement and considers the higher creative reality which makes suns and his own immediate God as well, and sees also that he is the victim of a purely gratuitous overlordship of which he is no more than a hypnotic victim, he may well be able to invent crawling and winged things with some primary system of nervous response and intelligence, quite as he was invented in the first place, which will serve him in some dull, hopeless way, just as he himself now serves a higher power. Already he has invented most complicated machinery, and what else may he not invent? For ions are ions, wherever found, in whatever form of life, amœba, or man or sun, and they are everywhere. Obviously they may not rule save in combination and by force, one combined group seizing on other uncombined and therefore helpless ions so to do, and is that not our method in all phases of life here on earth now? But once the ions of men finding themselves in combination, by whatsoever process contrived, it may not be so easy longer to control them. Rebellions may occur, and probably will. The great thing seems to be to get enough of them in combination. Time perhaps is the great factor in all these things. At the same time it might be true, and at present so appears, that the generative group of ions which evolved man and all of his so-called superior combinations and results here, might be so jealous of its own creative skill in this respect that, seeing man or his ionic content attempting to gain knowledge of how to proceed and do, it might at once set out to undo him. The fable of Prometheus and of Adam and Eve may not be so impossible, after all. Yet should his "God" not be able to completely destroy him he may yet well imitate his Creator and create.

But will he be allowed so to do?

LIFE, ART AND AMERICA

I do not pretend to speak with any historic or sociologic knowledge of the sources of the American ethical, and therefore critical, point of view, though I suspect the origin, but I am at least convinced that, whatever its source or sense, it does not accord with the facts of life as I have noted or experienced them. To me the average or somewhat standardized American is an odd, irregularly developed soul, wise and even froward in matters of mechanics, organizations and anything that relates to technical skill in connection with material things, but absolutely devoid of true spiritual insight, correct knowledge of the history of literature or art, and confused by and mentally lost in or overcome by the multiplicity of the purely material and inarticulate details by which he finds himself surrounded.

As a boy in the small towns of the middle West I had no slightest opportunity to get a correct or even partially correct estimate of what might be called the mental A B abs of life. I knew nothing of history, and there was not a book in any of the schools which I attended, labeled either history or science or art, containing the least suggestion of the rationale which I subsequently came to feel to be relatively true, or at least acceptable to me. If I remember correctly, in the history of the world which was labeled Swinton's, the defeat of Napoleon, not his career, was pointed out as having had a great moral if not Christian value to the world. His end on St. Helena, not the Code Napoleon or the hieratic and ultra-economic arrangement of his material forces, was supposed to have achieved something for society! Similarly Socrates and his death were descanted upon as having almost a religious if not a Christian import. His death was painted as having been brought about by his low private deeds, not his higher moral views. The true significance of the man as illustrated by the exact details of his life were utterly ignored.

Because my father was a Catholic and I was baptized in that faith, I was supposed to accept all the dogma, as well as the legends, of the Church as true. In the life about me I saw flourishing the Methodist, the Baptist, the United Brethren, the Christian, the Congregationalist, the what-not churches, each representing, according to its adherents, the exact historic and truthful development and interpretation of life or the world. As a fourteen- or fifteen-year-old boy I listened to sermons on hell, where it was, and what was the nature of its torments. As rewards for imaginary good behavior I have been given colored picture cards containing exact reproductions of heaven! Every newspaper that I have ever read, or still read, has had an exact code of morals by the light of which one may detect at once Mr. Bad Man and Mr. Good Man and so save oneself from the machinations of the former! The books which I was advised to read, and for the neglect of which I was frowned upon, were of that naïve character known as pure. One should read only good books—which meant of course books from which any reference to sex had been eliminated, and what followed as a natural consequence was that all intelligent interpretation of character and human nature was immediately discounted.

A picture of a nude or partially nude woman was sinful; a statue equally so. The dance in our home and our town was taboo. The theater was an institution which led to crime, the saloon a center of low, even bestial vices. The existence of such a thing as an erring or fallen woman, let alone a house of prostitution, was a crime, scarcely a fact to be considered. There were forms and social appearances which we were taught to wear, quite as one wears a suit of clothes. One had to go to church on Sunday whether one wished to or not. It was considered good business, if you please, to be connected with some religious organization; and, by the same token, this commercialized religiosity was transmuted into glistening virtue. We were taught persistently to shun most human experiences as either dangerous or degrading or destructive. The less you knew about life the better; the more you knew about the fictional heaven and hell ditto. People walked about in a kind of sanctified maze or dream, hypnotized or self-hypnotized by an erratic and impossible theory of human conduct which had grown up heaven knows where or how, and had finally cast its amethystine spell over all America, if not over all the world.

Now I have no particular quarrel with this save that it is so impossible, so inane. In my day there were apparently no really bad men who were not known as such to all the world, or at least quickly detected, and few if any good men who were not sufficiently rewarded by the glorious fruits of their good deeds here and now! Success—mere commercial success—was in its way all but synonymous with greatness. Positively, and I stake my solemn word on this, until I was between seventeen and eighteen I had scarcely begun to suspect any other human being of harboring the erratic and sinful thoughts which occasionally flashed through my own mind.

At that time I was just beginning to suspect that some of the things which had been laid down to me by one authority and another were not true. All so-called good men were not necessarily good, I was beginning to suspect, and all bad men not hopelessly bad. There were things in cities and town which, as I was coming to see, did not accord with the theories of the particular realm from which I had sprung and seemed to indicate another kind of human being, different from the type among which I had been raised. My mother, as I even then saw, admire her as I might, was a mere woman, not an angel; my father a mere, mere crotchety man. My sisters and brothers were individuals such as I soon began to find were breasting the stormy waters of life outside, and not very different from all other brothers and sisters, not perfect souls set apart from life and happy in the contemplation of each other's perfections. In short, I was beginning to find the world a seething, stormy, bitter, gay, rewarding and destroying realm, in which the strong and the subtle and the charming and the magnetic were apt to be victors, and the weak and the homely and the ignorant and the dull were apt to be deprived of any interesting share, not because of any innate depravity but rather because of the lacks by which they were handicapped and which they could not possibly overcome.

And there were other phases which previously I had scarcely suspected. The race was to the swift and the battle to the strong. All great successes, as I was beginning to discover for myself, were relatively gifts, the teachings of the self helpers and virtue mongers to the contrary notwithstanding. Artists, singers, actors, policemen, statesmen, generals, were born and not made. Sunday-school maxims, outside of the narrowest precincts, did not apply. People might preach one thing on Sunday or in the bosom of their families or in the meeting-places of conventional social groups, but they did not practice them except under compulsion, particularly in the marts of trade and exchange. Mark the phrase "under compulsion." I admit a vast compulsion which has nothing to do with the individual desires or tastes or impulses of individuals. That compulsion springs from the settling processes of forces which we do not in the least understand, over which we have no control and in whose grip we are as grains of dust or sand, blown hither and thither, for what purpose we cannot even suspect. Politics, as I found in working as a newspaper man, was a low mess; religion, both as to its principles and its practitioners, a ghastly fiction based on sound and fury, signifying nothing; trade was a seething war in which the less subtle and the less swift or strong went under, while the more cunning succeeded; the professions were largely gathering-places of weaklings, mediocrities or mercenaries, to be bought by, or sold to, the highest bidder.

The individual, as I found, was trying to do one thing: make himself happy principally; life was plainly trying to do another, or at least what it was doing involved no great concern for the welfare of any particular individual. He might live, he might die; he might be well fed, he might be hungry; he might, accidentally or by taking thought, ally himself with successful movements, or he might inherently, by some incapacity or fatality of disposition, involve himself in the drifts toward failure; he might be weak, he might be strong; he might be wise, he might be dull or narrow. Life in the large thrashing sense in which we see it to move about us cared no whit for him. Why so many failures? I was constantly asking myself; so many early deaths, so many accidents, crass and unexplained? Why so many fires? So many cyclones? So many destroying epidemics? So many breaks in health or in trade or by reason of vice or crime or mere increasing age and mood? So many, many individuals going down into the limbo of nothingness or failure, so few attaining to that vast and lonesome supremacy which all were seeking? Why? Why? I persistently asked myself; and I have yet to find the answer in any current code of morals or ethics or the dogma of any religion.

If you should chance to consult a Methodist, a Baptist, a Presbyterian, a Lutheran, or any other current American sectarian, on this subject you would find (which after all is a dull thing to point out at this day and date) that his conception of the things which he sees about him is bounded by what he was taught in his Sunday School or his church, or what he has stored up or gathered from the conventions of his native town. (His native town! Kind heaven!) And although the world has stored up endless treasures in chemistry, sociology, history, philosophy, still the millions and millions who tramp the streets and occupy the stores and fill the highways and byways and the fields and the tenements have no faintest knowledge of this, or of anything else that can be said to be intellectually "doing." They live in theories and isms, and under codes dictated by a church or a state or an order of society which has no least regard for or relationship to their natural mental development. The darkest side of democracy, like that of autocracy, is that it permits the magnetic and the cunning and the unscrupulous among the powerful individuals to sway vast masses of the mob, not so much to their own immediate destruction as to the curtailment of their natural privileges and the ideas which they should be allowed to entertain if they could think at all—and incidentally to the annoying and sometimes undoing of individuals who have the truest brain interests of the race at heart: vide Giordano Bruno! Jan Huss! Savonarola! Tom Paine! Walt Whitman! Edgar Allan Poe!

For after all the great business of life and mind is life. We are here, I take it, not merely to moon and vegetate, but to do a little thinking about this state in which we find ourselves, or at least to try. It is perfectly legitimate, all priests and theories and philosophies to the contrary, to go back, in so far as we may, to the primary sources of thought, i. e., the visible scene, the actions and thoughts of people, the movements of Nature and its chemical and physical subtleties, in order to draw original and radical conclusions for ourselves. The great business of the individual, if he has any time after struggling for life and a reasonable amount of entertainment or sensory satiation, should be this very thing. He should question the things he sees—not some things, but everything—stand, as it were, in the center of this whirling storm of contradiction which we know as life, and ask of it its source and its import. Else why a brain at all? If only one could induce or enable a moderate number of the individuals who pass this way and come no more apparently to pause and think about life and take an individual point of view, the freedom and individuality and interest of the world might be greatly enhanced. We complain of the world as dull. If it is so, lack of thinking by individuals is the reason. But to ask the poor, half-equipped mentality of the mass to think, to be individual—what an anachronism! You might as well ask of a rock to move or a tree to fly.

Here in America, by reason of an idealistic Constitution which is largely a work of art and not a workable system, you see a nation dedicated to so-called intellectual and spiritual freedom, but actually devoted with an almost bee-like industry to the gathering and storing and articulation and organization and use of purely material things. In spite of all our base-drum announcement of our servitude to the intellectual ideals of the world (copied mostly, by the way, from England) no nation has ever contributed less, philosophically or artistically or spiritually, to the actual development of the intellect and the spirit. We have invented many things, it is true, which have relieved man from the crushing weight of a too-grinding toil, and this perhaps may be the sole mission of America in the world and the universe, its destiny, its end. Personally I think it is not a half bad thing to have done; the submarine and the flying machine and the armored dreadnought, no less than the sewing-machine and the cotton-gin and the binder and the reaper and the cash register and the trolley-car if not the telephone, may prove in the end, or perhaps already have proved, as significant in breaking the chains of the physical and mental slavery of man as anything else. I do not know.

One thing I do know is that America seems profoundly interested in these things, to the exclusion of anything else. It has no time, you might almost say, no taste, to stop and contemplate life in the large, from an artistic or a philosophic point of view. Yet after all, when all the machinery for lessening man's burdens has been invented and all the safeguards for his preservation completed and possibly shattered by forces too deep or superior for his mechanical cunning, may not a phrase, a line of poetry, or a single act of some half-forgotten tragedy be all that is left of what we now see or dream of as materially perfect? For is it not thought alone, of many famous and powerful things that have already gone, that endures?—a thought most often conveyed by art as a medium?

But let me not become too remote or fine-spun in my conception of the ultimate significance of art itself. The point which I wish to make is just this: that in a land so devoted to the material, although dedicated by its Constitution to the ideal, the condition of intellectual freedom, let alone art, is certainly anomalous. Your trade and your trust builder, most obviously dominant in America at this time, is of all people most indifferent to, or most unconscious of, the ultimate and pressing claims of mind and spirit as expressed by art. If you doubt this you have only to look about you to see for what purposes, to what end, the increment of men of wealth and material power in America is most devoted. Stuffy, tasteless houses crowded with stuffy, tasteless antiques, safety deposit vaults stuffed with securities, the having and holding of purely material values always. In proof of which I may add that we have something like twenty-five hundred colleges and schools and institutions of various kinds, largely furthered by the money of American men of wealth, and all presumably devoted to the development of the mental equipment of man (or so we are told), yet nearly all set with flinty firmness against anything which is related to truly radical investigation, or thought, or action, or art. The inculcation of morality and patriotism are even now laid down as the true task and province of the so-called schools of higher learning by the educators themselves, or at least the presidents of most of the leading institutions—not the getting of knowledge at any cost, patriotic or other.

As a matter of fact, in spite of the American Constitution and the American oratorical address on all and sundry occasions, the average American school, college, university, institution, is as much against the development of the individual, in the true sense of that word, as any sect or religion. What it really wants is not an individual but an automatic copy of some altruistic and impossible ideal, which has been formulated here or elsewhere under the domination of Christianity or some other ism. I defy you to read any American college or university prospectus or address or plea which concerns the purposes or ideals of these institutions and not agree with me. They are not after individuals; they are after types or schools of individuals, all to be very much alike, all to be like themselves. And what type? Listen. I know of an American college professor in one of our successful State universities who had this to say of the male graduates of his institution, after having watched the output for a number of years: "They are all right, quite satisfactory as machines for the production of material wealth or for the maintenance of certain forms of professional skill, but as for ideas of their own or being creators or men with the normal impulses and passions of manhood they do not fulfill the requisite in any respect. They are little more than types, machines, made in the image and likeness of their college. They do not think; they cannot, because they are held hard and fast by the iron band of convention. They are afraid to think. They are moral young beings, Christian beings, model beings, but they are not men in the creative sense, and the large majority will never do a thing other than work for a corporation in a routine unindividual way, unless by chance or necessity the theories and the conventions imposed or generated by their training and surroundings are broken, and they become free, independent, self-thinking individuals."

In this connection I might say I know of one woman's college, an American institution of the highest standing, which since its inception has sent forth into life some thousands of graduates and post-graduates to battle life as they may for individual supremacy or sensory comfort. They are (or were) supposed to be individuals capable of individual thought, procedure, invention, development; yet out of all of them not one has even entered upon any creative or artistic labor of any kind. Not one. (Write me for the name of the college, if you wish.) There is not a chemist, a physiologist, a botanist, a biologist, an historian, a philosopher, an artist, of any kind or repute among them; not one. They are secretaries to corporations, teachers, missionaries, college librarians, educators in any of the scores of pilfered meanings that may be attached to that much abused word. They are curators, directors, keepers. They are not individuals in the true sense of that word; they have not been taught to think; they are not free. They do not invent, lead, create; they only copy or take care of, yet they are graduates of this college and its theory, mostly ultra conventional, or, worse yet, anæmic, and glad to wear its collar, to clank the chains of its ideas or ideals—automatons in a social scheme whose last and final detail was outlined to them in the classrooms of their alma mater. That, to me, is one phase, amusing enough, of intellectual freedom in America.

But the above is a mere detail in any chronicle or picture of the social or intellectual state of the United States. Turn, for instance, if you will, to the legislative and judicial phases of our Government—those grand realms in which only statesmen and judicial students of our economic and social condition are supposed to move and rule, and what do we find?

As long ago as 1875 Ernst Haeckel, the eminent German scientist, complained that the judges and legislatures of his day and country had "but a superficial acquaintance with that chief and peculiar object of their activity—the human organism and its most important function, the human mind," and that they had no time for anything save "an exhaustive study of beer and wine and the noble art of fencing." If that could be said of intellectual Germany in his day how much more and worse could be judicated of the American jurist and legislator in America to-day. The shabby mess which finance and trade rivalries make of our laws and our halls of legislation—the mental equipment of the average politician, his henchmen, the legislator and the judge—the hall boys of finance, and at the same time of religious and therefore arbitrary moral dogma which they have become, the petty ignoramuses we see on every hand legislating for the people or interpreting the laws once they are thus formulated! Haeckel wrote sadly of the judges and law enactors in his day: "No one can maintain that their condition to-day is in harmony with our advanced knowledge of this world"—and, certainly, in America to-day, fifty years later, not a week passes in which we do not read of legislative deeds and legal decisions which make a thinking man sigh. Consider the slavish acceptance of religious and moral and financial dictation from self-interested and equally ignorant people, the running here and there to find what is temporarily expedient—what will satisfy or quiet the public for an hour; what will keep them from losing their petty jobs—by the politicians and legislators and so-called statesmen and judges; the complete ignorance of every congressman and senator and state legislator and judge and lawyer as to the commonest facts of biology, psychology, sociology, economics, and history! One president, Roosevelt, admitted that he could in no way understand economics. Yet once the average country or city law student has mastered a few hundred paragraphs of law he is ready to hire out to the nearest corporation, to legislate for the people, to prefix "Hon." to his name and set up in business as a judge or a statesman.

On the other hand, and in the very teeth of all this, no country in the world, at least none that I know anything about, has such a peculiar, such a seemingly fierce determination, to make the Ten Commandments work. It would be amusing if it were not pitiful, their faith in these binding religious ideals. I have never been able to make up my mind whether this springs from the zealotry of the Puritans who landed at Plymouth Rock, or whether it is indigenous to the soil (which I doubt when I think of the Indians who preceded the white), or whether it is a product of the Federal Constitution, compounded by such idealists as Paine and Jefferson and Franklin and the more or less religious and political dreamers of the pre-Constitutional days. Certain it is that no such profound moral idealism animated the French in Canada, the Dutch in New York, the Swedes in New Jersey, or the mixed French and English in the extreme South and New Orleans.

The first shipload of white women ever brought to America was sold, almost at so much a pound. They were landed at Jamestown. The basis of all the first large fortunes was laid, to speak plainly, in graft—the most outrageous concessions obtained abroad. The history of our relations with the American Indians is sufficient to lay any claim to financial or moral virtue or worth in the white men who settled this country. We debauched, then robbed and murdered them; there is no other conclusion to be drawn from the facts covering that relationship as set down in any history worthy the name. As regards the development of our land, our canals, our railroads, and the vast organizations supplying our present-day necessities, their history is a complex of perjury, robbery, false witness, extortion, and indeed every crime to which avarice, greed and ambition are heir. If you do not believe this, examine the various congressional and State legislative investigations which have been held on an average of every six months since the Government was founded, and see for yourself. The cunning and unscrupulousness of American brains can be matched against any the world has ever known, not even excepting the English.

But an odd thing in connection with this financial and social criminality is that it has been consistently and regularly accompanied, outwardly at least, by a religious and a sex-puritanism which would be scarcely believable if it were not true. I do not say that the robbers and thieves who did so much to build up our great commercial and social structures were in themselves always religious or puritanically moral from the sex point of view, although in regard to the latter they most frequently made a show of so being; but I do say that the communities and the States and the nation in which they were committing their depredations have been individually and collectively, in so far as the written, printed and acted word are concerned, most loud in their pretensions. Why? I have a vague feeling that it is the American of Anglo-Saxon origin only who has been most vivid in his excitement over religion and morals where the written, printed, acted or painted word was concerned, yet who at the same time, and perhaps for this very reason, was failing or deliberately refusing to see the contrast which his ordinary and very human actions presented to all this. Was he a hypocrite? Is he one?

Your American of Anglo-Saxon or other origin is actually no better, spiritually or morally, than any other creature of this earth, be he Turk or Hindu or Chinese, except from a materially constructive or wealth-breeding point of view, but for some odd reason he thinks he is. The only real difference is that, cast out or spewed out by conditions over which he had no control elsewhere, he chanced to fall into a land overflowing with milk and honey. Nature in America was, and still is, kind to the lorn foreigner seeking a means of subsistence, and he seems to have immediately attributed this to three things: First, his inherent capacity to dominate and control wealth; second, the especial favor of God to him; third, to his superior and moral state (due, of course, to his possession of wealth). These three things, uncorrected as yet by any great financial pressure or any great natural or world catastrophe, have served to keep the American in his highly romantic state of self-deception. He still thinks that he is a superior spiritual and moral being, infinitely better than the creatures of any other land, and nothing short of a financial cataclysm, which will come with the pressure of population on resources, will convince him that he is not. But that he will yet be convinced is a certainty. You need no fear. Leave it to Nature.

One of the interesting phases of this puritanism or phariseeism is his attitude toward women and their morality and their purity. If ever a people has refined eroticism to a greater degree than the American I am not aware of it. Owing to a theory of the doctrinaire acceptance of the Mary legend possibly (Mary-olotry, no less), the good American, capable of the same gross financial crimes previously indicated, has been able to look upon most women, but more particularly those above him in the social scale, as considerably more than human —angelic, no less, and possessed of qualities the like of which are not to be found in any breathing being, man, woman, child or animal. It matters not that his cities and towns, like those of any other nation, are rife with sex; that in each one are specific and often large areas devoted to Eros or Venus. While maintaining them he is still blind to their existence or import. He or his boys or his friends go—but——

Only a mentally one-sided nature or race such as the Anglo-Saxon could have built upon any such asinine theory as this. One would suppose that as they did, so they would have the courage to say, or at least cease this endless pother as to superior virtue. But no. The purity, the sanctity, the self-abnegation, the delicacy of women in America—how these qualities have been exaggerated and dinned into our ears, until at last the average scrubby non-reasoning male, quite capable of visiting the gardens of Venus or taking a girl off the street, is no more able to clearly visualize the creature before him than he is the central wilds of Africa which he has never seen. A princess, a goddess, a divine mother or creative principle, all the virtues, all the perfections, no vices, no weaknesses, no errors—some such hodge-podge as this has come to be the average Anglo-Saxon, or at least American, conception of the average American woman. I do not say that a portion of this illusion is not valuable, but as it stands now she is too good to be true, a paragon, a myth! Actually, she doesn't exist at all as he has been taught to imagine her. She is nothing more than a two-legged biped like the rest of us, but in consequence of this delusion sex itself, being a violation of this paragon, has become a crime. We enter upon the earth, it is true, in a none too artistic manner (conceived in iniquity and born in sin, is the Biblical phrasing of it), but all this has long since been glozed over, ignored, and to obviate its brutality as much as possible the male has been called upon to purify himself in thought and deed, to avoid all private speculation as to women and his relationship to them, and, much more than that, to avoid all public discussion, either by word of mouth or the printed page.

To think of women or to describe them, especially in our printed or publicly uttered word, as anything less than the paragon previously commented upon has become, by this process, not only a sin but a shameful infraction of the moral code. Women are now so good, the sex relationship so vile a thing that to think of the two at once is not to be thought of. They are supposed to have no connection. We must move in a mirage of illusion; we must trample fact underfoot and give fancy, in the guise of our so-called better natures, free rein. How this must affect or stultify the artistic and creative faculties of the race itself must be plain, yet that is exactly where we stand to-day, ethically and spiritually, in regard to sex and women, and that is what is the matter with American social life, letters and art. Imagine a puritan or a moralist attempting anything in art, which is nothing if not a true reflection, emotional and intellectual, of insight into life! Imagine! And contrast this moral or art narrowness with the American's commercial or financial or agricultural freedom and sense, and note the difference. In regard to all the latter he is cool, skeptical, level-headed, understanding, natural, consequently well-developed in those fields; in regard to this other he is disillusioned, theoretic, religious. In consequence he has no power, except for an occasional individual who may rise in spite of these untoward conditions (to be frowned upon), to understand, much less picture, life as it really is. Artistically, intellectually, philosophically we are weaklings; financially and in all ways commercial we are very powerful. So one-sided has been our development that in this latter respect we are almost giants. Strange, almost fabulous creatures have been developed here by this process, men so singularly devoid of a rounded human nature that they have become freaks in the matter of money-getting. I refer to Rockefeller, Gould, Sage, Vanderbilt the first, H. H. Rogers, Carnegie, Frick.

America I fear can be most aptly pictured as the land of Bottom the Weaver; and by Bottom I mean the tradesman or manufacturer who by reason of his enthusiasm for the sale of paints or powder or threshing machines or coal has accumulated wealth, and in consequence and by reason of the haphazard privileges of democracy, has strayed into a position of counsellor, or even dictator, not in regard to the things about which he might readily be supposed to know, but about the many things about which he would be much more likely not to know: art, science, philosophy, morals, public policy in general. You recall Bottom, of course, in "A Midsummer Night's Dream," unconscious of his furry ears and also of the fact that he does not know how to play the lion's part; that it is more difficult than mere roaring. Here he is now, in America, enthroned as a lion, and in his way he is an epitome of the Anglo-Saxon temperament. Bottom is so wise in his own estimation. He never once suspects his furry ears or that he is not a perfect actor in the rôle of the lion—or, if you will take it for what it is meant, the arts. He is just a dull weaver really, made by this dream of our Constitution ("an exposition of sleep" come upon him) into a roaring lion—in his own estimation. No one must say that Bottom is not; he will be driven out of the country, deported or exiled. No one must presume to practice the arts save as Bottom understands them. If you do, presto, there is his henchman Comstock and all Comstockery to take you into custody. Men who have come here from foreign shores (England excepted) have been amazed at Bottom's ears and his presumption in passing upon what is a lion's part in life. Indeed he is the Anglo-Saxon temperament personified. He is convinced that liberty was not made for Oberon or Peaseblossom or Cobweb or Mustard, but for bishops and executives and wholesale grocers and men who have become vastly rich canning tomatoes or selling oil. The great desire of Bottom is for all of us to have furry ears and long, and to believe that he is the greatest actor in the world. He is bewildered by a world that will not play Pyramus his way. Quince, Snug, Flute, Snout and Starveling (all those who came over with him in the Mayflower) agree that he is a great actor, but there are others, and Bottom is convinced that these others are in error, trying to wreck that dream, the American Constitution, which brought this "exposition of sleep" upon him and made him into a lion, "marvelous furry about the face" and with great ears.

Alas, alas! for art in America. It has a hard, stubby row to hoe.

But my quarrel is not with America as a comfortable commercial and industrious atmosphere in which to move and have one's being, but largely because it is no more than that, because it tends to become a dull, conventionalized, routine, material world, duller even than its reputed mother, sacred England. We are drifting, unless most of the visible signs are deceiving, into the clutches of a commercial oligarchy whose mental standards outside of trade are so puerile as to be scarcely worth discussing. Contemplate, if you please, what has happened to one of the shibboleths or bulwarks of our sacred liberties and intellectual freedom, i. e., the newspaper, under the dominance of trade. Look at it. I have not the time here to set forth seriatim all the charges that have been made, and in the main thoroughly substantiated, against the American newspaper; but consider for yourself the newspapers which you know and read. How much, I ask you, if you are in trade, do the newspapers you read know about trade? How far could you follow their trade judgment or understanding? And if you are a member of any profession, how much reported professional knowledge or news, as presented by a newspaper, can you rely on? If a newspaper reported a professional man's judgment or dictum in regard to any important professional fact, how fully would you accept it without other corroborative testimony?

You are a play-goer: do you believe the newspaper dramatic critics? You are a student of literature: do you accept the mouthings of their literary critics or even look to them for advice? You are an artist or a lover of art: do you follow the newspapers for anything more than the barest intelligence as to the whereabouts of anything artistic? I doubt it. And in regard to politics, finance, social movements and social affairs, are they not actually the darkest, the most misrepresentative, frequently the most biased and malicious guides in the world of the printed word? Newspaper criticism, like newspaper leadership, has long since come to be looked upon by the informed and intelligent as little more than the mouthings or bellowings of mercenaries or panderers to trade; or, worse still, rank incompetents. The newspaper man, *per se,* either does not know or cannot help himself. The newspaper publisher is very glad of this and uses his half intelligence or inability to further his own interests. Politicians, administrations, department stores, large interests and personalities of various kinds use or control or compel newspapers to do their bidding. This is a severe indictment to make against the press in general, but is it not literally true?

Take again the large, almost dominant religious and commercial organizations of America. What relationship, if any, do they bear to a free mental development, a subtle understanding, art or life in its poetic or tragic moulds, its drift, its character? Would you personally look to the Methodist or the Presbyterian or the Catholic or the Baptist church to further individualism, or freedom of thought, or directness of mental action, or art in any form? Do not they really ask of all their adherents that they lay aside this freedom in favor of the reported word or dictum of a fabled, a non-historic, an imaginary ruler of the universe? Think of it! And they are among the powerful, constructive and controlling elements in government —in this government, to be accurate—dedicated and presumably devoted to individual liberty, not only of so-called conscience, but of constructive thought and art.

And our large corporations, with their dominant and controlling captains of industry so-called; what about their relationship to individuality, the freedom of the individual to think for himself, to grow mentally? Take, for instance, the tobacco trust, the oil trust, the milk trust, the coal trust—in what way do you suppose they help? Are they actively seeking a better code of ethics, a wider historic or philosophic perspective, a more delicate art perception for the individual, or are they definitely and permanently concerned with the customary bludgeoning tactics of trade, piling up fortunes out of which they are to be partially bled later by pseudo art collectors and swindling dealers in antiques and so-called historic art and literature? Of current life and its accomplishments, what do they actually know? Yet this is a democracy. Here, as in no other realm of the world, the individual is supposed to be permitted, even compelled, to seek his own material and mental salvation as best he may. Yet one trouble with a democracy, in so far as art and individual intelligence is concerned, as opposed to an autocracy with a line of titled idlers, is that the latter permits at least the gift of leisure and art indulgence to a few and there usually is a central force or group to foster art, to secure letters and art in their inalienable rights, to make of superior thought a noble and a sacred thing. I am not saying that democracy will not yet produce such a central force or group. I believe it may or can. It is entirely possible that when the time arrives it may prove to be better than any form of hereditary autocracy. But I am talking about the mental, the social, the artistic condition of America as it is to-day.

To me it is a thing for laughter, if not for tears; one hundred and twenty million Americans, rich (a fair percentage of them, anyhow) beyond the dreams of avarice, and scarcely a sculptor, a poet, a singer, a novelist, an actor, a musician, worthy the name. One hundred and forty years (almost two hundred, counting the Colonial days) of the most prosperous social conditions, a rich soil, incalculable deposits of gold, silver and precious and useful metals and fuels of all kinds, a land amazing in its mountains, its streams, its valley prospects, its wealth-yielding powers, and now its tremendous cities and far-flung facilities for travel and trade—and yet contemplate it. Artists, poets, thinkers, where are they? Has it produced a single philosopher of the first rank—a Spencer, a Nietzsche, a Schopenhauer, a Kant? Do I hear some one offering Emerson as an equivalent? Or James? Has it produced a historian of the force of either Macaulay or Grote or Gibbon? A novelist of the rank of Turgenev, de Maupassant or Flaubert? A scientist of the standing of Crookes or Röentgen or Pasteur? A critic of the insight and force of Taine, Sainte-Beuve or the de Goncourts? A dramatist the equivalent of Ibsen, Chekhov, Shaw, Hauptmann, Brieux? An actor, since Booth, of the force of Coquelin, Sonnenthal, Forbes-Robertson or Sarah Bernhardt? Since Whitman, one poet: Edgar Lee Masters. In painting a Whistler, an Inness, a Sargent. Who else? (And two of these shook the dust of our shores forever.) Inventors, yes; by the hundreds, one might almost say thousands; some of them amazing enough, in all conscience, world figures, and enduring for all time. But of what relationship to art, the supreme freedom of the mind?

The most significant, and to me discouraging, manifestation in connection with the United States to-day is the tendency to even narrower and more puritanic standards than have obtained in the past. I am constantly astonished by the thousands of men, exceedingly capable in some mechanical or narrow technical sense, whose world or philosophic vision is that of a child. As a nation we accept and believe naïvely in such impossible things. I am not thinking alone of the primary tenets of all religions, which are manifestly based on nothing at all and which millions of Americans, along with the humbler classes of other countries, accept, but rather of those sterner truths which life itself teaches: the unreliability of human nature; the crass chance which strikes down and destroys our finest dreams; the fact that man in all his relations is neither good nor evil, but both. The American, by some hocus pocus of atavism, has seemingly borrowed or retained from English lower middle-class puritans all their folderol notions about making human nature perfect by fiat or edict—the written word, as it were, which goes with all religions. So, although by reason of the coarsest and most brutal methods we as a nation have built up one of the most interesting and domineering oligarchies in the world, we are still not aware of the fact.

All men, in the mind of the unthinking American, are still free and equal. They have in themselves certain inalienable rights; what they are when you come to test them no human being can discover. Life here, as elsewhere, comes down to the brutal methods of Nature itself. The rich strike the poor at every turn; the poor defend themselves and further their lives by all the tricks which stark necessity can conceive. No inalienable right keeps the average cost of living from rising steadily, while most of the salaries of our idealistic Americans are stationary. No inalienable right has ever yet prevented the strong from tricking or browbeating the weak. And although by degrees the average American is feeling more and more keenly the sharpening struggle for existence, yet his faith in his impossible ideals is as fresh as ever. God will save the good American and seat him at His right hand on the Golden Throne.

With one hand the naïve American takes and executes with all the brutal insistence of Nature itself; with the other he writes glowing platitudes concerning brotherly love, virtue, purity, truth, etc., etc. A part of this right or left hand tendency, as the case may be, is seen in the constant desire of the American to reform something. No country in the world, not even England, the mother of folderol reforms, is so prolific in these frail ventures as this great country of ours. In turn we have had campaigns for the reform of the atheist, the drunkard, the lecher, the fallen woman, the buccaneer financier, the drug fiend, the dancer, the theatergoer, the reader of novels, the wearer of low-neck dresses and surplus jewelry—in fact every taste and frivolity, wherever sporadically it has chanced to manifest itself with any interesting human force. Your reformer's idea is that any human being, to be a successful one, must be a pale spindling sprout, incapable of any vice or crime. And all the while the threshing sea of life is sounding in his ears! The thief, the lecher, the drunkard, the fallen woman, the greedy, the inordinately vain, as in all ages past, pass by his door and are not the whit less numerous for the unending campaigns which have been launched to save them. In other words, human nature is human nature, but your American cannot be made to believe it.

Personally my quarrel is with America's quarrel with original thought. It is so painful to me to see one after another of our alleged reformers tilting Don Quixote-like at the giant windmills of fact. We are to have no pictures which the puritan and the narrow, animated by an obsolete dogma, cannot approve of. We are to have no theaters, no motion pictures, no books, no public exhibitions of any kind, no speech even, which will in any way contravene his limited view of life. Finally we even contrived a President who was to have no more war! A few years ago it was the humble dealer in liquor whose life was anathematized and whose property was descended upon with torch, axe and bomb. A little later, our cities growing and the sections devoted to the worship of Venus becoming more manifest, the Vice Crusader was bred, and we now have the spectacle of whole areas of fallen women scattered to the four winds and allowed to practice separately what they cannot do collectively. Also came Mr. Comstock, vindictive, persistent, and with a nose and taste for the profane and erotic such as elsewhere has not been equaled since. Pictures, books, the theater, the dance, the studio—all came under his watchful eye. During the twenty or thirty years in which he acted as a United States Postoffice Inspector he was, because of his dull charging against things which he did not understand, never out of the white light of publicity which he so greatly craved. One month it would be a novel by d'Annunzio; another, a set of works by Balzac or de Maupassant, found in the shade of some grovelly bookseller's shop; the humble photographer attempting a nude; the painter who allowed his reverence for Raphael to carry him too far; the poet who attempted a recrudescence of Don Juan in modern iambics, was immediately seized upon and hauled before an equally dull magistrate, there to be charged with his offense and to be fined accordingly. All this is being continued with emphasis.

Then came the day of the armed White Slave Chasers, and now no American city and no backwoods Four Corners, however humble, is complete without a vice commission of some kind, or at least a local agent or representative charged with the duty of keeping the art, the literature, the press and the private lives of all those at hand up to that standard of perfection which only the dull can set for themselves. When the White Slave question was at its whitest heat the problem of giving expression to its fundamental aspects was divided between raiding plays which attempted to show the character of the crime in too graphic a manner, and licensing those which appealed to the intelligence of those who were foremost in the crusade. Thus we had the spectacle of an uncensored, but nevertheless approved, ten-reel film showing more details of the crime and better methods of securing white slaves than any other production of the day, running undisturbed to packed houses all over the country; while two somewhat more dramatic but far less effective distributors of information via plays were successfully harried from city to city and finally withdrawn.

Shakespeare has been ordered from the schools in some of

the States. A production of "Antony and Cleopatra" has been raided in Chicago. Japanese prints of a high art value, intended for the seclusion of a private collection, have been seized and the most valuable of them destroyed. By turns, an artistic fountain to Heine in New York, loan exhibits of paintings in Denver, Kansas City and elsewhere, scores of books by Stevenson, James Lane Allen, Frances H. Burnett, have been attacked, not only, as in the case of the latter, with the airy weapons of the law, but in the case of the former with actual axes. A male dancer of repute and some artistic ability has been raided publicly by the Vice Crusaders for his shameless exposure of his person! No play, no picture, no book, no public or private jubilation of any kind is complete any more without its vice attack.

To me this sort of thing is dull and bespeaks the low state to which our mental activities have fallen. When it comes to the matter of serious letters it is the worst. In New York a literary region of terror has been and is now being attempted. The publisher of Freud's "Leonardo" is warned before he brings it out that he will be prosecuted—a work that probably has no more defect than that of being intelligent and true. Similarly, Mr. Przybyszewski's "Homo Sapiens," a by no means pornographic work, was at once seized on its appearance and the publishers frightened into withdrawing it. This was true of "Hagar Revelly," "Tess of the d'Urbevilles," "Sapho," "Jude the Obscure," "Rose of Dutchers Cooley," "A Lady of Quality," "A Summer in Arcady," and scores of others. Imagine banning a book like "A Summer in Arcady" from the public libraries! Even "The Sexual Question" by the eminent August Forel has been banned and of course all of Kraft-Ebling (Freud and Ellis are sold only on the written order of a doctor —a mental prescription as it were). Think of it—the work of a scientist of Freud's attainments!

This sort of interference with serious letters and science is to me the worst and most corrupting form of espionage which is conceivable to the human mind. It plumbs the depths of ignorance and intolerance; if not checked it can and will dam initiative and inspiration at the source. Life, if it is anything at all, is a thing to be observed, studied, interpreted. We cannot know too much about it because as yet we know nothing. It is our one great realm of discovery. The artist, if left to himself, may be safely trusted to observe, synchronize and articulate human knowledge in the most comprehensive form. Human nature will seek and have what it needs, the vice crusaders to the contrary notwithstanding. There is no compulsion on any one to read; one must pay to do so. What is more, one must have taste inherently to select, a brain and a heart to understand. With all these safeguards and a double score of capable critics in every land to praise or blame, what need really is there for a censor, or a dozen of them, each far less fitted than any of the working critics to indulge his personal predilection and opposition, and to appeal to the courts if he is disagreed with?

Personally I rise to protest. I look on this interference with serious art and thought and serious minds as an outrage. I fear for the ultimate intelligence of America, which in all conscience, judged by world standards, is low enough. Now comes a band of wasp-like censors to put the finishing touches on a literature and an art that has struggled all too feebly as it is. Poe, Hawthorne, Whitman and Thoreau, each in turn was the butt and jibe of unintelligent Americans, until by now we are well nigh the laughing-stock of the world. Where is it to end? When will we lay aside our swaddling-clothes, enforced on us by ignorant, impossible puritans and their uneducated followers, and stand up free-thinking men and women? Life is to be learned as much from books and art as from life itself—almost more so, in my judgment. Art is the stored honey of the human soul, gathered on wings of misery and travail. Shall the dull and the self-seeking and the self-advertising close this store on the groping human mind?

THE COURT OF PROGRESS

EDITORIAL NOTE: The following manuscript, recovered from one of the twenty-seven tombs of Federated Chairmen of the Post Federated Period of World Republics, A.D. 2760-3923, recently discovered in the debris centers of Exomia, Domas and Polos (Central Asia), plainly refers to some annual festival or period of congratulation which, according to the historian, Ruffstuff, who seems to have flourished toward the close of that period when the great Asiatic and American world floods (the shifting of the boundaries of the Pacific) ended the old order, was apparently held, first, at some point in Central South Africa; later in Middle Western North America, as the then continents were called. The author or dramatist, Theobromo, plainly of some period later than that of the Post Federated, when literature of all sorts, owing to the religious viewpoint of the Federation, was non-existent, was plainly familiar with records of this great court or festival, now non-existent. (See mention in closing paragraph of Moline-Emporia-Sedalia sittings, points or places which have not as yet been identified.) The translator, Can. Theodore Dreiser, of Cambo, North Dromio, begs to explain that owing to the peculiar difficulties of the language then used the exact rendition of certain phrases and passages is not guaranteed.

CHARACTERS

NOXUS PODUNKUS: *Grand Referendunce Chairman of the Federated Musnud of the World.*

SHISHMASH HASH HASH: *Master of Ceremonies to the Court of Progress.*

<table>
<tr><td rowspan="6">Of</td><td>Savants ....</td><td rowspan="6">One hundred</td></tr>
<tr><td>Moonshees ....</td></tr>
<tr><td>Roctor-Proctors ....</td></tr>
<tr><td>Pundits ....</td></tr>
<tr><td>Theorists ....</td></tr>
<tr><td>Seers ....</td></tr>
</table>

Of	*Zadkiels* ..... *Oracles* ..... *Solons* ..... *Nestors* ..... *Gamaliels* ..... *Daniels*	One hundred

Of	*Dizzards*	50
	Zanys	100
	Fuddys	100
	Hoddy-Doddys	100
	Loobies	1000
	Gaberlunzies	1000
	Nizys	5000

Of Descendant Sons and Daughters of Ancient and Honorable	*Anti-Vivisectionists* ..... *Anti-Vaccinationists* ..... *Anti-Contraceptionists* ..... *Anti-Saloon Leaguers* ..... *Anti-Vice Crusaders* ..... *Anti-Lewd Book Examiners* ..... *Eugenic Sires* ..... *Free and Accepted Boy Scouts* ..... *Professors of Christian Economy* .... *Feminists* ..... *Moral Prophylaxers* ..... *Non-Smokers' Social Unionists* ..... *Seventh Day Adventists* ..... *Sabbath Day Exclusivists* ..... *Holy Rollers* ..... *Evangelists* ..... *King's Daughters* ..... *Women Magazine Editors* ..... *Library Protection Association Guards* *Watch and Ward Society Guards*..... *Prohibitionists* ..... *Federated Philosophers* ..... *Union Astronomers* ..... *Socialists*	50,000

Of plaster or Ossified Specimens of Ancient and Degraded	*Gamblers*	One Each
	Saloon-keepers	
	Bartenders	
	Financiers	
	Thieves	
	Vivisectionists	
	Vaccinationists	
	Philosophers	
	Politicians	
	Astronomers	
	Magdalens	
	Madams	
	Novelists	
	Playwrights	
	Scenario Writers	
	Musicians	
	Painters	
	Poets	
	Cigarette Fiends	
	Dope Fiends	
	Sabbath Day Breakers	
	Pragmatists	
	Predatory Rich	
	Anarchists	
	White Slavers	
	Nietzscheans	
	Scientists	
	Chemists	
	Physicists	
	Stoics	
	Liars	
	Dogs	
	Scoundrels	

THE COURT OF PROGRESS

SCENE: *A great plain, filled with a vast multitude of people, Tents, pagodas, pavilions, booths, kiosks, scattered over a wide area and alive with a swarming mass. Overhead innumerable flags, banners, shields, emblems and insignia of all kinds, as well as a welter of decoration and bunting, all symbolic of peace, prosperity and progress. Innumerable alleyways and passages suggest a maze. In the center, behind a great open square or drill-ground, an enormous pink-and-green pavilion of silk, fluttering innumerable pinions and streamers of the most variegated hues. In the extreme west of this (center) and facing east (to suggest open-mindedness and a spirit of receptivity and progress) a giant Musnud or throne of dried mush, straw and the polished grains of the oyster plant, each with its spiritual, ethical and social significance. This same is richly carved and tinted to represent the dawn, while at the top, by a process of higher coloring, the floridity, variety and fecundity of tropic life, signifying fullness of development, is suggested. Over this a canopy of dried morning-glory vines stained to represent the pink glow of dawn and strung with innumerable papier-maché flowers representative of the bursting blooms of perfection. Beneath, a large assortment of pillows, rugs, bed-ticks, mats, cushions, hassocks and the like, tinted to suggest the variety, fecundity, beneficence and generosity of Nature. On these rest the one hundred Moonshees, Savants, Pundits, Roctor-Proctors, Theorists, Seers, Zadkiels, Oracles, Solons, Nestors and profound Daniels and Gamaliels, members of the High Court of Progress of the Federated Republics of the World for the years 3913-3923, and representing in themselves the world's farthest intellectual reaches as well as its peace, progress, perfection and plenty.*

On their heads tall cornucopias of green-and-yellow tinfoil, fluttering with ribbons. On their bodies flowing silk robes of green decorated with red, yellow and blue astrologic designs, each of special ethical, social and spiritual significance. In the center of this company, his body clad in yellow, green and blue cheesecloth, his head surmounted by a tall blue cornucopia (signifying peace and plenty), and resting on an immense stack of eiderdown pillows, NOXUS PODUNKUS, *Grand Referendunce Chairman of the Federated Republics of the World and President pro tem of the Court of Progress of the same. He is very fat and restful. Behind and among them, fifty Dizzards in sky-blue fleshings, jackets of yellow, and pink coal-scuttle helmets, who keep watch and ward by whistling between their teeth and laying about them with feather-stuffed clubs whenever the attention of the Moonshees is desired. Among the audience, one hundred thousand already admitted and in their seats, five thou-*

sand Nizys in pink fleshings and striped blue-and-green shawls, each carrying a tin wash-boiler full of orange and lemon souffle and doling out the same in ice-cream cones to all who signal. The latter are hung around their waists in long strings.

Before the Musnud one hundred Hoddy-Doddys, Ticklers Extraordinary to the Savants, Zadkiels, etc. These are arrayed in green fleshings and yellow silk overcoats, and carry yellow feather-dusters attached to long blue bamboo stalks. They assist the Dizzards in keeping the Moonshees awake. About the Hoddy-Doddys, ranged in a semi-circle, one hundred Zanys, Official Wing-Bag Rattlers to the Musnud. These same wear orange-and-green sweaters and running pants of black and orange, plus long-visored caps of green, and carry pear-shaped wind-bags containing dried watermelon seeds, the ethical symbol of receptivity, which they rattle whenever the attention of the audience is desired. Between the Hoddy-Doddys and the Musnud, and at the immediate base of the same, one hundred Fuddys, Wireless Telegraph Operators Extraordinary to the Court, in green silk uniforms and plug hats, who are busy sending out preliminary notices to the world of the assembling of the Court of Progress. Beyond the Zanys in the aisles and semi-circular passages between the seats, one thousand Loobies and one thousand Gaberlunzies, Official First and Second Readers to the Court, the First arrayed in blue-and-white, the Second in green-and-white polka-dot gowns and mortar-boards, and each carrying about his waist a chain to which is attached all the then permitted classics of the pre-Federated Period (A. D. 1897-1927)—Hamilton Wright Mabie, Orrison Swett Marden, Harold Bell Wright, Gene Stratton Porter, Ralph Waldo Trine and others—from which at all moments of undue excitement it is their duty to read soothing passages in unison.

Outside the principal entrance to the pavilion, on the Grand Concourse, separate companies or regiments of Descendant Sons and Daughters of Ancient and Honorable Anti-Vivisectionists, Anti-Vaccinationists, Anti-Contraceptionists, Anti-Vice Crusaders, Eugenic Sires, Feminists, Non-Smokers' Social Unionists, Anti-Saloon Leaguers, Free and Accepted Boy Scouts, Professors of Christian Economy, Seventh Day Adventists, Sabbath Day Exclusivists, Holy Rollers, King's Daughters, Watch and Ward Guards, Library Protection Association Guards, Union Astronomers, Federated College Philosophers, Evangelists, etc., each practicing their separate evolutions and class yells. A giant procession, fifty thousand in number, soon to start and file before the assembled Pundits and Zadkiels of the Court sitting on the Musnud within, is intended to demonstrate to it and to the Universe at large, via the assembled audience, the happy presence and persistence and strength of the forces of light and order and truth, as opposed to the quondom and now all but vanished remnants of darkness prevailing in the world before the Federation of the Commission-Governed Republics of the World. As the principal function of the Court is to catechise its adherents and delegates as to the reason for the faith that is in them, and to learn as to the present progress of truth, mercy, justice, etc. via a series of shrewd and now sacred questions (the Post Federated Tablets of the Law) especially calculated to bring forth the facts and shame the forces of darkness into silence, these same stand ready to answer all such questions as to the certainty of the final perfection of life and so to receive the approval of the Musnud and the assembled populace.

Some companies of these same are at present busy executing their preliminary maneuvers, walking on their hands, turning hand-springs and cart-wheels, whirling as dervishes and whistling and cat-calling. Others ask and answer each other the sacred questions of the Tablets; still others leap, run around in a ring, roll in the dust and kick. Still others meditate head in hand or stare in fixed absorption at Philosophers' targets fixed on posts at different points in the grounds. A general air of hope, sequacity, peace, content, well-being, ease, and other forms of human satisfaction, pervades each and every section of the field.

Hauled about by varying groups of Descendant Sons and Daughters of Free and Accepted Boy Scouts, Anti-Vivisectionists, Anti-Vaccinationists, etc., all in attractive and unforgetable raiment of cerise, purple, yellow and nile green, are the only remaining speciments or images of now all but extinct Gamblers, Saloon-Keepers, Financiers, Thieves, Vivisectionists, Vaccinationists, Philosophers, Politicians, Magdalens and Predatory Rich still in captivity or existence. It should be stated in passing that all Liars, Thieves, Scoundrels, Lechers, Anarchists and the like were finally exterminated during the all-memorable Federated Presidency of Bonehead X, A. D. 3409-3427, just five hundred years before. Saloons and all forms of illegal as well as commercialized vice departed this earth some seven hundred years before. The ladies of the Inner High Council of Descendant Sons and Daughters of Ancient Thirty-second Degree Anti-Vivisectionists have here (muzzled and chained) the only extant examples of a Vivisectionist surgeon of the former cult of inhuman experimentalists, captured in Greenland. The Federated Union of Descendant Sons and Daughters of Ancient and Honorable Vice-Crusaders of the World present in a drop-forged steel cage, painted yellow, blue and green, the only living specimen of a simon-pure Madam, recently captured in the outlying regions of Borneo. In other portions of the field, caged and dressed to represent now extinct types of Materialists, Scientists, Philosophers, Chemists, Nietzscheans, Pragmatists, Stoics and so forth, are one hundred volunteers of the East South African School of Christian Histrionic Culture, freely giving their services for this great occasion.

SHISHMASH HASH HASH

(Grand Secretary-Treasurer of the Indo-African group of Commission-Governed Republics, now in federation with the rest of the world, and Master of Ceremonies to the Court of Progress. He is a tall man, in a suit of red-and-green pajamas, slightly rubberized and inflated. His ears are pierced and hung with blue earrings and his cheeks are adorned with yellow lambrequins three feet long. Temporarily he is entertaining himself just outside the stage entrance to the main tent by doing back somersaults, but at the sight of five thousand Descendant Sons and Daughters of Free and Accepted Boy Scouts, Watch and Ward, and Library Protection Guards in marching order approaching the main or stage entrance, he executes nine hand-springs, three bounds and one back somersault, landing in front of the Musnud. At sight of him the assembled multitude stirs and quivers and he-haws with delight. The associated Moonshees, Pundits, Roctor-Proctors and others stir slightly but continue to snore. SHISHMASH HASH HASH, *executing a jig-step and tying his whiskers in a bow-knot.)* Your Referendunces! *(At this the fifty Dizzards directly in attendance on the assembled Moonshees of*

the Musnud, each over six feet tall and weighing exactly one hundred and twenty-seven pounds, stir the latter to wakefulness by whistling between their fingers and beating them with their feather-stuffed clubs.)

THE FIFTY DIZZARDS

Pfs-s-t!——Pfs-s-t!——Pfs-s-t! *(They lay about them mightily with their clubs.)*

THE FIVE THOUSAND NIZYS

(Bearers of orange and lemon souffle to the Court. Becoming greatly excited at sight of the platform Dizzards belaboring the Moonshees and beginning to jump up and down, at the same time ladling out cones of green and pink souffle.) Refresh yourselves, good people! Refresh yourselves! Ssh!—Ssssh!—Ssssssssh!

THE ONE HUNDRED HODDY-DODDYS

(Shaking their long-handled feather-dusters and whirling about in a ring.) Awake, your Referendunces! Awake! Awake! *(They tickle the noses, ears, chins and necks of the Moonshees, Zadkiels, etc., who stir feebly but continue to snore.)*

THE ONE HUNDRED ZANYS

(Rattling their wind-bags and jigging in unison.) Attention! Attention, good audience! Attention! Their Grand Referendunces of the Federated Musnud of the World are about to be awakened! Attention! Attention! *(They rattle their wind-bags vigorously and roll their eyes from left to right and back nine times.)*

THE TWO THOUSAND LOOBIES AND GABERLUNZIES

(Roaming nervously to and fro, reading.) "At this moment, the sun sinking low in the West, the faint West wind stirring in the leaves, the pellucid rill tinkling gently—so, for a heart-beat, he saw her." *(Each holds up a restful hand.)*

SHISHMASH HASH HASH

(Executing three steps to the left and four to the right and spinning on his right toe.) Your Referendunces! Most

Worthy and Grand Referendunces! Is the High Court of Progress of the Federated Republics of the World now ready to receive the reports of the various battalions of Law, Order, Peace, Justice, Truth, etc., accredited to this Court? They await your Referendunces' pleasure without. *(At this another herculean attempt is made to arouse the assembled judges of the Musnud. The fifty Dizzards who are in direct attendance on the Moonshees begin whistling between their teeth and striking them with their feather-clubs. The one hundred Hoddy-Doddys stir up the multitude in the front rows by dusting off their ears and noses with their long-poled feather-dusters. The one hundred Zanys rattle their wind-bags, and the two thousand Loobies and Gaberlunzies read intently and with vigor, each holding up a hand. The five thousand Nizys hurry here and there offering souffle to all.)*

THE ONE HUNDRED MOONSHEES, ROCTOR-PROCTORS, ZADKIELS, ETC.

(Stirring slightly and opening their eyes.) Souffle! Souffle! *(Great panniers of souffle are fed to them, and they relapse into slumber.)*

THE FIFTY DIZZARDS

(Seeing they have the Moonshees partially awake.) Your Referendunces! Most worthy Referendunces! The Secretary of the Honorable Court desires to know is it ready to receive the first division of the assembled Battalions of Knowledge now about to report as to the present state and progress of the world? *(A vast murmur of "Hee-haw!"—the 30th century expression of approval—passes over the assemblage. SHISH-MASH HASH HASH executes four more hand-springs, lights gracefully on his back and slowly draws his toes up to his fingers, thus gradually assuming a standing position, and bows. The fifty Dizzards whistle between their teeth and beat the Moonshees vigorously with their feather-clubs. The Zanys rattle their wind-bags lustily. Fifty of the one hundred Moon-*

shees awake and call for more souffle. Five hundred tons are at once distributed to the audience, and quiet is restored.)

THE MOONSHEES, ROCTOR-PROCTORS, ZADKIELS, ETC.

(Stirring feebly and pushing the feather-dusters out of their eyes. In chorus.) What is the question? What is the question? *(They sink back heavily on their pillows. SHISH-*MASH HASH HASH *throws four fits and attempts to insert his left foot in his mouth, then stands at attention while four Dizzards, lifting aloft silk banners on which are pictures of keys of knowledge and open books, fall to the ground and get up again. The one hundred Hoddy-Doddys tickle the noses of the Moonshees frantically. The five thousand Nizys throw handfuls of souffle in the faces of the audience and spin on one foot. The two thousand Loobies and Gaberlunzies rear and plunge, murmuring "Shush! Shush!" then read.)*

NOXUS PODUNKUS

(Chief Presiding Referendunce of the Federated Court of Progress of the World. Sitting up, opening one eye and gazing about.) Indeed! You say, do you? Well, let them enter! *(He collapses again.)*

SHISHMASH HASH HASH

(Spinning away to the stage entrance, at which the representatives of the various forces of Progress are waiting in parade array.) Are you ready? Are you ready? *(A shout goes up. He lifts both hands,and pirouetting gracefully backward toward the Musnud is followed by the 1st, 316th, 3727th, 4728th, 6914th and 7178th Divisions of Descendant Sons and Daughters of Ancient and Honorable Free and Accepted Boy Scouts, Watch and Ward and Library Protection Association Guards, King's Daughters, Sabbath Day Exclusivists, Seventh Day Adventists, and Holy Rollers in close formation. They are all in Empire Nicollet silk, striped with blue bombazine, ruched at neck and feet, and carry immense banners of green and yellow on which are pictured barred library doors, sealed books, bonfires of questionable or lewd books, and padlocked library*

safes. They are preceded by and interlarded with silver and gold harp bands in great numbers, as well as a small exhibition corps of Anti-Lewd Book Examiners, carefully examining lewd books after the manner of the years A. D. 1885-1921. *These last carry large red, yellow and green-blue pencils and wear horn glasses the size of saucers. They read, blush, and blue-pencil as they come. They are preceded by cage-cars containing* [*one each*] *Ossified Specimens of Ancient Lewd Novelist, Playwright and Poet. They pause and stand at attention before the Musnud, giving first an exhibition of lewd-book editing, then the Free and Accepted and Descendant yell, "Anti-Vice! Anti-Vice! Boy Scouts Forever!" after which they clog and whistle.)*

NOXUS PODUNKUS

(Scratching one ear and blinking his one open eye, the while the five thousand Nizys distribute souffle and the audience cheers vociferously.) Descendant Sons and Daughters of Ancient and Honorable Free and Accepted Boy Scouts, Watch and Ward Guards, King's Daughters, Sabbath Day Adventists, Holy Rollers *(whispers to a Dizzard, "Did I get them all right?")*—we have, as you know, as President and Referendunces of this great Court, founded so long ago by our worthy predecessor, Mush Mush I, a certain duty to perform, and that is the asking of our regular prepared and revered and revised Sacred Questions, the answers to which, given as we all know you will give them, constitute in themselves at once a record and a testimony to the wisdom, perfection, peace and plenty to which our vast Federated Republics and Peoples the world over have at last arrived. *(Great applause lasting one hour, during which transcripts of the proceedings and speech thus far are wirelessed by the Fuddys to all parts of the world.)* Once, as you well know and as we are sorry to remember, there existed a certain amount of vice and crime in the world *(vast and prolonged boo-ing and cat-calling)*—less and less, we will admit, as the forces of righteousness and order such as we represent

here to-day gained momentum *(a second burst of applause lasting one hour, during which this portion of the speech is wirelessed. The Zadkiels breathe heavily),* but plentiful enough—plentiful enough, I am glad to say—Souffle! Souffle! *(he sighs and is fed)*—as well as a tendency, disobedient in the extreme, to investigate and study and doubt everything, from stars to ant-hills, and even to make light of the revealed and divine facts of Nature, which as we all know are irrefutable and not to be questioned and to which our hearts are always and only our best guides. *(Enormous applause, lasting thirty minutes.)* Fortunately for us now, however, and happily, and owing, as I may say, to the benign activities of those noble workers in the cause of righteousness, Mush Mush I, Bonehead V, and Dish Rag III, who flourished A. D. 1970-2061 in America and elsewhere, the virtues of sobriety, justice, truth, mercy, industry and the like were, as we all well know, firmly and finally established. *(Tremendous applause, lasting one hundred and eight minutes, during which seven hundred wash-boilers of souffle are consumed. Wireless messages are sent to all parts.)* Thanks to them and their beneficent efforts, we do not attempt to investigate any more. *(Prolonged cheering.)* We do not seek to reason any more. *(Immense cheering, lasting two hours.)* Man, as you all well know, has seen the line of his duty and has followed it closely. *(More cat-calling.)* With the greatest care we have been able to eliminate not only those besetting vices which scarred the face of man with their hideous thoughts, but also those equally great vices of curiosity and speculation in regard to chemistry, philosophy, physics, astronomy, sociology, political economy, those low and evil so-called sciences which once so disturbed and irritated and afflicted the human mind. *(A burst of applause, lasting forty-three minutes.)* They have been done for, and instead we have strictly and sensibly confined ourselves, I am happy to state, to those more acceptable evidences of our place in Nature and our duties, as revealed by those renowned and profound teachers and thinkers, our noble and revered ancestors, Billy Sunday the Great, he of blessed memory *(applause, lasting one hour)*—Ralph Waldensicuss Trinecuss of Boston *(applause, lasting fifty minutes)*—Arise-and-Sweat Marden *(applause, lasting forty minutes)*—Erbert Goughman *(applause, lasting thirty minutes)*—Philip Dugmore Potts *(applause, lasting twenty minutes)*—and Edith Whiller Nox Nox *(applause, lasting ten minutes)*—revealers and thinkers all, the true forerunners and prophets of our present peaceful and happy state. *(Prolonged applause, enduring over seven-hundred minutes, during which NOXUS and the Moonshees snore and the two thousand Loobies and Gaberlunzies read long and refreshing passages from the works of the individuals mentioned. The Fuddys sizz at their task.)*

THE ONE HUNDRED HODDY-DODDYS

(As the applause subsides, feathering the face of the Moonshees.) Awake, your Referendunces, awake! *(They pole-vault in front of the Musnud.)*

THE FIFTY DIZZARDS

(Whistling between their teeth and striking with their feather clubs.) Oh, your Very Great Referendunces! Oh! Come to! Come to! *(They chatter and clog.)*

NOXUS PODUNKUS

(Batting an eye and being lifted to a sitting position.) Ah, yes! Ah, yes! Let me see . . . where was I? *(A Dizzard, prompted by a Fuddy, repeats his last sentence.)* Ah, yes! As I was saying, these, our revered leaders, taught us. It is to them, their patient and enduring labors, their deep, even profound, cogitations as to life, that we all owe all that we enjoy and revere so deeply to-day—our peace, our freedom from disturbing thought, from the besetting vice of questioning or investigating. All we have to do now is ask and re-ask and affirm and re-affirm our Sacred Questions, so ably asked and answered so many centuries since by our noble forerunners, Bonehead V. and Dish Rag III. *(Separate and prolonged applause at each*

name, during which Podunkus again slumbers, is feathered and clubbed and lifted to a sitting position.) Ah, yes! Ah, yes! The Questions—the Questions. *(He fumbles weakly about, while seven Dizzards hand him seven engrossed and gold-plated copies of the regulation Sacred Questions as made and provided for all such occasions. He stares at one feebly and continues.)* Ah yes! Now I have them! The Questions—the Questions, on which, as I was saying, are based, as on a rock, all our peace, security, freedom from thought; the very, indeed, pillows—I mean pillars—of our ease and comfort. The Sacred Questions! To be sure! Question One—let me see—Question One—Question One *(aside "Where is it?" A Dizzard points to it.)*—Question One is most important, the very corner-stone, I might say, of our undisturbed security and ease in thoughtlessness. *(Examines it closely.)* It reads—it reads—Ah yes! —Now I have it!—"Have you kept the faith?" That's it. "Have you kept the faith?" To be sure! Have *we* kept it, I might say? Almost the most sacred of all our Questions! Have *we* kept the faith? *(He mumbles feebly on.)* That's it! Have *we* kept the faith?

THE 1ST, 316TH, 3727TH, 4728TH, 6914TH, AND 7178TH

(Standing at attention and in unison.)

We have, we have!
We have, have, have!

(They clog. Immense applause from the audience, lasting thirty minutes. The First and Second Readers read soothing passages.)

THE MOONSHEES, ROCTOR-PROCTORS, GAMALIELS, ZADKIELS

(Turning on the other side and imbibing souffle.) Excellent! Excellent! Couldn't be better! They have kept the faith! Most comforting. Ah!

NOXUS PODUNKUS

(Reclining and imbibing souffle.) Charming! Charming! Most sweet of them! The dear, dear things! They would

keep anything we asked them to! It is really too wonderful! *(He sighs.)*

THE FEDERATED SPECTATORS

(One hundred thousand strong.) Hey! Hey! Hey! Rah! Rah! Rah! Federated Republics forever! Long live the Court of Progress! *(The cheering continues for fifteen minutes.)*

NOXUS PODUNKUS

(When comparative silence is restored, and blinking his open eye.) Beautiful! Beautiful! It is as I thought! A wondrous scene! Now for Question Number—let me see *(eleven Dizzards point to the place)*—Ah, yes! To be sure! *(Reads.)* Question Number Two—a wonderful question—a deep and subtly devised question—a question which, as I may say, has done as much as any of the others to persuade us to and keep us all in that happy and unquestioning frame of mind which, as we all know, we now so wisely seek to maintain—Souffle! Souffle! *(he imbibes)*—a question the like of which is not to be found in any other sacred code the world has ever known—and here, my dear fellow-Federationists *(he raises a hand)*, and here is it: Question Two—Ah, yes! *(reads)* "Is it not true that all men are now honest, kind, true, moral, virtuous and wise?" *(He pauses for breath and looks benignly about.)*

THE 1ST, 316TH, 3727TH, 4728TH, 6914TH, AND 7178TH

(Jigging vigorously.) They are! They are!
They rarr! rarr! rarr!

(They walk on their hands.)

NOXUS PODUNKUS

Beautiful! Beautiful! Never have I heard such perfect teamwork! It is wonderful! Not so, my fellow Moonshees? *(He turns.)*

THE MOONSHEES, PUNDITS, ZADKIELS, ETC.

(Turning over and snoring.) Excellent! Couldn't be better! They do perfect work! *(They each catch a wink of sleep.)*

NOXUS PODUNKUS

(Aroused and scratching the back of his neck, the while he eyes them feelingly.) It is too delightful! That I should have lived to have the exalted honor of presiding on so wonderful an occasion! But now for Question Three, my dears—Question Three—another beautiful question *(he fumbles foolishly about seeking the tablet. Seventeen Dizzards point to it.)*—Ah, yes! Ah, yes! Very difficult to manage all of these questions! But here it is!—And now for Question Three—a lovely question! A question lovely! I almost hate to read it and have it all over with! *(Reads.)* "And that all women are as pure as driven snow?" *(Pauses and gazes about ecstatically, one hand up.)*

THE 1ST, 316TH, 3727TH, 4728TH, 6914TH, AND 7178TH
(Executing cart-wheels in circles.)

Aye! Aye! Aye! Aye! Aye! Aye!
'Tis as easy to say as Pie! Pie! Pie!

(They end by waving with their feet.)

THE FEDERATED SPECTATORS

Hey! Hey! Hey! Hey! Hey! Hey!
The world's now safe for ever and a day!

(An hour of unbroken applause follows.)

NOXUS PODUNKUS

(As quiet is once more restored and he is dusted into semi-consciousness.) Quite so! Quite so! Forever and a day! Ah! And—and *(he looks about for his tablet and twenty-seven Dizzards hand him each a sacred plate.)*—and that—let me see—Ah, yes!—Question Four! Question Four! Here it is! *(Reads.)* "And that God is always on His Throne?" *(He collapses from exhaustion.)*

THE 1ST, 316TH, 3727TH, 4728TH, 6914TH, AND 7178TH
(Falling flat on their backs.)

He is! He is! It is so plain
Upon His Throne He doth remain!

By day or night, in dark or light,
We feel His presence shining bright!
All's well with the world!

(They roll to and fro in rows of one hundred each.)

THE ONE HUNDRED THOUSAND SPECTATORS

(Uproariously.)

Hey! Hey! What a glorious day!
Hey! Hey! What a glorious day!

(The cheering is resumed for fifteen minutes more, during which ten vanloads of souffle are distributed.)

NOXUS PODUNKUS

(After order has been restored and surveying his associates of the Musnud sleepily.) Perfect! Perfect!—or nearly so! Beautiful! I never saw anything so well done! Never! Such order! Such union! But—let me see—I believe these are all the questions to be asked of these divisions, are they not? *(Looks about him helplessly and yet benignly. The fifty Dizzards all rush together and confer. The Hoddy-Doddys ditto. The Zanys ditto. The Loobies and Gaberlunzies bite their nails, then rush together and mumble. The Moonshees sit up and confer with PODUNKUS. He proceeds.)* Ah yes! As I was saying! Quite so! Quite so! Since, then, it is the opinion of the Associated Members of the Musnud that the report of the Descendant Sons and Daughters of Ancient and Honorable Free and Accepted Boy Scouts and Anti- *(he reads the entire roster)* seems to accord with the progress of the year as reported to us from all outlying sections of the Federation, and it is their wish that it be accepted and offered and engrossed in the records of the Musnud as a true picture of the state and progress of the world for this year of our Lord A. D. 3913, they will signify as much by saying "Aye," contrary, "Nay." The "Ayes" have it. The report of these excelling representatives is accepted and they are excused. *(He falls back and into a deep sleep. The Moonshees do likewise.)*

THE ONE HUNDRED MOONSHEES

(Weakly, in their sleep). Souffle! Souffle!

THE ONE HUNDRED THOUSAND SPECTATORS

Hey! Hey! Hey! 'Tis a perfect day!
'Tis a perfect day! 'Tis a perfect day!
Hey! Hey! Hey! 'Tis a perfect day!

(They cheer for one solid hour.)

THE 1ST, 316TH, 3727TH, 4728TH, 6914TH, AND 7178TH

(Ricochetting and executing triple hand-springs, the while SHISHMASH HASH HASH sidesteps and returns to the main stage entrance, left.)

What pleasure, oh! What pleasure, oh!
To know the world is perfect, so
That never now by day or night
Need any one feel fear or fright.

(They zigzag gaily in ranks of one thousand and exit.)

SHISHMASH HASH HASH

(At the stage entrance, surveying one hundred and fifty divisions of Descendant Sons and Daughters of Ancient and Honorable Moving Picture Censors, Sabbath Day Observance Leaguers, Baptist and Methodist Evangelists, and Non-Smokers' Social Unionists, now ready and in marching order just outside the tent entrance. These have arranged themselves in battalions of two thousand each and are arrayed in snow-white frock coats, bright red silk hats, lavender pants or skirts, as the case may be, and carry bright brass drum-major batons. Numerous bands of Descendant and Amalgamated Sons and Daughters of Ancient and Honorable Anti-Saloon Leaguers and Billysundays are arrayed in pink-flowered business suits and silver-green capes, carrying hatchets and bearing aloft the portrait of their patron saint, Mrs. Carrie Nation, who flourished A. D. 1884-1913, *playing on silver and tin horns, wind instruments, hewgags and jew'sharps. These are preceded by cage-cars containing one each of Ossified Specimens of Ancient Cigarette Fiend, Simon-pure American*

Bartender, Lewd Scenario Writer, Sabbath Day Breaker. The bands begin playing "All Hail the Peace Which Now Prevails!" As they enter, preceded by SHISHMASH HASH HASH with his head between his legs and walking on his hands to the Musnud, forty thousand members of the audience rise and stand on their heads. Another forty thousand sink to the floor between their seats and gasp. The five thousand Nizys pass swiftly among them administering souffle. The first and second readers read rapidly. SHISHMASH HASH HASH, landing on his feet as he reaches the Musnud and beginning to jig.) Will the High and Mighty Referendunces of the Federated Musnud of the World deign to notice these humble instruments of moral intercession here gathered from all parts of the world to testify at this great review to the blessings of peace, morality, fecundity and other social virtues? *(As he says this he executes nine flip-flaps, whereat the great assemblage bursts into thunders of applause. The fifty Dizzards on the Musnud leap on each other's necks as they whistle between their teeth. The one hundred Zanys rattle their windbags furiously.* NOXUS PODUNKUS, *being simultaneously beaten by four stuffed clubs and tickled by four feather-dusters, while two Dizzards whistle in his ears, opens both eyes and looks blandly around.)*

NOXUS PODUNKUS

(With a fat, ingratiating smile, as the uproar continues.) Are we now beholding more divisions of the unconquerable forces of Truth, Virtue, Justice, Sobriety and Righteousness? Good! Good! *(He opens his mouth, which is immediately filled with souffle.)*

THE ONE HUNDRED AND FIFTY DIVISIONS

(Cakewalking, shamble-shuffling and tossing their hatchets, batons, musical instruments, etc., aloft.) Hail! Hail! The end of shame! *(They sing.)*

'Tis now that we with joy behold
The earth of virtue yield fourfold

Of truth and right the crop is great—
Indeed, enough the world to sate!

(Melody the same as "Behold the Power." To be sung without lining.)

NOXUS PODUNKUS

(Scratching one ear and making a supreme effort to think.) A charming sight! A charming sight! The world is indeed progressing! Allow us to congratulate you, my dears and dearesses! Allow us! Allow us! Perfection is at hand! It has been long in coming, but now, as I might say, it has reached its destination. Souffle! Souffle! *(A pannier is brought and fed him.)* As I was saying to those last dear battalions who so gracefully testified to our Peace and Progress, Security and the like, it now becomes my duty to read from our revered and Sacred Questions—the compendium, as you know, of all our Knowledge, Law, Intelligence—Questions Five, Six, Seven and Eight —I believe that is the allotted number, is it not? *(Thirty-one Dizzards nod.)*—and as I do so will you please answer in unison so that all may know—the world—the universe indeed—how well we understand, how firmly we know, believe, that which has brought us to our present state of peace and comfort, our ease of mind and body. *(Reads.)* Question Five—Question Five—ah yes! Just as I thought! *(Reads, one hand up.)* "There is a God, is there not? We know that, do we not?"

THE ONE HUNDRED AND FIFTY DIVISIONS

(Jabbing their batons into the ground, tossing them in the air and then catching them again.)

There is! There is! We do! We do!
What joy to know 'tis true, true, true!

(At this ninety-nine Moonshees, who have risen to a sitting position, fall back, murmuring "Splendid! Splendid! Wonderful!" The Hoddy-Doddys exclaim the same thing and practice at sword-play with their feather-dusters, while the Dizzards play at leap-frog and the Zanys beat each other with their empty wind-bags. The five thousand Nizys plunge their

heads into the soufflé but withdraw them quickly and ladle out cones to the mass. The two thousand Loobies and Gaberlunzies read many enchanting passages as the audience applauds, after which the Dizzards resume normal positions and lay about them with their stuffed clubs.)

NOXUS PODUNKUS

(Scratching his nose and making another great effort to think, the while he beats the railing before him.) Ah, yes! That is it! "There is! We do!" It is on our knowledge of that that we rest so peacefully, all else being of no importance. *(Reads.)* Question Six—*(pauses)*—"He is on His Throne, is He not? We know that, do we not?"

THE ONE HUNDRED AND FIFTY DIVISIONS

(Jigging) He is! He is! We do! We do!
This truth is ever new and true!

NOXUS PODUNKUS

(Sinking into his pillows and peacefully closing his eyes.) Quite so! Quite so! We need that knowledge to sustain us in our present ease. It is so comforting! As I often say, what would we do without our dear Questions? *(He falls asleep. Seven Dizzards and seven Hoddy-Doddys club and feather him. He resumes.)* And now for—ah yes!—let me see—Question—Question *(various Dizzards gather about him and point)* —Ah, yes! Seven—Question Seven! *(Ecstatically.)* Let me read this to you, this beautiful Question, the answer to which, as I so often say, reassures us all so much, keeps us all so sweet and content, always. *(Raises one hand.)* "All is well with the world, is it not? We know that, do we not? It is, is it not?" Come now, all together—One, Two, Three——

THE ONE HUNDRED AND FIFTY DIVISIONS

Yea ho! Yea ho! Yea, Bo! Yea, Bo!
A truer thing we do not know!

(They fall to the ground and roll rapturously to and fro.)

NOXUS PODUNKUS

(As wave on wave of applause sweeps over the pavilion and

bags out the sides and top, leaning forward and opening one eye.) 'Tis beautifully said! Beautifully said! A perfect answer to a perfect Question! A wonderful testimony to the ever upwardness and onwardness of things! It is almost more than one could hope for—than any one *can* hope for! And now, my dears and dearesses, comes Question—*(looks at the tablet while all the Dizzards lean and point)*—Question Eight, a very, very great Question, a Question which, as I always say, has undoubtedly more than any other Question brought us at last to this very perfect and peaceful state, in which we rest as, I might say, a babe in its cradle, as a—a—Souffle! *(he is fed).* Here it is: "How is it that we know that God is on His Throne and all is well with the world? How is it?" Can't you see how important that is, how wonderful? Come now! We must have a perfect and compelling answer to this! All together—One, Two, Three! *(Leans forward expectantly, intently.)*

THE ONE HUNDRED AND FIFTY DIVISIONS

Our hearts, our hearts, they tell us so—
What is it that our hearts don't know!

(Each places a hand over his heart.)

NOXUS PODUNKUS

(Falling back on seven pillows and taking a deep breath.) Beautiful! Beautiful! Even so! And given as it should be! Let me hear you say that again, my dears and dearesses! Let me hear it again! *(They repeat it, waving pink handkerchiefs. The audience bursts into deafening applause lasting seventy-eight minutes. The Loobies and Gaberlunzies leap in the air, turn three somersaults before landing, and fall on their feet. Five thousand wirelesses are sent. NOXUS PODUNKUS, falling back and strangling with joy.)* This is too much! Too much! Who can say now that the world has not progressed! *(He is lifted up, feathered and doused with souffle.)* With the consent of my fellow Moonshees *(looks about him affably at the sleeping Moonshees)*, I will now excuse these very good people. *(Feeble calls of "Beautiful! Beautiful!" and "Let them be ex-*

cused!" from the Moonshees.) You may go, my dears and dearesses! You may go! *(He collapses.)*

THE ONE HUNDRED AND FIFTY DIVISIONS

(Executing a flank movement and assuming an open formation five hundred abreast and marching briskly away, twirling their batons and wagging their heads.) All hail the power of Podunks' name! *(They exit. Enter seven thousand Union Astronomers and four thousand Federated College Philosophers in close formation, all in green knee pants, white spike tail-coats and blue silk hats. The Astronomers carry green telescopes instead of canes. The Philosophers are all chewing tutti-frutti. They are preceded by cage-cars containing each one Specimen of Ossified and Ancient and Unmoral Stoic, Nietzschean, Pragmatist, Anti-Christ, Chemist and Physicist.)*

SHISHMASH HASH HASH

(Preceding them and climbing up the feather pole of a Hoddy-Doddy he has seized.) The Union Astronomers, your Referendunces! The Federated College Philosophers, your Referendunces! *(He leaps and tumbles three times around the arena, holding his toes with his hands.)*

THE ONE HUNDRED HODDY-DODDYS

(Pole-vaulting over the procession as it approaches.) The Union Astronomers, your Referendunces! The Federated Moral College Philosophers! *(The Dizzards give an exhibition of feather-club swallowing. The five thousand Nizys each juggle nine ice-cream cones in the air.)*

THE SEVEN THOUSAND UNION ASTRONOMERS

(Marching to "Oh, Believe Me If All Those Endearing Young Charms," and doing a hop, skip and jump as they near the Musnud.)

The universe is moral! The universe is moral!
'Tis as true—'tis as true—
As that a green horse isn't sorrel!

(One-half the division stand on their heads, the others on their feet.)

THE FIFTY DIZZARDS

(Receiving souffle handed up by the Nizys below. In chorus.)

"The universe is moral! The universe is moral!
'Tis as true—'tis as true—
As that a green horse isn't sorrel!"

THE ELEVEN THOUSAND PHILOSOPHERS AND ASTRONOMERS

(In chorus) Hail! Hail! The Comet's Tail!
All is well! All is swell!
Never was there an age like this!

(They wave their feet or hands, as the case may be.)

NOXUS PODUNKUS

(Rising on one elbow and rubbing his eyes.) What! What! More? What have we here? The Union Astronomers, you say? The Federated College Philosophers? Excellent! A fine body of men, indeed! And, as you say, the universe *is* moral. Very, very, very moral. One of the most moral universes I have ever known. *(Scratches an ear and sinks into his cushions, but the nearest Dizzards lift him up.)*

SHISHMASH HASH HASH

(Excitedly touching his toes with his hands nine times.) The Questions, your Noble Referendunce! The Sacred Questions!

NOXUS PODUNKUS

(Heavily and benignly.) Ah, yes! Ah, yes! The Sacred Questions! It is not intention, but memory, that seems to fail me. Quite so—the Sacred Questions! *(He takes one of fifty plates offered him and examines it closely.)* Ah yes! Here it is! One of the most significant and wonderful questions that has ever been planned, I think, to ease our minds and comfort us. *(Reads.)* Question Nine: "Is it not true that the universe is ordained for Truth, Justice, Virtue, Mercy, Tenderness, Purity?" *(His voice trails off in utter exhaustion.)*

THE SEVEN THOUSAND UNION ASTRONOMERS

(Doing a light come-all-ye and waving red bandana handkerchiefs.)

It is! It is! We know! We know!
The stars we see, they tell us so!

THE FOUR THOUSAND COLLEGE PHILOSOPHERS

(Masticating their gum vigorously.)

It is! It is! Hail, loud and long!
Our works, they sing the same sweet song!

(Loud and prolonged cheering by the audience. Wirelesses are sent to the waiting world. The Dizzards gnaw excitedly at their feather-clubs, then do a double-quick clog. The two thousand Loobies and Gaberlunzies read many, many soothing passages. The Nizys dole out souffle.)

NOXUS PODUNKUS

(Biting his nails and crossing his legs.) So! Quite so! The stars tell us! It couldn't be different! And now, my dears *(sighs from weariness)*, for the Tenth Great Question—one of those beautiful things that I always love to read and re-read. The most important one, I always think, in so far as astronomy is concerned, that has ever been devised. A Question so perfect that, when we pause to consider its absolute truthfulness and perfection, answers fully—oh, so fully!—all our astronomical needs. *(Reads.)* "Are not the stars maintained in their courses in order that man may progress and be moral?" *(He contemplates a fly which has lit on the end of his nose.)*

THE UNION ASTRONOMERS

(Juggling their telescopes after the manner of a shillalah and doing a come-all-ye.)

They are! They are! The stars, they say
That man to truth is on his way!

THE COLLEGE PHILOSOPHERS

(Catching hands and dancing around in a circle.)

The Universe was made for man—
And man for good, by God's dear plan!

(They slap each other on the back.)

NOXUS PODUNKUS

(Rolling back in ecstasy and smearing his face with souffle.) Lovely! Lovely! "The stars they say!" This certainly is the most inspiring session we have ever had! Such unity of feeling! Such innate wisdom! Surely the waiting world must realize now how completely we have progressed—how absolutely—*(he sinks to his pillows and is lifted to a sitting position by the Dizzards, who place the tablet in his hand, while the Moonshees turn over and murmur "Excellent! Excellent!" The wireless operators send out five thousand messages. PODUNKUS pulls himself together and continues.)* And now, my dear children—and now comes one of the keenest, the most searching really, of all the Great and Sacred Questions made and provided for these immortal occasions and handed down to us by our renowned and dear bygone leaders and saints, Bonehead V. and Dish Rag III. Really, when I stop to think of their great work for mankind, when—*(he sinks back and the Hoddy-Doddys proceed to dust him off)*—Ah yes! Ah, yes! Question Eleven—almost the most wonderful, the most important of all—*(reads)*—"How—how," so it reads, "do we know that, me good men? How? *(He smiles and waits expectantly, one finger up.)* How do we know? That is the famous, the keenest and most searching of all the Twelve Sacred Questions. How?

THE SEVEN THOUSAND UNION ASTRONOMERS

(Telescope to eye and weaving in and out in a wild dance.)

Our hearts, they tell us! We can hear
This truth they whisper, year by year!

(They kiss each other on each cheek.)

THE FOUR THOUSAND COLLEGE PHILOSOPHERS

(In chorus, and doing a hop, skip and jump.)

Our hearts do tell us! We do know—
Besides, our Astronomers do say so!

(They swallow their gum. The multitude breaks into tumultuous applause, which lasts for one hour, during which one

thousand messages are sent out and five thousand more wash-boilers of souffle are consumed.)

NOXUS PODUNKUS

(Aiming at the fly and missing it.) Ah! Ah! Could the world wish for anything more—more enlightening? Our hearts tell us! Oh, dear! Our dear Astronomers and College Philosophers stand in absolute accord as to this! Wonderful! Wonderful! *(Turning to the Musnud.)* I am sure that you, my dear fellow Moonshees and Savants, must be greatly impressed and inspired by this! It is what we all so much wish to hear, always! *(PODUNKUS rolls over on his side, while the Moonshees turn over and murmur "Excellent! Exquisitely put! Couldn't be better!" The Union Astronomers and College Philosophers now march off singing, "Hail! Hail! The Gang's all here!" the Philosophers weeping on each other's necks for joy while the Astronomers wig-wag the song with their telescopes. The Moonshees, Zadkiels, etc., squeak feebly for souffle.*

(Enter forty-eight divisions of five hundred each of Descendant Sons and Daughters of Ancient and Honorable Anti-Vice Crusaders, Prison Visitation Leaguers, Moral Prophylaxers, Anti-Contraceptionists, Eugenic Sires and Women Magazine Editors, in green, yellow and blue burnouses and pink papier-maché casques, fox-trotting as they come. An immense banner of Chinese silk and Australian wool mixed [symbolic of the general sequacity, tranquillity, plasticity, yet not to say florescence or flaccidity which now hovers over all the world] is carried before. This same contains a pale representation of a jail, such as existed in former centuries when the world was evil, but now [in the picture], in order to symbolize the present peace and progress of the world, crumbled and covered with vines and spiderwebs, while four angels of peace, one at each corner, hold up palms of victory. They are preceded by cage-cars containing each one Specimen of Ossified and Ancient White-Slaver, Gambler, Thief and Predatory Rich. As they approach,

the Loobies, Gaberlunzies, Nizys and Zanys bustle hither and thither among the audience, the former reading, the latter calling for silence and explaining the exact significance of the symbol while they ladle out souffle. On and before the Musnud the Hoddy-Doddys and Dizzards hover over NOXUS and the Moonshees, who have fallen into a sound sleep. Two thousand members of the Inter-Federated Association of Inter-Asiatic Descendant Sons and Daughters of Ancient and Honorable Eugenic Sires approach first, the men wearing green Zouave trousers, white silk overcoats and blue shakos. They carry lilies. The ladies are wrapped in nine layers of pink asbestos each one inch thick and carry poisoned hatpins. After charging and counter-charging they form a square in front of the Musnud, the ladies stacking hatpins, the men presenting lilies.)

SHISHMASH HASH HASH

(Tumbling back from the entryway where he has been supervising the general formation of the new division.) Your Referendunces! Your Referendunces! Look, oh look! The Inter-Federated Association of Inter-Asiatic Descendant Sons and Daughters of Eugenic Sires crave the honor of approaching and testifying before this great Court as to what Progress has done for them! Your Referendunces!

THE ONE HUNDRED HODDY-DODDYS

(Ranging in a line and presenting arms with their feather-dusters.)

Oh, never, never has there been
A sight to equal this, we ween!
Glorious!

(They clog, and chatter their teeth.)

THE MEMBERS OF THE INTER-FEDERATED ASSOCIATION OF INTER-ASIATIC DESCENDANT SONS AND DAUGHTERS

(Pirouetting and bowing to each other.)

'Tis six full centuries at least
Since un-Eugenic weddings ceased;

And now each youth and maid you see
Is married full Eugenic-ly.
In us behold the perfect fruitage
That followed on the former brute-age!

(They ring-around-the-rosy.)

NOXUS PODUNKUS

(Lifted to a sitting position by the Dizzards, tickled with feather-dusters, beaten with wind-bags and doused with ice-water until he opens his eyes.) What a sight!—A beautiful sight, I mean! My word! O never, my celebrated and associated Referendunces *(he turns to them)* have I seen so much beauty and virtue! Never! So much modesty! So much—much—everything! Really this is the worst—I mean best—I ever saw! This in itself is a complete refutation of that foul charge, once so common, that the world was in danger of not progressing. Look! Behold! O Progress, where is thy sting? *(He collapses, calling for soufflé, but is bolstered up and ice-water poured over him.)*

ONE HUNDRED EUGENIC MAIDS

(In pink Mother Hubbards and green Quaker bonnets. Stepping forward and sinking on one knee, hands on their chins. They sing.)

It is our duty to attest
How by Eugenics we are blest!
O 'tis a wondrous art divine,
Which causes all the world to shine!

NOXUS PODUNKUS

(Leaning over the railing and eying them closely.) Really! This is the limit—I mean almost too much—too much! Sweet maids! Dear sweet maids! This spectacle of the perfect fruitage of Progress under the great moral care of our forefathers—blessed be the name of the ever-to-be-remembered Anthony!—*(he bows, and the audience with him)*—is all but too much! Progress can do no more! I would, if any service which the mere sight of you does not render—could render—

ask you the Twelfth and final Question, but what would be the use? How well we know the import of your message, even before you speak! How well we know the import of you yourselves—wonderful creatures that you are! *(They bow their heads.)* This vast assemblage, which in itself is a testimony to the value of Eugenics, understands full well that by the practice of Eugenics alone all weakness, vice, crime, art, philosophy *(except that which our dear Union Astronomers and Federated Philosophers instinctively know and proclaim)*, the need of white-slave laws, saloons, the theater—all, all have long since been done away with, so that we have now—the most of us, I am glad to say—not even so much as an historic memory of them. Indeed, as we all know, on this once most unsafe but now safest of planets *(applause lasting seventeen minutes)*, men and women are now as safe and perfect and pure as ever our worthy forefathers could have dreamed of or desired. Why, to look at you alone is enough! *(He sighs and rests.)*

Dear Eugenic citizens and citizenesses, without taxing you further with these deep and brain-racking questions, so sacred to us all of course, the one message of this great Court to you is to go and do as you have always done: think no more than is absolutely necessary. Don't tax your brains. This, our great Federation of Commission-Ruled Republics, is here to do all that for you *(the Moonshees stir)*. The less we know the better, as we all know. *(Long and loud applause lasting eighteen minutes.)* In former and darker, and therefore sadder, times, there were many who thought differently. But they and all those who were a part of them have long since been disposed of. *(Long and uproarious applause.)* And is not, I now ask you, the world happier, fairer, sweeter to the eye and the mind? *(Cries of "Hear! Hear!" and "Yea! Yea!" lasting two hours.)* Now, dear Eugenic citizens, you need only consider how thoughtless you are and therefore how happy in these sweet exercises and games such as we see here to-day which contribute only to the sustenance, docility and fertility of man, to know how true all this is. Be thoughtless. Be happy. And by so being, as I always think, you contribute and testify to the efficiency of Truth, Virtue, Justice, Mercy, Sobriety, Love, Beauty, Simplicity, Peace—*(he collapses from sheer exhaustion.)*— Souffle! Souffle! *(A bucket of souffle is brought and administered.)*

THE ONE HUNDRED MAIDS

(Wishing not to tire their noble Referendunces, singing in chorus.)

O, sweet Eugenic thought—to know
That our dear Noxus loves us so!

(They fall back in the ranks.)

(Enter fifteen thousand Descendant Sons and Daughters of Ancient and Honorable Anti-White Slavers of the pre-Federated Period (A. D. 1870-1927), *in green-and-white kilts and galligaskins, with perukes and billy-cocks on their heads. They march swiftly forward, an expression of grim determination—historically correct—on their faces, and pause before the Musnud. Over their left arms, after the fashion of the world's great Anti-White-Slave Leaders and in accordance with historical descriptions of the same, hang immense mantles of dark green bed-ticking intended to shield naked fleeing white slaves. Over their shoulders are carried papier-maché broadaxes of the kind known to have been used by all Anti-White-Slavers, male and female, in felling the enemy. These they occasionally brandish as they walk. At their belts hang lanterns, files, skeleton keys, medicine kits containing concentrated food pills, digitalis and the like, all intended for the rescue and resuscitation of overcome white slaves. Their eyelids and mouths are painted a bright cerise to give a look of extra vigor and force, and as they walk, one hundred abreast, they peer to right and left in the most searching and secretive and yet detecting way from beneath their hands, and occasionally flash their dark lanterns on the surrounding spectators.)*

SHISHMASH HASH HASH

(Leaping up and cracking his heels nine times before descending.) Your Referendunces! Your Referendunces! We have here the only living Descendant Sons and Daughters of Ancient and Honorable American Anti-White Slavers—the organization which in its day gave rise—laid the foundation, as it were, of our present great and perfect World Federation, over which at present your Referendunces are so ably presiding. It claims to be the only existing organization that preserves in all their purity the customs, manners and instincts of the original pre-Federated Anti-White-Slavers of seven and eight centuries since. I beg of your Referendunces—I beg of you!—on this very special occasion—I know you are tired—Will your Referendunces be pleased to receive them? *(He runs swiftly around in a ring and falls over three extended feather-dusters. NOXUS PODUNKUS groans. The Moonshees moan.)*

THE ONE HUNDRED ZANYS

(Dancing on before them and rattling their wind-bags.) The Anti-White-Slavers! The Anti-White-Slavers! Look! Behold!

THE FIFTY DIZZARDS

(Beating the Moonshees with feather-clubs and whistling between their teeth.) Awake! Awake! *(The Moonshees stir feebly and call for souffle. By the aid of a dozen gallons of ice-water* NOXUS PODUNKUS *is once more aroused and now surveys the approaching procession, which marches about the arena and back to the Musnud.)*

NOXUS PODUNKUS

(Scratching his left ear and surveying the assembled throng.) What—more? Oh! Well, welcome, noble citizens! Welcome! I see by your brows that you possess the unconquerable love of Liberty, Virtue, Truth, Justice, Beauty, etc., so necessary to the happy maintenance of our present Federated condition. *(He collapses and more souffle is administered. Recovering.)* Stick to it! What supreme comfort it must be to you and your exceedingly courageous ancestors to know that our very happy

present condition is almost entirely due to them—their noble deeds of valor performed in order that we might become so—so—*(he coughs)*. What supreme deeds would not you now, I am sure *(they brandish their battleaxes)* gladly perform were it not that fortunately all provocation had long since been done away with. *(Loud cheering. All the Nizys, Zanys, Hoddy-Doddys, etc., walk on their hands.)* Night after night in the wilds of the great cities of those far-off centuries, now so happily past, did your forefathers fearlessly and tirelessly seek out the enslavers of resisting and lovely womanhood and battle to the death with those who would have corrupted our worthy sires—I mean siresses—Souffle!—*(he imbibes)*—performing astounding and now almost unbelievable feats of valor, felling the vile and rapacious enslaver to the plain and chopping him to bits, leaving us, their humble descendants, little if anything to do save revere and historically represent the marvels which they then performed. *(Immense and prolonged cheering. Eight thousand wireless messages are sent forth.)* Literature, by their aid, as we all well know, has at last been completely done away with. *(Riotous applause.)* Profane art in all its forms and all its seductive wiles has long since ceased. *(The audience shouts for one hour.)* The vile newspapers of ancient days *(innumerable swells of booing and cat-calling)*, wont to chronicle only the private and social vices of unregenerate man, now, thanks to the unremitting toil of those who had only the moral regeneration of the world in view, its true spiritual progress *(prolonged and enduring applause)*, chronicle only the sweet messages of hope and cheer by which we sustain each other in our happy state—Souffle! Souffle! *(He dips his head in a pannier. The audience cheers for one hour.)* Now we are not troubled with politics, armies, or any vile evidences of commercial strife and contest. *(More applause.)* Nothing disturbs us in any way! Could we ask more? *(Cries of "Hear! Hear!")* As I was saying to those dear creatures who just left, our beloved Eugenic citizens and citizenesses, we need now only concern ourselves with the simple arts of peace and pleasure as we here see manifest in this great assemblage. On you, therefore, more than on any other group which at this time could come before this august Court to testify to the Truth, Peace, Virtue, Sequacity and Docility of our present world-realm, devolves, as lineal descendants of these our great sires, the sweet task of keeping bright the memory of their great deeds. I am sure that you, my dears and dearesses, by maintaining so earnest a stand against all thought of any kind, by persisting in your aversion to moral heresies of all sorts and indeed learning and science in every form, and by your persistent and industrious mutilation and destruction of all profane facts, so long the curse of society *(loud cries of "Down with all facts!")*, will succeed—I know you will!—in keeping the world as fresh and pure and innocent as on the day it was made. *(Cries of "Yes, yes," and "we will, we will." Applause for one hour.)* Souffle! Souffle! *(He is fed.)*—Cruel, disturbing thought, that one great curse of humanity in its earlier ages must never be allowed to trouble us again. *(Immense applause.)* And since, by what processes of hardy non-thinking only our revered ancestors know, profound peace has at last been reached, I caution you, O my fellow-citizens, let not a single irritating disturbing fact ever again impinge upon the sweet idealism and mental slumber which now reigns. Behold our happy Dizzards! *(They wiggle their stuffed clubs.)* Could any of the so-called and boasted mental processes of former ages have produced them? *(They walk on their hands.)* And our dear Zanys! *(They rattle their wind-bags.)* What would our great peaceful Federation be without them? *(They beat each other over the head.)* Or our graceful Nizys! *(They take up wash-boilers of souffle and ladle it right and left solemnly.)* The gentility and wholeheartedness of their service! *(They playfully pelt each other with cones filled with souffle.)* Or our kindly Hoddy-Doddys! *(They vault.)* What more could humanity desire in the shape of perfect and helpful men? *(They leap on each other's backs and fall gracefully to the floor.)* When I contemplate these, and this great audience *(profound applause lasting seventeen minutes)*, and these our assembled cohorts of Virtue, Truth, Justice, Mercy *(more applause, lasting one hour)*, come here from all parts of the known world to testify to the great fundamental truths which have made them so, I—*(At this point the great audience rises en masse and cheers for one hour, seventeen and one-half minutes and thirteen seconds. Rival groups of Descendant Sons and Daughters of Ancient and Honorable Anti-White-Slavers, Anti-Vivisectionists, Anti-Contraceptionists, Billysundays, Eugenic Sires, Anti-Saloon Leaguers, Watch and Ward Guards, King's Daughters, Free and Accepted Boy Scouts, etc., rush forward and seize upon the cages containing the only remaining specimens of Gambler, Saloon-keeper, Predatory Financier, Philosopher, Magdalen, Vivisectionist, Madam, Nietzschean and other early examples of now nearly or quite extinct miscreants or papier-maché representations of the same, and haul them before the Musnud amid the cheering, hee-hawing, cat-calling of the audience. The Zanys, Nizys, Dizzards, Loobies, Hoddy-Doddys, Gaberlunzies and Fuddys, forgetting their regular duties, spin, squeal, play at leap-frog, beat each other with feather-dusters and wind-bags. Various regiments of Descendant Sons and Daughters of Ancient and Honorable Feminists, Professors of Christian Economy, Prohibitionists, Socialists, etc., who have not yet had the privilege of parading and testifying before the Musnud, crowd the entryways, swarm the aisles and so obstruct the peaceful and orderly development of the proceedings of the Court that, in view of this and because ordinarily the proceedings consume from twenty to thirty days anyhow, so great is the anxiety of all to testify to the magnificent progress of the world since vice and crime have been done away with,* NOXUS PODUNKUS, *now thoroughly awake and after due counsel with the ninety-nine other Moonshees, Savants, Roctor-Proctors, Pundits, Theorists, Zadkiels, Seers, Oracles, Solons,*

Nestors, Gamaliels, Daniels, etc., also disturbed in their slumbers, decides that, all things considered, and notwithstanding, it were as well if the taking of testimony were to be discontinued for this day, and to this end, after various signs, grunts, squeals, motions to the Zanys, Dizzards, Nizys, Loobies, Hoddy-Doddys, Gaberlunzies, Fuddys, etc., the latter are brought to their senses and through them the audience calmed.

(It was then that NOXUS PODUNKUS, *speaking for the Musnud, announced that the proceedings for this day were hereby ended and that the Court stood adjourned until the following morning at ten o'clock; after which SHISHMASH* HASH HASH, *as Master of Ceremonies, Chairmaster, etc., led the outgoing throng with a magnificent example of rotary hand-spring motion. At this point, also, owing to lack of space and by reason of the fact that enough is as good as a feast, the humble recording Dramatist quits and the curtain is hereby drawn on this historic scene. For those, however, who desire a fuller report of the same, it may be found in Volumes MMCCCIII, MMMMMMMMCCCLLVI, Proceedings of the Federated Court of Progress [Moline-Emporia-Sedalia Sittings] for the years* 3913-'14-'15, NOXUS PODUNKUS *presiding;* SHISHMASH HASH HASH, *Secretary and Master of Ceremonies.)*

Curtain.

www.ingramcontent.com/pod-product-compliance
Lightning Source LLC
LaVergne TN
LVHW011200110826
845150LV00006B/1278

* 9 7 8 1 4 2 5 5 7 2 8 2 2 *